Macmillan International Political Economy Series
General Editor: Timothy M. Shaw, Professor of Political Science and Director of International Development Studies, Dalhousie University, Nova Scotia

The global political economy is in a profound crisis at the levels of both production and policy. This series provides overviews and case studies of states and sectors, classes and companies in the new international division of labour. These embrace political economy as both focus and mode of analysis; they advance radical scolarship and scenarios.

The series treats polity-economy dialectics at global, regional and national levels and examines novel contradictions and coalitions between and within each. There is a special emphasis on national bourgeoisies and capitalisms, on newly industrial or influential countries, and on novel strategies and technologies. The concentration throughout is on uneven patterns of power and production, authority and distribution, hegemony and reaction. Attention will be paid to redefinitions of class and security, basic needs and self-reliance and the range of critical analysis will include gender, population, resources, environment, militarisation, food and finance. This series constitutes a timely and distinctive response to the continuing intellectual and existential world crisis.

John Ravenhill (*editor*)
AFRICA IN ECONOMIC CRISIS
Stephen Riley (*editor*)
THE POLITICS OF GLOBAL DEBT
Garry Rodan
THE POLITICAL ECONOMY OF SINGAPORE'S INDUSTRIALIZATION
Patricia Ruffin
CAPITALISM AND SOCIALISM IN CUBA
Roger Southall (*editor*)
LABOUR AND UNIONS IN ASIA AND AFRICA
Sharon Stichter and Jane L. Parpart (*editors*)
WOMEN, EMPLOYMENT AND THE FAMILY IN THE INTERNATIONAL
    DIVISION OF LABOUR
Fiona Wilson
SWEATERS: GENDER, CLASS AND WORKSHOP-BASED INDUSTRY IN
RURAL MEXICO
David Wurfel and Bruce Burton (*editors*)
THE POLITICAL ECONOMY OF FOREIGN POLICY IN SOUTHEAST ASIA

Democratic Transition and Consolidation in Southern Europe, Latin America and Southeast Asia

Edited by

Diane Ethier

Assistant Professor of Political Science
Université de Montréal

MACMILLAN

First published 1990

Published by
THE MACMILLAN PRESS LTD
Houndmills, Basingstoke, Hampshire RG21 2XS
and London
Companies and representatives
throughout the world

Typeset by Footnote Graphics,
Warminister, Wilts
Printed in Hong Kong

British Library Cataloguing in Publication Data
Democratic Transition and Consolidation in Southern
Europe, Latin America and Southeast Asia. (Macmillan
International Political Economy Series).
1. Democratisation
I. Ethier, Diane, *1948–*
321.09

ISBN 0–333–52128–5

Contents

v

PART III DEMOCRATIC CONSOLIDATIONS

List of Figures and Tables

Preface

Between 1975 and 1986, academic work focusing on the democratization of authoritarian regimes was almost exclusively centred on single case-studies or comparative studies of democratic transitions in Southern Europe and Latin America. In the following two years, three new lines of research developed: the analysis of democratic transitions in other regions, in particular, in Southeast Asia; the critical examination of the theoretical and methodological foundations of the existing studies; and the evaluation of the conditions and prospects of consolidation of the new democratic regimes in Southern Europe and Latin America.

The importance of these new concerns encouraged us to unite the principal specialists in the field, in the context of an international symposium in the autumn of 1988, to examine these questions in more detail. The texts put together in this volume largely draw their inspiration from the presentations and discussions at that symposium.

Concentrating on theories of processes of transition and democratic consolidation, the introduction tries to delimit points of agreement and of divergence. At the same time, it attempts to delineate links between these theories and the approaches that have dominated the analysis of political change since 1950.

Taking comparative analysis of the democratic transitions in the Southern Cone of Latin America as his basis, C. Gillespie critically examines the principal explanatory paradigms of the causes and modalities of democratic transitions.

Referring to the democratic transitions of the Second French Empire and the German Empire, G. Hermet tries to shed light on the causes of the recent democratic transitions in Greece, Spain, and Portugal. As in the case of C. Gillespie, this line of thought leads him to examine critically the explanations on the subject put forward by different schools.

Focusing on the study of democratic transitions in Ecuador, Bolivia, and Chile, C. Conaghan and V. Montecinos insist on the crucial role of certain actors, such as business, technocrats, and economic counsellors. These actors have been neglected so far by most authors, as they are apparently excluded from the political decision-making process.

David Wurfel, an ex-advisor of the Aquino government, analyses in detail the process of democratic transition in the Philippines. At the same time, he compares it to the scenarios of democratization in Southern Europe and Latin America. This comparison is of great interest, since it shows that the Philippine case constitutes in certain ways an exception to the dynamic of recent transitions in the West.

Based on single and comparative case-studies, the texts in the second part evaluate the possibilities of consolidation of the new democratic regimes, mainly in Southern Europe and Latin America. Despite the diversity of the situations studied and of the criteria favoured by the authors – modalities of economic development (K. Vergopoulos), party system and constitutions (T. Bruneau, A. MacLeod), ideologies of dominant groups (L. C. B. Pereira), institutions and political attitudes (R. Boschi, G. Ducatenzeiler), electoral system (A. Blais, S. Dion) – a similar diagnosis emerges from each of these analyses. Except perhaps for the Spanish case, the prospects for the consolidation of the new 'peripheral' democracies are hardly encouraging, due to the absence or the fragility of the social consensus within these societies.

Diane Ethier

Acknowledgments

Certain texts in this volume draw their inspiration from the presentations given at the symposium 'The Internationalisation of Political Democracy: Problems and Perspectives', which was held at Université de Montréal from 28 September 1988 to 2 October 1988. We would like to thank all those who participated in the organisation of this meeting, in particular, Denis Monière, chairman of the Department of Political Science at Université de Montréal, and the organisations which financed it: the Social Sciences and Humanities Research Council of Canada (SSHRC), the Fonds pour la formation de chercheurs et l'aide à la recherche (FCAR), and the Université de Montréal. We also express our gratitude to Nicole Laberge, Jocelyne Dion, Liette Bonin, and Chantal Villeneuve, who standardized the final presentation of the manuscript, and to Clay Suddath, who revised the English translation of certain texts.

Notes on Contributors

André Blais is full professor in Political Science at the Université de Montréal. Research coordinator for the Royal Commission on the Economic Union and Development Prospects for Canada (1983–85), he has published extensively on public policies, political institutions and electoral systems. His more recent publications include: 'The Classification of Electoral Systems', *European Journal of Political Research*; 'The Impact of Electoral Formulae on the Creation of Majority Governments', *Electoral Studies*; 'Government, Special Interest Groups and Economic Growth', *Public Choice*; and 'The Political Economy of Public Subsidies', *Comparative Political Studies*.

Renato R. Boschi is assistant professor and researcher at the Instituto Universitario de Pesquisas do Rio de Janeiro (IUPERJ). He is the author of 'Bureaucracia, Clientelismo e Oligopolio: O Conselho Interministerio de Precos' in Lima and O. Abranches, eds., *As Origens da Crise: Estado Autoritario e Planejamento no Brasil* and 'Social Movements and the New Political Order in Brazil' in W. J. Nunes and T. Bogerschild, eds., *State and Society in Brazil: Continuity and Change*.

Thomas C. Bruneau, former professor of Political Science and director of the Center for Developing Area Studies at McGill University, is currently full professor of National Security Affairs at the Naval Postgraduate School in Monterey. He has published extensively on Portuguese and Brazilian politics. He is the author of *The Church in Brazil: the Politics of Religion;* and *Politics and Nationhood: Post-Revolutionary Portugal*; co-author (with A. MacLeod) of *Politics in Contemporary Portugal: Parties and the Consolidation of Democracy*; and co-editor (with P. Faucher) of *Authoritarian Capitalism: Brazil's Contemporary Economic and Political Development*.

Catherine M. Conaghan is associate professor in Political Science at Queen's University. She has recently published 'Party Politics and Democratization in Ecuador' in James Malloy and Mitchell A. Seligson, eds., *Authoritarians and Democrats, Regime Transition in Latin America* and a book on democratic transitions in Bolivia and Ecuador.

Stéphane Dion is associate professor in Political Science at the Université de Montréal. His publications include: *La politisation des mairies*; 'Les politiques municipales de concertation: néo-conservatisme et démocratie', *Sociologie du Travail*; and 'Pouvoir et conflits dans l'organisation: grandeur et limites du modèle de Michel Crozier', *Revue canadienne de Science politique*.

Graciela Ducatenzeiler is associate professor in Political Science at the Université de Montréal and co-director of the Groupe de Recherche sur l'Amérique latine (GRAL). She has carried out much research on social movements and politics in Argentina and has published *Syndicats et politique en Argentine* and 'Ouverture politique, transition démocratique et classe ouvrière en Argentine', *Politique*.

Diane Ethier is assistant professor in Political Science at the Université de Montréal. Her field of research is economic development and political change in newly industrialized countries. She has published, among others, 'L'adhésion à la CEE et ses incidences sur l'économie espagnole' in M. Couture and C. Deblock, *Un marché: deux sociétés*; 'Gunnar Myrdal et la modernisation du sud-est asiatique' in G. Dostaler, D. Ethier and L. Lepage, *Gunnar Myrdal et son oeuvre*. She is co-editor of *F. Hayek, Philosophie, Economie et Politique* and has recently completed a book on democratic transition in Spain.

Charles G. Gillespie, formerly visiting assistant professor at Yale University is now assistant professor in Political Science at the University of Wisconsin. He has published many articles on political change in Latin America, in particular, 'Uruguay's Return to Democracy', *Bulletin of Latin American Research*; 'Uruguay's Transition from Collegial Military–Technocratic Rule' in G. O'Donnell, P. Schmitter and L. Whitehead, eds., *Transitions from Authoritarian Rule: Prospects for Democracy*; and 'Uruguay: the Challenge of Democratic Consolidation', *Latin American Research Review*.

Guy Hermet is director of research at the Fondation nationale de sciences politiques and full professor at the Institut d'etudes politiques de Paris. Former director of the Centre d'etudes et de recherches internationales and founder of the Institut colombien des hautes etudes de développement, he has published extensively on comparative politics of European and Latin American societies and is one of the well-known specialists on Spain. He is the author of *Aux*

Frontières de la démocratie; Totalitarismes; L'Espagne au XXe siècle; and *Sociologie de la construction démocratique* and *La Guerre d'Espagne.*

Alex MacLeod is full professor in Political Science at the Université du Québec à Montréal. Former director of the Centre interuniversitaire d'etudes européennes, he was involved in many research projects on Southern European economics and politics. He is the author of *Portugal in Development: Emigration, Industrialization, the European Community* and co-editor (with T. Bruneau) of *Politics in Contemporary Portugal: Parties and the Consolidation of Democracy.*

Veronica Montecinos, former fellow of the Helen Kellogg Institute for International Studies, Notre-Dame University, is currently visiting professor in Political Science at Pittsburgh University. She has recently completed important research on the role of economists in the process of democratic transition in Chile.

Luis Carlos Bresser Pereira, formerly president of the Banco do Estado de Sao Paulo, Chief of Staff for the Governor of the State of Sao Paulo and Minister of Finance of Brazil, is at present Secretary of Science and Technology of the State of Sao Paulo, full professor at the Getulio Vargas Foundation (Sao Paulo) and editor of the Revista de Economia Politica. His numerous books include: *Development and Crisis in Brazil 1930–1983; Economia brasileira: Uma introducao critica; Inflacao e Recessao; A Divida e a Inflacao, Pactos Politicos – Do Populismo a Redemocratizacao;* and *Lucro, Acumulacao e Crise.*

Kostas Vergopoulos is full professor of Political Economy at the Université Paris VIII. Coordinator of various major research projects on Latin American and Mediterranean countries, in particular, the Project 'Méditerranée', supported by the Italian Government and UNITAR, he has published many books and articles, especially: *Le Capitalisme difforme et la nouvelle question agraire; La question paysanne et le capitalisme;* and *Nationalisme et développement économique.*

David Wurfel is full professor of Political Science at Windsor University. Former special advisor to the Aquino government during the democratic transition in the Philippines, he is one of the best-known specialists of Southeast Asia. His more recent books are *Filipino Politics: Development and Decay* and (co-editor with Bruce Burton) *The Political Economy of Foreign Policy in Southeast Asia.*

Part I
Introduction

Introduction: Processes of Transition and Democratic Consolidation: Theoretical Indicators[1]

Diane Ethier

The comparative analysis of the recent processes of transition and democratic consolidation in Southern Europe, Latin America and East Asia brings up several methodological problems stemming from the complexity of these phenomena, the heterogeneity of the cases studied and the diversity of the paradigms employed by researchers. The collation of the numerous works published since the end of the 1970s, in particular on the democratic transition of authoritarian regimes, nevertheless permits a certain theoretical consensus susceptible of shedding light on the causes, outcome, modalities, conditions, and perspectives of these political changes. This introduction is intended to give an account of that consensus so that the reader may grasp both the common and the particular characteristics of the scenarios studied in this work. It provides, at the same time, a comparative grid of the approaches favoured by the authors.

DEMOCRATIC TRANSITION OF AUTHORITARIAN REGIMES

Studies of recent democratic transitions of authoritarian regimes between 1978 and 1986, largely founded on the observation of cases in Southern Europe (Greece, Spain, Portugal) and Latin America (Peru, Bolivia, Ecuador, Uruguay, Argentina, Brazil), led to the formulation of a series of hypotheses on the outcome, causes, and development of these processes of political change. These hypotheses were then used in the framework of several studies on processes of late democratization (in Turkey, Chile or Southeast Asia – the Philippines, South Korea, Thailand).

The collation of these models shows that hypotheses which can be verified empirically are the subject of a fairly broad consensus among specialists, whereas those of a speculative nature vary considerably from one author to another. Thus, propositions relating to the *outcome* of these transitions, attempting to define the type of democracy targeted by these changes, and those serving to specify their *scenario*, that is, the juridical-institutional reforms that constitute their different phases, are relatively convergent. They follow from the observation of concrete phenomena such as the constitutions of current Western democracies and the modification of laws, institutions and the behaviour of political actors in countries touched by the transitions. However, hypotheses relating to the causes of these changes – origins and dynamic of the crisis of authoritarian regimes, conditions for the emergence of democracy – constitute an important source of divergence. They refer to either abstract processes (perceptions and psychological strategies of individual actors) or complex processes (cultural, ideological, social and economic changes) that cannot be apprehended in a satisfactory way by empirical methods. In so far as the explanation of these changes remains founded by and large on speculation, the possibilities for theoretical, normative and ideological choices by the researchers increase. This is the reason why the analysis of the causes of recent democratic transitions, as in the case of earlier research on other forms of political change, remains riddled with controversy.

Outcome and Origins of Democratic Transitions

As indicated by O'Donnell and Schmitter (1986, IV, 7), several authors attach a similar meaning to the expression 'democratic transition'. This expression designates an *interval* between an authoritarian and a democratic regime, while the notion regime generally refers to:

> the ensemble of patterns, explicit or not, that determines the forms and channels of access to principal governmental positions, the characteristics of the actors who are admitted and excluded from such access, and the resources or strategies that they can use to gain access. This necessarily involves institutionalization, i.e. to be relevant the patterns defining a given regime must be habitually known, practiced and accepted, at least by those which these same patterns define as participants in the process. (O'Donnell and Schmitter 1986, IV, 73)

This definition clearly specifies the *political nature* of the changes, their autonomy with regard to any significant modification of the existing economic and social structures, as well as their *outcome*, which is the installation or the restoration of political democracy. In several studies, this notion refers to the concept of *polyarchy* formulated by Dahl (1971) on the basis of De Toqueville's (1835) and Schumpeter's (1942) theses. According to Boudon and Bourricaud (1982, 421), this concept designates the particular shape democracy takes in contemporary Western industrial societies and the evolutionary forms that could bring less developed societies closer to this ideal type. The principal characteristics of polyarchy are (a) *pluralism* or the existence of multiple socio-economic strata tending to alleviate conflicts of interest and to favour consultation; (b) *multipartisanism*, which implies competition and alternation in power of pluralist rather than class-based political parties and assumes an evolution of the party system towards a certain type of centrist bipartisanism; (c) *effective guarantees of fundamental individual and collective rights and freedoms*, implying, in particular, the election of leaders by universal suffrage, parliamentary responsibility of government, and juridical control of the rulers.

These essential, but not exclusive, characteristics of polyarchies constitute the principal criteria that define the starting point of transitions, that is, authoritarianism – which, whatever its specific forms, always constitutes a negation of pluralism, multipartisanism and the rules permitting effective recognition of the principle of citizenship. They also define their outcome, that is, the institutionalization of democratic rules.

As emphasized, in particular, by Moore (1966), Rustow (1970), Dahl (1971), Stepan (1986), and Share and Mainwaring (1987), there exist several possible scenarios of democratic transition: (1) transitions driven by external forces (conquests, putschs masterminded from abroad, foreign interventions, wars) which are similar to the democratic restorations that occurred in several European countries and in Japan following the Second World War; (2) transitions resulting from violent intervention by certain internal socio-political forces (revolutions, civil wars, coups d'état) to which most of the processes of the emergence of democracy in the West in the 17th, 18th and 19th centuries belong (Hermet, this volume, chapter 1); (3) evolutionary or continuing transitions initiated by an internal crisis of the political regime. According to all studies on the subject, the recent democratic transitions in Southern Europe, Latin America and Southeast Asia belong to this third category.

Most authors, following the lead of O'Donnell and Schmitter, believe that these transitions originate within an *internal crisis* of authoritarian regimes. The crisis is marked by a rupture of consensus between actors controlling (protagonists) or partaking (supporters) in political decision-making. This rupture is linked to the emergence of tensions or contradictions between conservative (*duros* or hardliners) and reformist elements (*blandos* or softliners).

> ... we assert that there is no transition whose beginning is not the consequence – direct or indirect – of important divisions within the authoritarian regime itself, principally along the fluctuating cleavage between hard-liners and soft-liners. (O'Donnell and Schmitter, 1986, IV, 19)

According to the same authors, the emergence of this conflict results from a modification in the calculations and strategies of a certain number of actors who, at a given moment, judge that their interests in the future are more threatened by the maintenance of the status quo than by a democratization of the political system.

Nevertheless, researchers favour different interpretations concerning the identification of the different groups in conflict, the analysis of the configuration of the balance of power characterizing the crisis, as well as the causes for the psycho-political changes. As was pointed out before, these divergences stem in large part from the fact that it is not possible to verify concretely the motivations and subjective strategies of each actor. The same can be said about the impact of any given series of variables on this psychological dynamic.

However, the interpretations of the configuration of the crisis are not exclusively related to the speculative nature of the hypotheses formulated by the authors. They are equally determined by the various theoretical models (typologies) serving to specify the characteristics of each authoritarian regime. Some authors, such as O'Donnell (1973), Cardoso (1979), and Martins (1982), associate the dominant group of 'bureaucratic-authoritarian regimes' with civil and military technocrats. Others associate it with representatives of the state, and of international and local capital (Pereira, 1985; Faucher, 1981), with the various factions of the internal and comprador bourgeoisies (Poulantzas, 1975), or with representatives of the ruling classes and various categories of actors belonging to the state apparatus (Giner and Sevilla, 1980). However, these divergences remain somewhat secondary, since they do not call into question the postulate that the crisis follows from a conflict between the actors occupying a dominant position within the regime. *This implies that the transition to democracy is controlled by the state rather than by the forces of civil society.*

The hypotheses relative to the causes of the crisis, despite their heterogeneity, draw their inspiration from three distinctive approaches. The first one favours internal political factors. The second one puts the accent on external economic factors. The third one, in an eclectic fashion and to a degree varying from case to case, attributes equal importance to internal and external political and economic factors.

Some of the interpretations inspired by the first approach insist on the fact that the emergence of a reformist current within the regime is linked to the perception that the costs of repression have become higher than the risks inherent in the adoption of a more tolerant and liberal attitude. This is based on the assumption that the government is no longer able to impose its authority on the opposition by means of physical coercion. Depending on the case, this loss of the monopoly of coercion is the result of various factors: (a) the emergence of conflicts within the repressive bodies (army, police corps, intelligence services) and between these bodies and the government. These conflicts can be related to military defeats of the regime (Greece, Argentina, Portugal), to struggles over the succession of the chief of state (Brazil, Philippines, Spain), or to the inefficiency of the repressive mechanisms; (b) the depoliticization of the repressive forces; (c) the decline of fear within civil society. (On this type of explanation, see in particular Linz, 1979 and 1982; Cardoso, 1979; Martins, 1982; Rouquié, 1983; Coverdale, 1979; Menges, 1978.) Nevertheless, several of these analyses acknowledge that pressures from Western governments and international non-governmental organizations, such as the Second Socialist International, also had a significant impact on the analysis of the costs and benefits of repression among the regime actors. (On this question, see White-head, 1986, among others.)

More specifically, other authors attribute the decline of the re-pressive capacity of the state to a legitimacy crisis. This crisis is characterized by the development of more or less important opposi-tion movements among the supporters of the regime (high-ranking technocrats, the church, junior officers, foreign and local enterprises) and within the social groups excluded from or oppressed by the regime (workers, unemployed, ethnic minorities, students, peasants). The legitimacy crisis is itself related to various factors, such as military defeats of the regime, decline of fear among the citizens, and an economic crisis. At first glance, this type of analysis seems to call into question the internal nature of the regime crisis and the postulate that the transitions were essentially initiated and controlled by the regime. For example, Stepan (1986), Gillespie (this volume, chapter 2), and Share and Mainwaring (1987) distinguish three types of transition: (1) *transitions by abandonment of power* (Greece, Portugal, Argentina), where the regime has no control over the process of change due to the force of the popular opposition movements; (2) *transitions by transfer of power* (Peru, Bolivia, Uruguay) – a category to which one could associate the cases of Korea and the Philippines (see Wurfel, this volume, chapter 5) – where the regime has a tenuous control over the modalities of change due to the relative importance of the opposition movements; (3) *transitions by transaction* (Spain, Brazil) entirely initiated and controlled by the regime in view of the absence of significant opposition movements within civil society. However, a more thorough comparative analysis of the popular opposition movements characterizing these various transitions shows that in all the countries concerned (with the possible exception of the Philippines) these movements were by and large directed, if not propelled, by regime supporters across political parties, pressure groups, professional associations and other interest groups. This acknowledgement tends to confirm the fact that the crisis at the origin of the transitions was largely confined to the actors of the political regime. Moreover, the limits of the democratic reforms adopted during the transitions seem to indicate that theses processes were in fact more or less controlled 'from above'.

While supporting the analyses based on internal political factors, O'Donnell, Schmitter (1986, IV) and Przeworski (1986) insist on the relative value of these explanations. Their remarks bring out the multitude and the uncertainty of choices confronting the actors and the immense diversity of variables susceptible of influencing their choice. According to these authors, it therefore remains difficult to specify the causes of the crisis of authoritarian regimes and its impact on the transitions other than by deduction from empirical observations of the political reforms adopted during the transitions.

The second type of approach puts the accent on external economic determinants of the crisis of authoritarian regimes. To that effect, three relatively different explanations are proposed by researchers. The first one, employed mainly by economists (Pereira, 1985; Furtado, 1981; Vergopoulos, this volume, chapter 6), establishes a relation between the crisis of authoritarian regimes (in Southern Europe and Latin America) and the consequences of external economic shocks during the period from 1973 to 1983 (oil crisis in 1973, recession in the centre in 1974–75, second oil crisis in 1979 followed by a rise of interest rates and a second recession in the centre between 1981 and 1983) on the evolution of development policies in the countries concerned. According to this line of argument, the consequences of the external upheavals imposed more liberal and outward-looking economic orientations on these countries. At the same time, they provoked important dissensions within the dominant coalition between those in favour of opening up and the defenders of the previous, more inward-looking, protectionist and interventionist, development model. The second explanation associates the crises of the Greek, Spanish, and Portuguese authoritarian regimes with the accentuation of inter-imperialist contradictions (European capital versus American capital). This is seen in the context of the crisis of accumulation at the beginning of the 1970s and its effects on the comprador and internal factions of the local bourgeoisie. According to Poulantzas (1975), the principal representative of this current, the downfall of dictatorship in the three countries, is linked to the victory of the pro-European forces (internal bourgeoisies) in favour of the consolidation of European capitalism by means of a southward enlargement of the European Community (EC) against the pro-American forces (comprador bourgeoisie). The third explanation (see, in particular, Lipietz, 1985; Giner and Sevilla, 1980) attributes the crisis of authoritarian regimes and their democratization to the modernization of economic and social structures that accompanied the industrialization of newly industrialized countries in Southern Europe, Latin America, and Asia. This industrialization was itself created by the delocalization of multinational firms from the centre and North–South transfers of capital and technology during this period. Inspired by neo-positivism and modernization (as below), the argumentation holds that these changes brought about a Westernization of cultural and ideological values of the majority of the population, thus creating favourable conditions for the re-emergence of democracy and the emergence of a liberal current within the authoritarian regimes.

As to the eclectic and pluralist approaches, they explain the crisis of authoritarian regimes by a combination of various external and internal political and economic factors. Dahl's (1971) analysis, which serves as a reference for some recent studies on democratic transition, may be classified in this group. Dahl notes that a government becomes more tolerant and open when the costs of repression seem higher than those of liberalization to certain regime actors. In addition, two circumstances favour this modification in the leaders' evaluations: the loss of the governmental monopoly on coercion and the growing dependence (notably, economic) of the state on external forces. Huntington (1984) attributes the crisis of authoritarian regimes to external pressure in favour of democracy and to the internal economic development of the societies concerned. He stresses that since 1973, successive American governments have geared their foreign policy towards the democratization of authoritarian regimes, because of the growing interdependence of socialist and capitalist systems and the unification of the world market. In such a context, political democracy seemed more desirable than authoritarianism. On the one hand, political democracy is based on a less centralized decision-making system and is therefore more adapted to the rules of economic liberalism; on the other hand, since it favours the adherence to capitalist values, it serves the interests of the USA and their Western allies better. According to Huntington, the economic development experienced by several peripheral societies since 1950 further strengthens possibilities of democratization of authoritarian regimes, in so far as it allows the democratic objectives to be more easily reconciled with those of national security, social justice, national independence, and political stability.

In the final analysis, all these explanations have only relative and approximate value, as their hypotheses can neither be conclusively verified with certainty nor generalized across all cases. Nevertheless, it must be recognized that only the eclectic approaches which take into account links between internal and external variables, allow light to be shed on possible common causes of the successive crises experienced by several authoritarian regimes in Southern Europe, Latin American and Southeast Asia in the post-1973 period.

Phases and Modalities of Democratic Transitions

Continuing democratic transitions constitute the only logical solution to the internal crisis of authoritarian regimes. In a context characterized by external pressures favouring reformist leaders and the absence of an insurrectionary movement, the likelihood of an external intervention or the overthrow of the regime by a revolution is indeed extremely remote. Furthermore, every attempt to consolidate the authoritarian regime can only perpetuate or aggravate the political crisis, as the Chilean case shows (see Montecinos and Gillespie, this volume, chapters 4 and 2).

However, the comparison of democratic transitions in Southern Europe, Latin America or Asia in the last fifteen years shows that their development can take on a wide range of forms from one country or region to another. In most instances, the re-establishment of polyarchic democratic institutions was preceded by a phase, which varied in duration from case to case, of opening up or liberalization (see Malloy, 1987; Baloyra, 1987; Kaufman, 1986; Gillespie, this volume, chapter 2). In other instances (Greece, Argentina, Portugal), the crisis of the authoritarian regime led very rapidly to the installation of democracy (see Diamandouros, 1986; Viola and Mainwaring, 1984; Bruneau and MacLeod, 1986). An analysis of the objectives and characteristics of the phases of liberalization and democratization can put the importance of these differences into perspective.

As was already emphasized, the outcome of the transitions is the installation of polyarchic democracy. This assumes the prior negotiation of a *compromise* or pact between moderate elements of the regime and 'loyal' forces of the opposition. Given the largely secret nature of these negotiations, only a comparative analysis of the reforms adopted during the transitions allows us to deduce the approximate terms of this compromise. Such an analysis shows that these terms vary according to the specific balance of power between opposition and regime in each country. Nevertheless, it seems that in all cases, four demands were formulated by the regime in exchange for the re-establishment of democratic liberties and institutions. These were: (a) an amnesty for offences committed by representatives of the authoritarian regime; (b) the exclusion of radical (in particular, communist) parties from future governments; (c) continued repression against 'disloyal' forces; (d) postponement of social and economic reforms and acceptance of the liberal capitalist model. The conclusion of such a compromise marks the beginning of the actual democratic phase, which is characterized by the *institutionalization* of the rules and procedures guaranteeing the exercise of fundamental rights and freedoms, election of the rulers by universal suffrage, party competition and alternation in power, and the accountability of the governing. As emphasized by Rustow (1970), and Schmitter and O'Donnell (1986, IV), among others, the notion of institutionalization denotes the *effective recognition* (notably in the form of constitutional laws) and the *acceptance* of these rules and procedures by most interest groups.

Conversely, the phase of *opening up* or *liberalization* is characterized by the absence of a compromise and thus by reforms which, while similar to the ones of the democratization phase – lifting of emergency measures, recognition of individual and collective rights, and, in some cases, re-establishment of universal suffrage and multipartisanism – are neither guaranteed by the state nor formally accepted by the various interest groups. Thus, these reforms have a provisional and arbitrary character. They can be annulled at any time by the regime without any legal recourse against this decision on the part of the opposition. The 'abertura' is a strategy that aims at evaluating the inherent risks of the re-establishment of democratic freedoms (Przeworski, 1986). Furthermore, it tries to put in place conditions favourable to a compromise between duros and blandos, on the one hand, and blandos and reformist organizations of the opposition, on the other hand (see below). Consequently, this period is characterized by great uncertainty and by contradictory measures and decisions. As far as it can effectively lead to a consolidation of authoritarianism, some authors have associated it with a remodelling of the façade of the regime rather than an exploratory phase aiming at an evaluation of the costs and possibilities of democratization (see Cardoso, 1979; Martins, 1982; Wurfel, this volume, chapter 5).

The foregoing specifications permit the character of the diverse scenarios of democratic transition to be viewed in perspective. According to several authors, the rapid but apparent re-establishment of democratic liberties and institutions is imposed by the seriousness of the legitimacy crisis or the social crisis accompanying the internal crisis of the regime. However, if one admits that the institutionalization of democracy begins with the conclusion of a compromise between the regime and the moderate forces of the opposition, one has to recognize that the said developments do not indicate that the process has reached its end point. Thus, the scenarios of abandonment of power (Argentina, Greece, Portugal) or of transfer of power (Peru, Bolivia, Uruguay, Philippines, for example) constitute a form of opening up which is designed to prepare the conditions for the conclusion of a new social pact as well as for the effective recognition of the rules of polyarchy.

CONDITIONS FOR THE EMERGENCE AND CONSOLIDATION OF DEMOCRACY

The analysis of the conditions for the installation and consolidation of the new democracies in Southern Europe, Latin America, and Asia draws its inspiration largely from theories of the emergence and stabilization of polyarchies. These theories were developed by American and European sociologists during the 1960s and 1970s. Two common traits characterize these theories: on the one hand, they associate the installation of this type of democracy with the conclusion of a *compromise* between the dominant actors and social groups. This compromise centres on the definition of collective objectives of power and the modalities of participation in the decision-making process. On the other hand, they link the *stabilization* of polyarchies to the development of a *social consensus*. However, the links between these two processes constitute an important point of divergence among sociologists, in particular, after the publication of Moore's (1966) and Rustow's (1970) works.

According to these two authors, most sociological theories (neo-positivist modernization theories, psycho-cultural theories, structuralist theory) confuse the conditions of installation and consolidation of democracy, since they claim that the conclusion of the democratic pact is *preceded* by the development of a social consensus. The authors emphasize that this thesis follows from the fact that these theories attribute the emergence of a new democratic regime (or any other political change) to objective (economic and social) or subjective (psycho-cultural) variables (transformations). However, the emergence of democracy (as any other political change) is exclusively founded on political factors, that is, on a struggle or balance of power between different classes (or social groups). Consequently, socioeconomic and/or cultural transformations leading to the development of a social consensus can only be considered as consequences of a democratic pact, or conditions for its consolidation.

The comparative analysis of democratic transitions in Southern Europe and Latin America shows that most authors refer to Moore's and Rustow's conceptions. Some of them subdivide these processes into three distinct phases: the phase of emergence or apparent installation of democracy (opening up) which is characterized by a struggle with uncertain outcome between the dominant actors and groups; the phase of effective installation of democracy which is characterized by a compromise among the moderate elements of the dominant groups (protagonists and supporters); and the phase of consolidation which is based on the development of a social consensus (see O'Donnell, Schmitter and Whitehead, 1986; Malloy, 1987; Baloyra, 1987). Basically, the question is tackled from two angles: the origins of the social consensus and the organizational and institutional forms through which it is realized.

Origins and forms of the social consensus

Although the notion of social consensus has been employed frequently by sociologists since its formulation by A. Comte, it has taken on several different connotations. Some authors (among them Dahrendorf, 1959) refuse to associate it with democracy, since it implies a limitation of free expression of conflicts of interest. Others also object to its use because it presents an analogy with the notion of corporatism. This concept denotes the existence of an organic relation between state and interest groups and, thus, the control of the state over civil society.

Nevertheless, it can be noted that in the few studies on the consolidation of new democracies in Southern Europe and Latin America, most authors attach a relatively similar meaning to the term. It designates the alleviation of conflicts of interest or a convergence of interests (of individuals or groups), represented by more civilized forms of competition and the emergence of different forms of collaboration (solidarity) between the members of society. Conforming to the theses of M. Weber and E. Durkheim, the origin of this consensus is generally associated with the adherence of a majority of citizens to the cultural values and forms of behaviour of modern democratic (or Western) societies. These values and this behaviour – individualism, rationalism, respect for others, moderation, etc. – are inherited from the Judaeo-Christian tradition and the philosophy of the Enlightenment.

The analysis of the mechanisms through which the diffusion of these cultural elements takes place plays a somewhat minor role in the studies on the consolidation of the new democracies in Southern Europe and Latin America. Without doubt, this is due to methodological problems (see Boudon and Bourricaud, 1982, 601). Nevertheless, three types of explanations are invoked.

According to the first explanation, the penetration by Western norms and models of behaviour, in particular, of the upper and middle classes of the countries in these regions, was linked to the progressive economic and political opening up of these societies in the post-1945 period.

According to the second explanation, the adherence of an important proportion of the citizens to Western cultural values is a consequence of the modernization of economic and social structures that took place in these societies during the 1950s, 1960s, and 1970s. This explanation (see Giner and Sevilla, 1980; Lipietz, 1985; Hermet, this volume, chapter 1), is largely inspired by modernization theories (Lipset, 1959, 1960; Deutsch, 1961; Gerschenkron, 1962; Adelman and Morris, 1967; Apter, 1965). According to these theories, there exists a causal relation between the modernization of economic structures, the differentiation of social structures, and the stability of democratic political institutions. On the basis of a series of statistical indicators (per capita income, percentage distribution of the active population according to economic sectors, number of media sources and doctors per capita, percentage of students enrolled in primary, secondary and post-secondary education, and so on) these approaches tried to prove this link by establishing correlations between levels of income, industrialization, urbanization, and education in a society and the degree of legitimacy and efficiency of its democratic institutions. The fact that this type of explanation occupies a relatively marginal place in the recent studies on the consolidation of new democracies in Southern Europe and Latin America is without doubt due to the numerous criticisms it provoked (see Moore, 1966; Rustow, 1970; Dahl, 1971; O'Donnell, 1973; Przeworski, 1986; Schmitter, 1980; Touraine, 1987). The reason for this was the arbitrariness of these correlations and the impossibility to generalize them across all cases. However, one has to acknowledge that several examples brought forward to prove the non-validity of the modernization theories – democratic underdeveloped countries (for example, India, Turkey, Philippines) or developed or underdeveloped authoritarian countries (USSR, GDR, Argentina, Uruguay, Paraguay, Indonesia, and others) – no longer apply, for the very reason of attempts at democratization (successful or in process) in these countries. Consequently, certain authors, among them Huntington (1984), consider it necessary to reassert the value of this paradigm.

The third explanation associates the adherence to democratic values (and institutions) with the evaluation done by every individual on the potential of the democratic system to satisfy his aspirations, needs, and interests. The basis of this is the individual's place (or role) within the system and the influence on his perceptions exerted by the positions and attitudes of the social groups (family, professional association, church, etc.) to which he belongs.

On the whole, the authors are more concerned with the effects of these cultural changes on the stabilization of the democratic political institutions than with the modalities of their diffusion. However, in so far as it is very difficult to delimit concretely the process through which values and behaviour influence the transformation of political and social institutions (see on this point Eisenstadt, 1966, 7), the authors generally centre their analyses on the second aspect, that is, on the transformations that convey or embody the social consensus and determine the consolidation of political democracy. In this respect, one finds a fairly broad-based agreement on the fact that six principles and categories of transformation favour the consolidation of polyarchic systems.

(1) *Free expression of divergent interests due to the autonomization of civil society.* This autonomization is linked to the creation and institutionalization of a series of organizations aiming at the representation or defence of economic, cultural, religious, professional, or other interests of the various *latent* or *nominal* social groups (see Dahrendorf, 1959 and Schmitter, 1988).

(2) *Formation of majority governments and peaceful alternation in power due to the development of political parties that are pluralist* in their ideological orientation, *unified* as organizations, and *legitimate* due to the enlargement of their territorial, sectorial, and social bases.

(3) *Enhancement of the legitimacy of organizations belonging to civil society and of the efficiency of political representation of interests due to the deepening of relations between political parties and interest groups* (see Schmitter, 1988).

(4) *Acceptance of the constitution by a majority of citizens, interest groups, and political parties.*

(5) *Setting up of mechanisms, be they formal or informal, limited or permanent, of consultation (concertation) between the state, the political parties, and the principal interest groups* (in particular, trade unions and employers' associations).

(6) *Deepening of effective recognition of the principle of citizenship* (administrative and territorial decentralization of the decision-making process, broadening of access to governmental information

protection of minority rights, etc.) (see O'Donnell, Schmitter and Whitehead, IV, 1986).

The Prospects of Consolidation of the New Democracies in Southern Europe and Latin America

The few studies focusing on this subject (among them the texts in the third part of this volume) reveal that at this point in time, only post-Franco Spain corresponds to the criteria that suggest the consolidation of democracy. Recent publications insist, in particular, on the profound transformation of ideology and cultural values, the establishment of a pluralist two-party system, the autonomization of civil society, and the development of relations between parties and interest groups that have characterized the evolution of this society since the end of the 1970s (see, in particular, Rodriguez and Enrique, 1987; Diaz, 1987; Share, 1986). In all other countries, the prospects for consolidation of the new democratic regimes appear rather gloomy due to the fragility and the limits of the social consensus. All but some authors (Vergopoulos, this volume, chapter 6; Lipietz, 1985) maintain that this situation cannot be related to the economic and financial crisis that puts a break on economic development and social reform in these societies, although it renders the adoption of measures suited for a solution of this crisis much more problematic (see Touraine, 1987; Pereira, this volume, chapter 9; O'Donnell, 1988).

The factors mentioned most often in this respect are: (a) the persistence of archaic or traditional political attitudes or ideologies (nationalism, populism, clientelism, corporatism) hindering the establishment of mechanisms of social consultation and the adoption of realistic collective objectives (a problem of particular importance in Brazil, Argentina, and in the Philippines – see Boschi; Pereira; Ducatenzeiler; Wurfel, this volume, chapters 10, 9, 11 and 5); (b) the weakness or absence of organizations representing interests within civil society (in particular, in Brazil, Argentina, Greece, Turkey, and Portugal) and/or the absence of relations between these organizations and the political parties (Chile, see Montecinos, this volume, chapter 4; Brazil, see Boschi and Bruneau, this volume, chapters 10, 8). In this respect, Gillespie emphasizes (this volume, chapter 2) that in certain countries (Brazil and Uruguay) the absence of links between civil society and the political parties is compensated by relations between the political parties and the military, which tend to increase the possibilities for a stabilization of democracy; (c) the institutionalization of conflict and/or the upholding of corporatist and clientelist forms of consultation blocking the installation of truly democratic consultation (see Boschi and Ducatenzeiler, this volume, chapters 10, 11); (d) internal and external division of the political parties, in particular in Brazil and Portugal, favouring the adoption of pluralist rather than majoritarian electoral systems (see Blais and Dion, this volume, chapter 12) and constitutions that slow down the consolidation of the political system (see Bruneau and MacLeod, this volume, chapters 8, 7). However, MacLeod maintains in his study that the emergence of a centrist two-party system in Portugal, favouring the election of a majority government in 1987, opened the way to new constitutional reforms susceptible of furthering the liberalization of the economy and the stabilization of polyarchic political institutions.

In conclusion, several elements of a consensus emerge from the comparative analysis of the studies on processes of transition and democratic consolidation in Southern Europe, Latin America, and Southeast Asia, despite the diversity of cases examined and paradigms employed. In particular, one can list the following points: (1) The democratic transitions were initiated and controlled by the authoritarian regimes in place. (2) Their essential goal was the establishment of polyachic democratic regimes and not the modification of the existing social and economic structures. (3) These transformations were made possible because of the negotiation of a (political and sometimes economic) compromise between the dominant social groups (protagonists and moderate supporters). (4) Except for Spain, the consolidation of this compromise and of the democratic political institutions established on this basis remains precarious due to the absence or weakness of the social consensus.

Note

1. This chapter was translated by Gerd Schönwälder.

References

Adelman, I. and Taft Morris, C. (1967) *Society, Politics and Economic Development: A Quantitative Approach* (Baltimore: Johns Hopkins University Press).

Apter, D. (1965) *The Politics of Modernization* (Chicago: Chicago University Press).

Baloyra, E. (1987) *Comparing New Democracies* (Boulder: Westview Press).

Boudon, R. and Bourricaud, F. (1982) *Dictionnaire critique de la sociologie* (Paris: Presses Universitaires de France).

Bruneau, T. and A. MacLeod, (1986) *Politics in Contemporary Portugal: Parties and the Consolidation of Democracy* (Boulder: Lynne Rienner).

Cardoso, F. H. (1979) 'Les impasses du régime autoritaire : le cas brésilien', *Notes et Etudes documentaires*, no. 45–46, pp. 89–107.

Coverdale, J. (1979) *The Political Transformation of Spain after Franco* (New York, Toronto: Praeger).

Dahl, R. (1971) *Polyarchy: Participation and Opposition* (New Haven, London: Yale University Press).

Dahrendorf, R. (1959) *Class and Class Conflict in Industrial Society* Stanford: Stanford University Press.

De Tocqueville, A. (1835) 'De la démocratie en Amérique' in: *Oeuvres complètes* (Paris: Gallimard, 1952–70).

Deutsch, K. (1961) 'Social Mobilization and Political Development', *American Political Science Review*, vol. 55, pp. 463–515.

Diamandouros, P. N. (1986) 'Regime Change and the Prospects for Democracy in Greece: 1974–1983' in: G. O'Donnell, P. Schmitter and L. Whitehead (eds), vol. 1, pp. 138–65.

Diaz, E. (1987) *La transición a la democracia : clanes idelógicas, 1976–1986* (Madrid: EUDEMA).

Eisenstadt, S. N. (ed.) (1966) *Readings in Social Evolution and Development* (Toronto: Pergamon).

Faucher, P. (1981) *Le Brésil des militaires* (Montréal: Presses de l'Université de Montréal).

Furtado, C. (1981) *O Brazil pos milagre* (Rio de Janeiro: Paz e Terra). French translation: *Le Brésil après le miracle* (Paris: Maison des Sciences de l'Homme, 1987).

Gerschenkron, A. (1962) *Economic Backwardness in Historical Perspective* (Cambridge: Cambridge University Press).

Giner, S. and Sevilla, E. (1980) 'From Despotism to Parliamentarism: Class Domination and Political Order in the Spanish State' in: R. Scase (ed.), *The State in Western Europe* (London: Croom Helm).

Huntington, S. (1984) 'Will more Countries become Democratic?' *Political Science Quarterly*, vol. 99, no. 2, Summer, pp. 193–219.

Kaufman, R. R. (1986) 'Liberalization and Democratization in South America: Perspectives from the 1970s' in G. O'Donnell, P. Schmitter and L. Whitehead (eds), Vol. III, pp. 85–108.

Linz, J. C. (1979) 'Europe's Southern Frontier: Evolving Trends Toward What?', *Daedalus*, vol. 1, pp. 175–209.

Linz, J. C. (1982) *The Transition from Authoritarian Regimes to Democratic Political Systems and the Problems of Consolidation of Political Democracy*, paper prepared for the International Political Science Association Tokyo Round Table, 29 March–1 April.

Lipietz, A. (1985) *Mirages et miracles* (Paris: La Découverte).
Lipset, S. M. (1959) 'Some Social Requisites of Democracy: Economic Development and Political Legitimacy', *American Political Science Review*, vol. 53 pp. 69–105.
Lipset, S. M. (1960) 'Economic Development and Democracy' in *Political Man* (New York: Doubleday).
Malloy, J. (ed.) (1987) *Authoritarians and Democrats* (Pittsburgh: Pittsburgh University Press).
Martins, L. (1982) 'Le régime autoritaire brésilien et la "libéralisation" politique', *Notes et Etudes documentaires*, no. 4657–4658, pp. 9–26.
Menges, C. C. (1978) *Spain: the Struggle of Democracy Today* (London: Center for Strategic and International Studies, Sage).
Moore, B. (1966) *The Social Origins of Dictatorship and Democracy* (Boston: Beacon Press).
O'Donnell, G. (1973) *Modernización y autoritarismo* (Buenos Aires: Padós).
O'Donnell, G., Schmitter P. and Whitehead, L. (eds) (1986) *Transitions from Authoritarian Rule: Prospects for Democracy* (Baltimore: Johns Hopkins University Press). Four volumes (in paperback): I *Southern Europe*, II *Latin America*, III *Comparative Perspectives*, IV *Tentative Conclusions about Uncertain Democracies*.
O'Donnell, G. (1988), communication presented at the Conference 'Internationalization of Political Democracy: Problems and Perspectives' (Montreal: Université de Montréal) 28 September–2 October.
Pereira, L. C. B. (1985) *Os pactos políticos* (São Paulo: Brasiliense).
Poulantzas, N. (1975) *La crise des dictatures* (Paris: Maspero).
Przeworski, A. (1986) 'Some Problems in the Study of the Transition to Democracy' in: G. O'Donnell, P. Schmitter and L. Whitehead (eds), Vol. III pp. 47–64.
Rodriguez, I. and Enrique, J. (1987) *Después de una dictadura : cultura autoritaria y transición política en España* (Madrid; Centro de Estudios Constitucionales).
Rouquié, A. (1983) 'Demande démocratique et désir de révolution', *Projet*, no. 176, pp. 603–14.
Rustow, D. A. (1970) 'Transitions to Democracy', *Comparative Politics*, April, pp. 337–63.
Schmitter, P. (1980) *Speculations about the Prospective Demise of Authoritarian Regimes and its Possible Consequences*, paper prepared for the project 'Prospects for Democracy: Transitions from Authoritarian Rule', Woodrow Wilson Center for International Studies, Washington DC.
Schmitter, P. (1988) *Organized Interests and Democratic Consolidation in Southern Europe*, paper presented at the Conference 'Internationalization of Political Democracy: Problems and Perspectives (Montreal, Université de Montréal) 28 September–2 October).
Schumpeter, J. (1942) *Capitalism, Socialism and Democracy* (New York: Harper).
Share, D. (1986) *The Making of Spanish Democracy* (New York: Praeger).
Share, D. and Mainwaring, S. (1987) 'Transitions through Transaction: Democratization in Brazil and Spain' in: W. A. Selcher (ed.) *Political Liberalization in Brazil* (Boulder: Westview Press) pp. 175–7.

Stepan, A. (1986) 'Paths Toward Redemocratization: Theoretical and Comparative Considerations' in: G. O'Donnell, P. Schmitter and L. Whitehead (eds), Vol. III pp. 64–85.
Touraine, A. (1987) *La Parole et le sang* (Paris: Odile Jacob).
Viola, E. and Mainwaring, S. (1984) *Transitions to Democracy: Brazil and Argentina in the 1980s*, working paper no. 21, Helen Kellogg Institute for International Studies, Notre-Dame University, July.
Whitehead, L. (1986) 'International Aspects of Democratization' in: G. O'Donnell, P. Schmitter and L. Whitehead (eds), Vol. III, pp. 3–47.

Part II
Democratic Transitions

1 From One Europe to the Other: From Liberal Authoritarianism to Authoritarian Democratization[1]

Guy Hermet

BETWEEN MEMORY LAPSES AND IMPROPRIETY

'Internationalization of Political Democracy: Issues and Prospects.' The simple title of this conference[2] could furnish ample subject matter for commentary when we consider the sub-themes that it inevitably implies. Without, however, going that far, the ideas that it suggests allow us to introduce the several preliminary and historical questions asked in these pages. These questions essentially concern the modest lessons to be learnt from historical European experience in evaluating at the present time the chances of democratization in what we will call, for convenience's sake, the Third World.

Use of the expression 'internationalization of democracy' is a reflection of our times. The day before yesterday, democracy was the universal value offered for the enlightenment of all peoples, a virtually unavoidable and indefensible model that represented the only political modernity, wherever it may be. Yesterday, on the contrary, it was no longer perceived to be anything but a sham, developed in a ethnocentric manner by those industrialized societies marked by Western Christian tradition. A prerogative of the rich, it was not exportable. Besides, it would have been unjust and tyrannical on the part of Western nations to imagine that it could be suitable for other peoples, peoples whose destiny was to invent their own modernity. And today the cycle has come full circle, and ethnocentrism transforms itself into philanthropy. People's Power has triumphed well in Manila on the basis of a very Western inspired model. Why should it not soon prevail, in accordance with this same model, in Seoul, Taipei, Algiers, even Rangoon and elsewhere in the tropics?

However, recourse to the term 'internationalization' does not only translate a certain veiled general optimism. It implies a somewhat inexpressible interrogation. If, really, democracy finds itself on the way to spreading even further throughout the world, can it spread everywhere in an identical fashion? Above all, must it spread not so much in conformity with the real history of democratization, but as seen in the popular image of national liberation to which history these days has reduced it? Should we not, on the contrary, rediscover that which was once this liberation in Western Europe or in North America, without shirking the brutal irony of past events and their often harmful linkages. That is, the multiplicity of our own – Western – advance towards democracy, as well as the starting points so often paradoxical and almost shameful because of their often authoritarian pathways.

After all, England, mother of parliamentary government and, thus, of democracy as we normally understand it, invented it to the beat of the furious reactionary outburst that followed its revolution in the second half of the 17th century. Inspired by John Locke and the lawyers of the landowners, the Bill of Rights of 1689 was hardly anything more than a charter of suppression of economic and political rights of the humble but boundless population of non-landowners. Parliamentarianism, creator of the *politeia* of our times, merged together at its origin with the imposition of suffrage based on property qualifications and increased repression of the poor. Similarly, French revolutionaries of the 1790s rapidly understood that potential voters were in no better a place than on the European battlefields where they sent them to be massacred. Then, for good measure, they opened the way for modern dictatorships by entrusting the role of arbiter of a government that eluded them to generals of whom the most well known would later be Napoleon Bonaparte. Besides, the adjective 'political' placed side by side in the title of the conference with the term 'democracy' enlightens, all in all, these false paradoxes for the use of conformists. It appears almost as a restrictive label.

In a strict sense, however, democracy can be nothing but political. On the other hand, it is precisely from this formal democracy so criticized during the next-to-last ideological mode that democracy progresses, a democracy, however unreal, that men of flesh and blood can enjoy. Only the existence of rules, even very superficial rules, shows itself capable of guaranteeing a minimal degree of liberty. On the other hand, the word 'democracy' itself only refers, on its own, to a formula for government. This being the case, either it is understood without an adjective, such as when Plato writes: 'let us see with what traits tyranny arises, because, as to its origin, it is fairly obvious that it comes from democracy' (Plato, 1966, 321); or it is qualified by the adjective 'political' to mean, according to common sense, that it is a matter of a democracy that is not ideal nor in the end totalitarian in its design for the creation of the New Man, but a democracy held back by the limiting rules of the majority's changing momentum; in short, of a kind of non-democracy, pleasant in the long run, called however democracy. But to speak for example of economic democracy amounts to referring to a more equal allocation of goods with inappropriate language, that is, to conjure up units of production managed quite plainly by producers, consumers, and non-consumers who would even have the right to want to do away with such units. The perspective is long term, just as with school board democracy or democratic unions that are currently managed by rather irremovable leaders (but as Plato said: and if the people want tyrants?). This is not to mention municipal democracy or voluntary associations that Jacques Godbout (1987) has shown to essentially correspond (only in Montreal?) to a relationship of domination of the users by permanent activists even more devoid of humour than old-style politicians.

Consequently, there is no pleonasm when speaking of political democracy in the sense that is of particular interest to us here. In a rather confusing yet essentially exact acceptance, the two last centuries were, in the Western area and in a larger universe, those of ever increasing rejection of pre-established hierarchies – say, at the beginning of the *ancien régime* – and of the conspicuously hereditary ways of legitimatization (of course, it is not a question here of alluding to the political dynasties of the democratic societies). People see themselves more and more as equals under whatever government, 'democratizing' the confusion between liberty and equality, following the example set by scholars. They took great pleasure, increasing daily, of the spectacle of the notables' waltz and then final removal, forgetting – to paraphrase De Tocqueville – that regimes on their last legs generally are worth more than those that immediately follow.

What we could thus call a democratic urge characterized and provided for modernity in Western Europe, North America, and elsewhere. And it developed largely by contravening the institutional differences existing between governmental regimes, provided that they all be new or 'modern', that is, to say, at least partially escaping the long past of hereditary legitimatization. It is here that our problems arise. Political democracy is born of this generic democracy that, in certain cases, has succeeded in spite of obstacles erected by the aristocratic representative regimes, as well as by the representative regimes that were inequitable in their initial practice as well as in their underlying inspiration. Elsewhere, political democracy had just as easily become the desired or unforeseen outgrowth of regimes that were rather indifferent or hostile to the electoral principal, regimes that were dictatorial, or to a greater or lesser extent, authoritarian. In sum, they had been rather severely at odds with the *ancien régime*, sort of 'discreditors' of established hierarchies, egalitarian in language, in short, liberal in the vague sense of the word.

When all is said and done, as Marc Augé notes, all of this comes down to the fact that spectators of the big political theatre chronically expect that their governments should give the illusion of a 'fresh start' (Augé, 1985, 31). The new-style semi-dictatorships have been able to give that impression, first in Europe and then elsewhere. There was a time, in France or in Germany, when Louis-Napoleon Bonaparte or Bismarck quite wholeheartedly fulfilled this expectation by shouting (in substance): 'The kings are dead! Long live the Emperor (of France or of the German people)!' Later, outside Europe, the group of Mexican bourgeois revolutionaries, Colonel Perón, and the Ortega brothers of Nicaragua have also repeated this behaviour to nearly general applause, as well as the Nehru dynasty in India (their slogan could have been: 'The Raj is dead! Long live us!'). Even so, since 1975 and the almost painless obliteration of the dictatorship in Spain, the authoritarian model of democratization has found itself rediscovered as if it were a surprising novelty. Moreover, everyone is already striving to erase from their memory the impure origins of the political liberation of the Spanish in the same way that lapses of memory had previously buried the role that liberal authoritarianism played in the democratic opening up of Europe of the last century. Today, as it doubtlessly was yesterday, the label on the democratic transition's bottle matters more than its actual content. It is advisable that, at any cost, democracy should appear to be born of itself, in accordance with a kind of peculiar immaculate conception. We should shout: 'The authoritarian King is dead! Long live the democratic King!'

Of course, this vision of Cassandra is completely barren of any impact on the practical political level. On this level, the remarks from the imperial balcony are precisely those that are the most important in instilling the obligation to follow the dictates of governments. The truly useful democratic truth comes from the mouth of those professionals who give the most flamboyant speeches, in much the same way that historical truth flows from the historians' inkwell. In our days, it ensures the self-satisfaction of Westerners, for it allows Europeans to forget that, of its own avail, authoritarianism ceased to be liberal during the interwar years; that it was then transformed with the connivance of certain national majorities into fascist or Nazi-style totalitarian tyranny, crushing minorities and proving Plato right. Today, their belief in democracy's immaculate self-birth similarly lets them forget that this form of government did not really consolidate itself in the greater part of the Western half of their continent until between the years 1945 and 1980, thus hardly being earlier – should that be hoped for – than in Latin America. Finally, this way of seeing things opportunely justifies the fury of Western Europeans, in their role as often neophyte democrats, who were only yesterday enthralled by Hitler, Mussolini, Dolfuss, Salazar, Primo de Rivera, Franco, Quisling, Degrelle or Pétain, by allowing them to make a clean sweep of their own dubious past. Their democratic systems, having reached rather belatedly a smooth cruising speed after inadmissable failures, Europeans – like North Americans – henceforth require that democracies built among other peoples should somehow sprout fully equipped. They want them without bonds and in absolute contrast with the prior non-democracy, springing up from the sole virtue of their citizens and leaders, in the total fulfilment of the respect of human rights.

Once again, it is not a question of doubting for one second that everything is not for the better in the best of democratic worlds. This philanthropy, indifferent to the real situation of men, includes one of the most appreciable advantages, that of assuring that our indignation escapes to the outside. It even brings a new and essential legitimacy, in opposition to Western democracies' frantic search for values: that of the 'non-democracy of others', furnishing, in short, the proof of our domestic democracy.

However, at the risk of appearing improper and insufficiently cooperative, it remains that we should also admit that the real history of whichever democracy – past, present, and probably to come – has nothing to do with the angelic concept of political liberation. For a long time, democratic regimes, or if not, then the longing for democracy, have emerged less as the fruit of a deliberate project to extend citizenship than as a function of non-premeditated impulses.

Moreover, up to the start of the 20th century and, again, in the middle of it, authoritarianism traced out one of the new political pathways of Western modernity, a quite distinct one, in the same way as the parliamentary or presidential regimes that planned the other of these pathways and, later, as a phase of political transformation that opens into present-day democracy. Of course, reviving the memory of this cutting episode is of no interest for those amongst us who make democracy their profession, and perhaps it is the same for their electoral supporters. This, however, should not motivate political analysts to restrain themselves to lucidity even when it is abrasive. This can represent its modest contribution to the difficult birth of political modernity outside the comfortable area of the advanced industrialized societies. This process almost necessarily proceeds amidst noise and fury. To want to hide it through some sort of ideological prudishness hinders the process more than it helps it.

THE FOUNDING AUTHORITARIANISM: SECOND EMPIRE AND GERMAN EMPIRE

In short, since we must rediscover the memory of the shocking experiences of the old democracies in order to better understand those that are only now emerging, it does not suffice to state, as does Barrington Moore (Moore, 1969), that there exists a 'reactionary capitalist', or authoritarian, pathway for Western political modernization. It is advisable to admit, furthermore, at least as a hypothesis, that it can involve a path leading to democratic modernity. Evidently, writers take it for granted that pre-democratic representative regimes have contributed to the production of practices, habits, environments, hazards, and wanted or contrary effects from which arise ulterior democratic developments as well as their accidents or their failures. There is no reason that the same proposition should be blacklisted in the case of at least some of the dictatorial governments of the last one hundred and fifty years, be they far or close in time. These have also generated both positive and contrary effects, going either in the direction of an expansion of political participation, or against it. Hardly any less than the representative governments, they also partake of the dynamics that emerge into democracy and its failures. At best, the democratic product of governments that are elected, or supposedly elected by some variable fraction of the population, would then appear more directly discernible. As for the rest, both the representative and authoritarian pathways can run parallel courses or be in conflict according to circumstances. Pushing things to their limits, for example, why not admit that the French Second Empire's ultimate legacy reveals itself as being generally 'democratizing', whereas that of the Weimar Republic can hardly be perceived to be anything but negative in this matter (on the other hand, the Weimar Republic is certainly the 'mother of dictatorship', like the Popular Unity government in Chile).

Of course, there is no discovery in this. Marx and his successors said it long ago, when studying what they called the Bonapartist phenomenon and likening it to a simple variant of the government of capitalist or bourgeois societies (the other form, more frequent in their view was, as we know, the parliamentary regime). What is more, Friedrich Engels went further than Marx in a letter that he sent him in 1866 (Rudel, 1960, 120). Of course, Engels took care to employ Marxian propositions concerning the global origins of the Bonapartist mechanism. However, when compared especially with Chancellor Bismarck's experience in Imperial Germany, this Bona-partism, made into a political category, appeared to him not as a regressive episode aroused by the momentary disarray of a dominant capitalist and bourgeois class that was scared by the social con-sequences of its own principled liberalism, but as a separate and complete form of the liberal strategy (a polysemous strategy since its normal framework does not confine itself to the parliamentary option). Going further, Engels apprehended the 'Bonapartist semi-dictatorship' as 'the true religion of the modern bourgeoisie, [...] which is not made to rule directly'. In his mind, it tended in reality to become the most authentic form of the State that he denoted as capitalist. It ceased to be 'the bourgeoisie's Special State' as Marx wanted it. On the contrary, it was the parliamentary and electoral path to Western political modernity that took on a special character, whereas the authoritarian and plebiscitary path of this modernity transformed itself almost into the norm.

At the start of the last third of the 19th century, at a time when universal suffrage had not really consolidated itself but in the two large continental European countries subjugated by strong govern-ments (France and Germany) and when the parliamentary regimes of the northern periphery of the same continent (among them, Great Britain) doggedly resisted the invasion of the electoral masses, Engels' remarks could be put down to simple common sense in view of the circumstances of his times. In addition, it came within the later perspective of growing personalization of top leadership of democratic government and the indefinite reinforcement of its executive machinery against parliamentary institutions. It was henceforth democracy itself that has become plebiscitary. However, Engels hardly foresaw the irony of a situation which he only thought of denouncing in order to further blacken the picture of capitalist and bourgeois domination. For him, there was no question of giving any credit to the Bonapartist dictatorships from some element of contribution to the opening up of democracy.

The French Second Empire and the German Empire clearly appear, however, as the authoritarian fathers of some of modern democracy's contents (Hermet, 1983). Common thinking is such that the evaluation of Napoleon III's regime remains generally negative. Be that as it may, the imperial government's policy of plebiscitary mobilization constituted in fact the counterweight to its dictatorial practices.

From this viewpoint, the personal deeds of the Emperor were clever, and would have generally born fruit if it had not been for the military defeat at Sedan. His Machiavellian nature allowed him in the end to present himself as the artisan of the re-establishment of universal male suffrage. Established in 1848, this law had in effect, been rapidly denatured by the Republican law of 31 May 1850 – adopted by the Assembly's liberal and conservative majority – that reduced the number of voters from 9.4 million to 6.8 million. Abiding by the constitution that compelled him to promulgate the text, the President Prince and future Emperor then had the foresight to ask the members of the Assembly for its repeal. They committed the blunder of rejecting the presidential request. This miscalculation provided the head of state with an unexpected – or carefully ripened – opportunity to become the defender of universal suffrage, which was re-established following the coup of 2 December 1851.

Arising under such auspices, the Second Empire's electoral strategy revealed itself to be no less effective later on. It conveyed first of all the new regime's additional concern to appeal to a parliamentary legitimacy wronged by its plebiscitary beginnings. Above all, it allowed the regime, thanks to the shrewdness of imperial commands and to the talent of the prefects, to mobilize a very broad popular support and in so doing laid the foundations for the modern running of French elections. The Emperor apparently absorbed the dominant characteristics of his middle and petty bourgeois supporters. He instructed the prefects to charm those who had some property (the 'parvenus') to push back the notables, who, more often than not, were held in contempt by the other social classes, and to present his power as a mixture of equality, law and order. At the same time, he tried to win over Catholics hurt by republican and revolutionary anticlericalism, notably through the legal recognition of confessional schools. In all, these precautions allowed the Second Empire's elections – referenda as well as legislative polls – not to be handicapped by massive abstentionism, as were those of the Weimar Republic. In turn, this broad participation rendered election rigging useless or marginal, since most electioneering is carried out before rather than during or following the poll. Furthermore, it appears that this participation increased with the years, and that it became more authentically representative of informed opinion to the extent that opposition votes increased to the point of indirectly consolidating the democratic nature of the imperial regime.

It was also the first regime in Europe, in 1867, to recognize the right to strike. Even before this recognition, it also showed a benevolent attitude with respect to the propagators of the First Internationale, in order, it is true, to counter the leaders of the pre-socialist movement lead by Blanqui. However, the Second Empire's durable imprint on the French democratic system is not found on this level, and remains of an electoral nature. Although unsuccessful in its attempt at institutional consolidation as with its plan to reconcile the two Frances, Jacobinic and Catholic, the Empire bequeathed on this level two essential elements of the political temperament of France.

The implanting of universal suffrage in the rural areas represents the first of these elements. In his *Tableau politique de la France de l'Ouest sous la Troisième République*, André Siegfried (Siegfried, 1913) showed how French peasants learned their role as voters thanks to the imperial regime. He also showed that the new generation of the victorious rural elected representatives of the notables class was born under the aegis of this regime, even if it was against them. Besides, most of the electoral control techniques proceed, similarly, from traditions established by the imperial prefects. This contribution to electoral skills can be seen in various ways. Be that as it may, however, Republican France is indebted to the Second Empire in that the extension of suffrage was not accompanied by a parallel development of abstentionism. Hardly a damaging development, if it remains temporary as in Great Britain, but one which leads to and aggravates the disrepute of the representative regime if it persists, as in Southern Europe or in Latin America. To avoid this danger, France had, it is true, to pay the price of State clientelism established by the administrative authorities in the rural regions. But this type of clientelism was probably less harmful, from a democratic perspective, than the private clientelism that it replaces.

On the other side, the persistence of a Bonapartist temperament in the French political make-up represents the second enduring mark left by the Second Empire (it being understood that the expression does not refer to some sort of dynastic loyalty, but support for a concept of national union, assertion of hostility towards 'divisive' parties, and admission of a preference for a strong but essentially republican government, and also a sign of the citizens' need to identify with the person of a democratically elected head of state). René Rémond (Rémond, 1977) was not the first to notice that this temperament leads to Gaullism (without a doubt it is also found in the support for President Mitterrand). Along with the liberal temperament and the Jacobin temperament – democratic or socialist – it forms one of the three major components of French political culture. It is, moreover, the most specific component of this culture, its democratic content probably explaining why its authoritarian counterpart never could give rise to a really intense version of fascism in France. When M. Chirac is accused of Bonapartism, it is basically a question of a compliment; no one has the idea of accusing M. Le Pen of the same.

In the Europe of the last century, the other classical example of authoritarianism begetting modernity is supplied by the German Empire, modelled in its political lay-out by Chancellor Bismarck from 1862 to 1890. Of course, and even if it resembles in many respects the Bonapartist plan, the 'Bismarckian' project exhibits distinct features. Partly, it is the product of a specific, somewhat topographical, Bonapartism, thanks to which a bourgeois and western liberal Germany 'handed off the sceptre' to a military, aristocratic and eastern agrarian Germany in order to accelerate the process of national unification. And partly, but in view of what preceded it, it represented in the same way a formula for an emerging government whose dominant authoritarian style simplified, as it were, the strictly political debate in order to save stored energies first and foremost for industrial development and cultural construction of a barely unified nation. Elsewhere in Europe, the emergence of political modernity was achieved through a series of sequences, generally separated by long intervals, going from the formation of territorial states, the posturing of elites towards central power, and on to the admission of the masses into the electoral game. In Germany, on the contrary, these sequences sped up during the last third of the 19th century, with a privileged position granted to the national unification venture.

But in spite of this kind of precipitation, similar to that of the Second Empire, the Bismarckian experience left a deep and lasting mark on the political modernity of Germany. Certainly, this mark was hardly at the electoral level, even if Bismarck also instituted universal suffrage in 1867 and if the origins of both German Christian and Social Democracies go back to that era. Bismarck's strategy of electoral mobilization ended in failure. The electoral systems remained too unequal and heterogeneous – according to the regions – to win the support of the masses, all the more so since the small non-industrialized German states remained strongly over-represented until 1918. Moreover, a cultural obstacle played against the electoral mobilization of Germans in favour of the Empire.

It certainly seems that Bismarck would have wished, following Napoleon III, to win the support of the independent farmers. But this plan came up against the socio-religious reality of the country. In effect, the small and medium independent farmers were mostly concentrated in the south-west, notably in Bavaria, and they reacted negatively to the Protestant-sounding policy on cultural identification – the *Kulturkampf* – lead by the Chancellor. As an indirect consequence, the fact that they were rallying around either the big Catholic party (the *Zentrum*), which integrated them in a kind of confessional counter-society, or the Agrarian Party frustrated any vague plebiscitary desire of the imperial regime. Consequently, the political socialization of Germans continued to be primarily performed in the framework of martial apprenticeship imposed by conscription rather than through elections. But it is true that conscription soon saw itself reinforced by another instrument of integration, which represented the alternative to direct electoral mobilization. This instrument could have been called the 'Welfare State' if that expression had existed at the time. In any case, it prefigured and even invented the expression, both as an essential resource and as the most cherished product – much more than suffrage – of the masses of the future modern democracies.

The social security policy initiated by the imperial state supplied, in effect, this alternative. At the start, a favourable terrain was quickly opened up by the radicalization of the German workers' movement (a radicalization that emerged particularly during the Gotha Congress of 1875, with the unification of the socialist movement under the aegis of its Marxist faction). Bismarck profited from this phenomenon by inspiring the repressive laws of 1878 that subjected social democratic militants to a form of siege. He further exploited it by borrowing from it most of the elements of the moderate socialist's programme.

Social democracy's revolutionary alignment allowed the imperial government to contrast it with its own reassuring option of paternalistic protection of workers. An option that aimed at the same time at making them dependent on the State, and at offering them a vital security supposedly capable of diverting them from political action, or from autonomous, or even radical, union activities. Even more than the vague worker impulses of the Second Empire, this state paternalism brings to mind certain aspects of the populist experiences of 20th-century Latin America. Even if the economic resources employed were infinitely more important in the German case, and even if the style of this paternalism seems rather bureaucratic and only slightly demagogic in its language, the ultimate demobilization was the same. It tended to temper the proletariat, to hem the unions in the network of jointly managed protective institutions, in short, to orient the workers' movement in the direction of a peaceful democracy to come.

The revolutionary convulsions of 1918 and 1919, the fall of the Weimar Republic and the rise of Nazism remind us that this strategy was for the moment not enough to insure the democratic socialization of Germans. In spite of the paternal care of the Iron Chancellor and his successors, or rather because of them, the German working class stayed in a *de facto* minority situation, without the possibility of a decisive electoral victory. This freeze explains the success of the idea of a social rupture defended by the Communist Party during the 1920s, and therefore the weakness of the republican regime's popular foundations during the same period. For their part, the middle class did not easily find their democratic status under the Empire, this being a persistent shortcoming of the Weimar party system, too close to the imperial aristocratic model in its conservative element and too marked by the communist shadow in its popular element. From this arose the attraction of the Nazi Party, and later regime, with a large segment of the middle class, finally convinced of having found a political position and rank.

In the long term, however, the Bismarckian contribution to democratic modernity cannot be denied in spite of these catastrophic accidents. Hidden child of Imperial Germany, the Welfare State is today to government what gold is to currency, even if the democracies try hard to believe or to have others believe that their legitimacy comes from suffrage rather than from welfare benefits or food stamps. Or at least, if democracy still has two teats, universal suffrage and the material security that democracy guarantees, it owes them as much to the dictatorships of the last century as to the post-1914 democratic regimes.

AUTHORITARIAN DEMOCRATIZATION AT THE PRESENT TIME

Basically, the incongruity of this assertion really comes only from the scandal that it later incites, when authoritarianism ceased to be liberal in the interwar period and transformed itself into Nazi-style racist and totalitarian tyranny. It is another thing for the fascist dictatorship. Many agree that it decisively modernized the economic structure of Italian society.[3] Some even acknowledge that it broke the abstentionist tradition of Italians with the aid of their forced but much accepted enlistment in the single party (Christian democracy or the Communist Party later replacing it as frameworks of political activity).[4] But to give the Hitlerian abomination a kind of commendation in view of certain of its eventually 'democratizing' consequences is evidently beyond all understanding, even decency; and this even though it indisputably and irreversibly crushed the old landed military oligarchy that had hindered German democracy up until 1930, and whose disappearance goes hand in hand with the successful post-1948 democratization.

Whence the heuristic difficulties that later appeared during the 1970s, when the Franco dictatorship appeared to make itself, intentionally or not, the forerunner of Spanish democratization, and when the 'Spanish transition' came to be taken as a model of a new political technology of controlled extinction of authoritarianism led by the authoritarians themselves. Of course, the model does not exist in a premeditated way and finds itself amply rebuilt and idealized after the event. But the Spanish experience effectively suggests new ideas about the contributions of dictatorships to democratic modernity, to the point that conservatives of the last 15 years seize upon it to calm their apprehensions in the face of the progressive disappearance of Latin American authoritarianisms, particularly in Brazil, Uruguay and now in Chile. All things considered, does not the consolidation of democracy continue to appear as the almost fortuitous result of mechanisms that could well be authoritarian in their origins as well as in their primary intentions? And conversely, are not the most zealous and hurried architects of uncompromising democratization ending up, in certain cases, with exactly the opposite result to what they were looking for, namely, a military coup that they indirectly brought about?

However, this time, contrary to what happened in the case of the Bonapartist or Bismarckian strategies, the direct electoral intentions of the leadership remains of secondary importance and even ineffectual on many levels. In Franco's Spain, repeated recourse to popular referenda used from 1945 onwards on the initiative of the Catholic ministers siding with Franco remained a simple mockery, largely barren of the emotional value of Napoleon III's plebiscites. Later, the non-competitive election of some members of the *Cortes* also left little trace on the Spanish mentality, if it was not perhaps as a perverse example of what non-democratic elections can be. Similarly, towards the 1960s and 1970s, the attempt by conservative Christian Democrats to create political associations as substitutes for, or parodies of, parties ended in an absolute fiasco. Finally, after the death of Franco, the failure of the government of Arias Navarro and of the ministers Fraga Iribane and Areilza proved itself no less obvious than when it was a matter of imposing on the budding Spanish democracy the yoke of a party system that excludes the extreme left, and especially the Communist Party. With the exception of the fascist regimes, almost all the authoritarian governments born during the last one and a half centuries in the West set out immediately, or later in their existence, to arrange new conditions for democracy, in restricting the legal political pluralism to only those sectors devoid of programmes of social upheaval. But this limited pluralism being nothing other than that which persists in an unofficial way under the dictatorship, it is not enough to legalize it in order to achieve the legitimization of a democracy true to the wishes of its authoritarian patrons. This legitimacy cannot be reconciled with the explicit exclusion of a segment of the political spectrum. It is born, on the contrary, from the almost total inclusiveness of the new democratic system, with the slight difference that its initial effectiveness in the post-dictatorship years depends on the moderation of the voters, on the power or absence of power of the extreme leftist parties, and even on that kind of manoeuving called the regulation of electoral systems.

On the strictly political or institutional level, the authoritarian leadership of Spain had, only when all is said and done, but one stroke of genius: that which consists of making the Franco dictatorship into a monarchy without a king, and above all designating and imposing at the right moment Prince Juan Carlos of Bourbon as General Franco's successor. Without truly being genial, the old dictator himself perceived, at the very least, that there were advantages in providing his country with a head of state who would be above the risks of political quarrels after his disappearance and who would also manage to impose his authority over a potentially putschist army. In the same way, the infinitely more enlightened merit of the young ministers, vilified on the left as on the right under the name 'Opus Dei technocrats', consisted in managing the optimal calendar of the process of naming a successor. In a country where the monarchist principle had been anachronistic, it was agreed to 'preposition' the prince neither too early, in order that he would not in the eyes of the Spanish wear himself out by his compromises with Franco, nor too late, in such a way that he should have the time to be accepted by the army, or quite simply, to be in place at the moment of the dictator's death.

This strategy centring on the restoration of the monarchy underlines in fact the peculiarity of the Spanish case. Because, if the absence of an obviously democratic leadership represents the common pitfall of most departures from dictatorships, as in Chile today, the application of the formula that consists of imposing a royal leadership on the political marketplace requires a network of rather unobtainable conditions. Its use appears inconceivable in Latin America. In Europe, it would have been theoretically imaginable in Portugal and above all in Greece. However, the monarchist sentiment was even more faint in Portugal than in Spain, and President Salazar had, what is more, stressed the republican continuity of his government. Moreover, in Greece, the available pretender had already worn himself out while in power and could hardly be dressed up in new clothes.

Other less specific points however are worth mentioning. Still on the political game level, but this time concerning the leadership personnel and not the institutions, the Spanish example provides the illustration of a democratic transition led for six years by men descended from the authoritarian enclosure and not from the professional milieux of the dictatorship's opposition. The King himself and Adolfo Suarez symbolized this continuity, which was also asserted until 1982 by all the wheels of the governmental and administrative organization and by the 'transition party', that is, the Union of the Democratic Centre. Obvious in Spain, this phenomenon can occur elsewhere with fewer difficulties than the monarchist operation. This is borne out in particular by Brazil beginning in 1985, notably with President Sarney. At least in the Spanish case, it entails the advantage of reassuring the state managers as well as the business community. It also spares the societies in democratic transition the risks of the somewhat demagogic urges of professional democrats (it is true that their spectacle, if not their impact, can become necessary under certain circumstances). However, to be fruitful, this initial solution requires the connivance of the democratic opposition. In Spain, this was rendered possible by the agreement made between Adolfo Suarez and Santiago Carrillo in 1976 that was vital, as it were, to recalcitrant socialists. On the other hand, nothing of the sort occurred in Brazil.

In any case, writers generally refer to another field than that of direct practical politics when pondering over the democratic impact of bureaucratic-authoritarian regimes, modernizing conservative dictatorships, and other 'neo-Bismarckian' authoritarianisms of the present day. In this case, their remarks consist, more often than not, of appreciating to what extent these dictatorships modified the economic and social bases that, in a given country, appeared up until then as obstacles to democratization.[5] Essentially, the most basic idea is that the implanting of democracy depends on the one hand on the expansion of the urban middle classes concerned about stability and marked by 'political reason', and on the other hand on the sufficient contraction of the masses of landless peasants prone to revolutionary outbursts and on the passing of the agrarian problem to the background. At the same time, a more elaborate concept of these processes is put forward by David Collier (Collier, 1978) and James Kurth (Kurth, 1979), along the lines of Alexander Gerschenkron's (Gerschenkron, 1962) and Karl De Scweinitz's (De Scweinitz, 1964) work on the industrialization and the democratization of 19th-century Europe.

Rather than summarizing yet again the major features of their interpretative paradigm, we will content ourselves with mentioning those of its elements that are relevant here. The first is linked to the acknowledgement that the old English-type spontaneous and precocious industrialization adapted perfectly to political liberalism and parliamentary transparence, while the later and massive industrialization of the French, German, Russian, Italian or even Spanish style, was accompanied, in most circumstances, by strong State intervention. Yet, without the dictatorship being exactly required to accelerate the industrial take-off in the countries where it hardly happened spontaneously, it appears that somewhat authoritarian govenments like the Second Empire, the imperial government of Germany, or the Franco regime can facilitate the intervention of the State and coincide more or less partially with this take-off.

Furthermore, Kurth and Collier consider as a corollary what it would be useful to call the 'technocratic syndrome'. Massive industrialization at a forced pace hurts not only little people but also the small and medium-sized industrial or agricultural entrepreneurs. It damages even the landed oligarchy, who see the peasant workforce escape to the manufacturing centres and who loose, what is more, their economic superiority to the new industrial, financial and administrative class. In other words, this form of industrialization unites the greater part of the society in opposition to it, from society's base and petty bourgeois layers to its summit. For this reason, it gives rise to more difficulties in a representative system open to the expression of a multiplicity of interests than in an authoritarian regime, whose opaqueness allows both private and public technocrats to agree secretly to elude the social environment's anti-industrializing pressures.

These considerations refer, it is true, to the development of authoritarianism rather than to the development of democracy, at least at first. Briefly, the leaders' preoccupation thus consists of escaping from the contingencies of the political marketplace in order to:

1. have farmers and salaried agricultural workers bear the cost of industrialization;

2. accelerate the rural exodus, supplier of industrial labour, by necessarily disrupting the heretofore privileged status of the essentially landed traditional elites;

3. rapidly increase the relative importance of the urban population, and in particular that of the middle classes, who are consumers of finished products;

4. centre the political equilibrium on these urban masses, by expecting that the legitimacy of the economic performance of the authoritarian governments will mean more in their eyes than the ineffable but abstract legitimacy of polls.

Secondly, however, Kurth and Collier notice on the basis of the Spanish example that the effect of authoritarian modernization reverses itself and plays in favour of a democratic expectation. On the one hand, industrialization re-enforces the relative weight of the proletariat and brings about an extension or a resumption of social agitation. That being the case, there is only a question of choosing between an indefinite intensification of police repression and denial of political rights, and an opening up of political power that would legalize unions and labour parties in order to supply interlocutors to company presidents and to permit social distension through negotiation. Situated in a competitive international environment where this last mechanism is almost the only one to be in current use and to have supplied proof of its efficiency, they most frequently end up desiring the second situation and hoping for the end of the authoritarian government.

On the other hand, the improvement in standard of living of the urban populations tends perhaps to temporarily alleviate their political demands. However, this kind of satisfied passiveness appears very delicate since it too is linked to a context of major economic circumstances (if crises arise, as in Brazil, and the precarious consensus collapses, authoritarian governments have only to move out of the way as they have actually done). Moreover, the rise to a certain material well-being is rapidly taken for granted by its beneficiaries. It inevitably gives rise to expectations of an immaterial kind that are, above all, democratic. From that moment on, the summit and the base of the society join in their rejection of the dictatorship, all the more so since the menace of a great agrarian uprising disappears to the rhythm of industrialization and the marginalization of the agricultural sector. At the same time, the authoritarian technocrats discover that they have been made not the forerunners but rather the sorcerer's apprentices of democracy.

If we must end on this point, it appears in reference to the Spanish example – and also Chilean – that authoritarian democratization exists today less as a deliberate political strategy than as an economic strategy capable of relegating the 'dangerous' peasant and working classes to the background and propelling the middle classes and the new entrepreneurial class to the forefront. In this way, the democratic perspective no longer appears as the antechamber of great social upheaval. It ceases to scare the greater part of the population (the urban or rural proletariat having become a minority). Also, in these conditions, this mass of democrats without deep convictions, or converted to political realism, do not see an inconvenience in benefiting from a supplementary guarantee in leaving the initial management of the transition in some of the most capable hands of the authoritarian leadership. Minus the provisional continuity of the political personnel, the old democracies have also known the process of extinction of the quite beautiful democratic passions, passions that are however open to possible accidents. It could be, that the remodelled modernizing dictatorship in Spain after 1956 had accelerated it.

Conversely, the experience of the Popular Unity between 1971 and 1973 in Chile perhaps killed this passion in another way, this time profitable for General Pinochet's dictatorship. By consistently governing with only minority support while carrying out a deep-seated upheaval in the whole of the Chilean population, President Allende committed, at the same time, an abuse of power and irremediably hurt the democratic sense of a large part of the population (the 43 per cent for 'yes' at the recent referendum). In effect, he broke in this way the egalitarian momentum of his country, opened up the way for the military, until then confined to their barracks, and transformed for a long time the nature of the political expectations of his fellow citizens. There is no doubt that the democratic process sometimes follows a roundabout path, and that the best intentions in the world are not inevitably the most efficient.

Notes

1. The English translation is © 1989 by André Bzdera.
2. Title of the conference organized by the Department of Political Science of the Université de Montréal, 28 September to 2 October 1988, at which this paper was originally presented.
3. The view of even a Marxist writer such as Mihaly Vajda (Vajda, 1979).
4. *Ouaderni dell'Osservatorio elettorale*, vol. 15, July 1983.
5. Obstacles related to poverty, the scandalously unequal allocation of wealth, illiteracy, the influence of the rural population and the clientelist domination that it encourages – basically following in the perspective of the quantitative indicators proposed originally by S. M. Lipset (Lipset, 1959).

References

Augé, M. (1985) *La traversée du Luxembourg* (Paris: Hachette).
Collier, D. (1978) 'Industrialization and Political Change', *World Politics*, vol. 38, pp. 593–614.

Gerschenkron, A. (1962) *Economic Backwardness in Historical Perspective* (Cambridge, Mass: Belknap Press of Harvard University Press).

Godbout, J. (1987) *La démocratie des usagers* (Montréal: Boréal Express).

Hermet, G. (1983) *Aux frontières de la démocratie* (Paris: Presses Universitaires de France).

Hermet, G. (1986) *Sociologie de la construction démocratique* (Paris: Economica).

Kurth, J. R. (1979) 'Industrial Change and Political Change' in: D. Collier (ed.), *The New Authoritarianism in Latin America* (Princeton: Princeton University Press), pp. 319–63.

Lipset, S. M. (1959) 'Some Social Requisites of Democracy: Economic Development and Political Legitimacy', *American Political Science Review*, vol. 53, pp. 69–105.

Moore, B. (1969) *Les origines sociales de la dictature et de la démocratie* (Paris: Maspero).

Plato, (1966) *La République*, trans. and ed.: R. Baccou (Paris: Garnier-Flammarion) (Plato, Book VIII).

Rémond, R. (1977) 'Bonapartisme et Gaullisme' in: K. Hammer *et al.* (eds), *Le bonapartisme* (Munich: Artemis Verlag).

Rudel, M. (1960) *Karl Marx devant le bonapartisme* Paris: Mouton.

De Scweinitz, K. (1964) *Industrialization and Democracy* (London: Free Press of Glencoe).

Siegfried, A. (1913) *Tableau politique de la France de l'Ouest sous la Troisième République* (Paris: Armand Colin).

Vajda, M. (1979) *Fascisme et mouvement de masse* (Paris: Le Sycomore).

2 Models of Democratic Transition in South America: Negotiated Reform versus Democratic Rupture

Charles G. Gillespie

AUTHORITARIAN REGIMES IN COMPARATIVE PERSPECTIVE

If the paths from authoritarian regimes (ARs) to polyarchy are diverse, this is not merely because there exist many different AR types (Linz, 1975), but also many different modes of transition. Alfred Stepan, for example, has delineated no less than ten. (Stepan, 1986). Even regimes which apparently shared many similarities, such as the military-technocratic ARs of Brazil and the Southern Cone during the past two decades, were inaugurated by very varied processes, and in quite dissimilar political contexts. There is therefore no reason to imagine that the manner of their demise will be any more uniform. Three very general alternatives may, in fact, be contrasted regarding the mode of transition from authoritarianism to democracy. The first is a controlled process of re-institutionalization 'from above' in which the AR closely determines the major parameters of regime reform, and a great deal of legal and institutional continuity is ensured. The outcome of such a process may well be a restricted form of democracy which the opposition finds quite unsatisfactory, though they are unable to do anything to change the situation. At the opposite extreme lies a second alternative, that of complete rupture of the AR, the dismantling of its institutions, and the rapid passage of power into the hands of the opposition. In this second case, the demise of the AR occurs under circumstances in which it is powerless to affect the course of events, or the institutions and leaders which will replace it. Between these two polar cases lies the third hybrid situation of negotiated reform in which neither

45

power-holders nor opposition leaders are able to determine the course of regime mutation. Though at first this may lead to stalemate, eventually the pressures for some form of understanding between the two sides may reach a point at which they agree to compromise on the rules governing the transition.[1]

Bearing in mind the two dimensions of democracy distinguished by Robert Dahl (Dahl, 1971) – participation and opposition – we may imagine two polar types of regime transition away from ARs. On the one hand, there might be increasing toleration for contestation, expressions of opposition, and autonomous organization by social groups. This movement corresponds to regime liberalization, or the inauguration of what Schmitter refers to as a *dictablanda* ('soft dictatorship') (Schmitter, n.d.). By contrast, the transition to what Schmitter dubs a *democradura* ('hard democracy') involves a move toward a regime with greater, but still limited, electoral accountability.

The first part of this chapter is an exploration of how four crucial cases of authoritarian regimes in South America – Argentina, Brazil, Chile and Uruguay – attempted to institutionalize, and the different paths that they took in the 1980s. In no case did these 'Bureaucratic-Authoritarian' situations lead to stable regimes – though the degree of success in this regard ranged from significant (in Chile) to non-existent (in Argentina). In order to understand why authoritarianism failed, the chapter turns to five types of explanation that have often been put forward by theorists of regime change. It argues that the usefulness of these approaches varies according to whether we are trying to explain the reasons for authoritarian breakdowns or the paths that transitions to democracy follow. In a nutshell, an attempt is made to distinguish the questions of why and how transitions occur. The penultimate section attempts to apply the five theoretical approaches in order to explain the diverging paths these regimes took in the 1980s, and the differential speed with which they reached democracy.

As we shall see, the Southern Cone ARs chose very different paths in their attempts to pursue renewed political institutionalization. Brazil, for example, evolved in the direction of a *dictablanda* after 1974, while in 1980 Uruguay attempted to inaugurate a *democradura*, but failed. In the same year Chile's AR was able successfully to lay plans for its own eventual transformation into a form of *democradura*. Argentina's AR, by contrast, remained the least institutionalized of the four and no sustained effort was ever made to transform it from a 'state of exception' into something more permanent.

SOUTHERN CONE MILITARY-TECHNOCRATIC REGIMES:
SIMILARITIES AND DIFFERENCES

The 'new authoritarian' regimes which came to power in the Southern Cone[2] in the 1960s and 1970s had much in common, not least the high levels of repression that they inflicted on their populations.[3] According to Guillermo O'Donnell's famous ideal type definition. 'Bureaucratic-Authoritarian' (BA) states[4] correspond to:

(1) A form of domination by a highly oligopolized and trans-nationalized bourgeoisie;
(2) Their institutions are controlled by the military and economic technocrats dedicated to the restoration of 'order' and economic 'normalization';
(3) The BA politically excludes a previously activated popular sector;
(4) Political exclusion of the popular sector requires the destruction of representative democratic institutions;
(5) The BA also excludes the popular sector from the benefits of economic growth by suppressing labour unions;
(6) BA policies favour the transnationalization of the economy;
(7) Attempts are made to 'depoliticize' social and economic issues;
(8) Only the heads of the armed forces and large corporations retain access to decision makers (O'Donnell, 1979b, 292–4).

The four regimes we are considering – Argentina 1976–83, Brazil 1964–85, Chile 1973–?, and Uruguay 1973–85 – all shared the characteristic of a shift in the political behaviour of the armed forces toward a new type of permanent rule (Stepan, 1973). Nevertheless, each regime was inaugurated following specific political crises reflecting national circumstances.

Argentina's (second) BA (see O'Donnell, 1988; Gillepsie, 1989) was inaugurated in the midst of: extremist violence approaching a state of civil war; total chaos in the ruling Peronist party, which was divided into feuding left and right wings; an economy paralysed by trade union militancy; and extreme economic instability and long-term decline. Brazil's BA, on the other hand, had arisen against a background of: belated political mobilization of urban labour and peasants; a very weak party system and weak unions; and dynamic late development leading to major social strains (Stepan, 1971). In both of these countries, military intervention had been endemic since 1930 – by contrast in Chile, and especially Uruguay, it had been unknown. The breakdown of Chilean democracy was the product of a failed attempt to construct a socialist society by democratic means which produced a major counter-revolution (Valenzuela, 1978). In Uruguay, military intervention was born of: a reaction to a powerful urban guerrilla movement (the Tupamaros); a stalemate of the traditional party system; long-term economic decline leading to mounting social tensions and fiscal crises (Gillespie, 1984).

The precise institutional organization of military-technocratic rule in these four countries differed in significant ways. The second Argentine BA (unlike the first) was based on a pattern of semi-collegial rule in which the three service chiefs formed a *de facto* legislature, while the Commander-in-Chief of the Army invariably occupied the Presidency. The government suffered constant internal strains as a result of inter-service rivalries and friction between the President and the Commander-in-Chief of the Army, and it was entirely without party support. By contrast the Brazilian BA consisted of a broader and more subtle military–civilian coalition in which conservative politicians were successfully co-opted into a pro-regime party, ARENA. With only temporary interruptions, Brazil retained a façade of elections and a domesticated Congress throughout over twenty years of military rule. Like Argentina, Chile's BA abolished all party activity (and the parties of the right went so far as to dissolve themselves, while calling for the support of the military). However, Chile was to develop the most personalist dictatorship of any of the four cases we are examining. General Pinochet combined the office of President with that of Commander-in-Chief, preventing the emergence of the clashes between the armed forces as institution and the government which were to cripple Argentina's BA. Finally, Uruguay develped the most collegial form of military rule of all: the President was merely a figurehead, while the country's top 26 generals, admirals and airforce brigadiers closely oversaw the workings of the government. Some attempt was made to co-opt civilian politicians, but with little success.

Argentina, Chile and Uruguay pursued broadly similar 'neoliberal' economic policies during the 1970s which involved liberalization of trade and finance, and the promotion of market-mechanisms (see Foxley, 1983; Ramos, 1986; Hartlyn and Morley, 1986). Technocrats in all three countries believed in the doctrine of comparative advantage and encouraged exports of non-traditional products while allowing a contraction of import-substituting industries. While the result in all these cases was 'de-industrialization', Brazil's economic model was very different. There the state promoted heavy industrialization by means of a partnership among state enterprises, multinational corporations, and large local firms. Whereas much of the foreign debt contracted by the other three countries leaked away in the form of capital flight or was squandered on a surge of luxury manufactured imports, a greater proportion of Brazil's loans were actually used to pay for large infrastructural investments. It therefore experienced far more sustained growth than the other three.

If the four BAs examined here were comparable during their heydays, the subsequent patterns by which they evolved and eroded were crucially different. We turn now to a comparison of their divergent paths.

The fate of military-technocratic rule: reform versus rupture

It has often been argued that the major factor in the Argentine transition was the military's decisive defeat in the 1982 South Atlantic war, but it is equally true that the regime's days were already numbered by the time the fateful decision was taken to invade the Falklands–Malvinas. President Galtieri's adventure, in other words, was also a *symptom* of crisis. The interest of the military institution was to avoid handing over power for as long as possible due to their fear of trials for past human rights violations. Yet they were in a 'Catch-22' situation: the longer they stayed the more they risked a social explosion and an internal confrontation between rival military factions of the kind which had put an end to their previous period of rule in 1973. In effect, the South Atlantic was was a desperate gamble which General Galtieri took, and lost – thereby precipitating an even more reluctant and disorderly retreat to the barracks than had occurred ten years earlier.

Argentina's neoliberal technocrats had created an economic disaster born of exchange rate overvaluation, capital flight, and indebtedness. Gross Domestic Product fell 13 per cent between 1981 and 1983. Popular protests were increasingly strong, leading to the resurgence of a wave of strikes and the activation of many different social movements such as squatters' associations and the Madres de la Plaza de Mayo, whose call for the investigation of past disappearances was particularly powerful (Navarro, 1989). No breakdown of law and order of the type seen in cities such as Cordoba after 1969 occurred. However, this was clearly an anticipated possibility. Little attempt had been made by governments after 1976 to seek legitimacy – but its absence began to be felt after the economic growth of the first five years gave way to slump with the massive devaluation of 1981. As in 1973, the strategies of Argentina's major parties prevented the military from achieving any negotiated guarantees on their future prerogatives. Politicians simply refused any dealings with the military. The only pacts that they entered were *among themselves*, particularly the so-called *Multipartidaria*'s insistence of a full transition to democracy and free elections. Argentina thus underwent a decisive democratic rupture – moving rapidly from dictatorship to democracy with almost no institutional continuity.

The situation of the Brazilian military in the two decades after they seized power in 1964 was strikingly different. Unlike Argentina, where human rights violations had been far more widespread, the interests of Brazil's armed forces no longer necessarily ran counter to democracy, given the reciprocal amnesty for guerrillas and military enacted in 1978. The military budget had remained quite low under the BA, while the armed forces were becoming increasingly interested in geostrategic concerns, not just domestic national security. Furthermore, a variety of structural factors and established prerogatives suggested that the Brazilian military would be able to retain a significant role in any civilian government. On the other hand, large sectors of the officer corps appear to have become concerned at the growing power of the Servico Nacional de Infomaçães, the secret service.

When the process of political 'opening' began in Brazil after 1974, the comparative success of the regime made the costs of tolerating more opposition rather low. On the other hand, significant business discontent had emerged at what was seen as the excessive growth of state enterprises and economic interventionism, leading to what became known as the 'anti-statism' (*Desestatizasão*) campaign by industrial associations and the sympathetic press. Coupled with a prosperity that seemed to make labour demands more negotiable and frustration at the lack of access to government policy-making, mistrust of the military caused large sections of domestic business to swing behind the idea of an orderly return to a more democratic system. Paradoxically, in the 1980s, economic crisis actually *threatened* the continuation of the transition by renewing the spectre of zero-sum class conflicts, just as Brazil experienced greatly increased labour mobilization.

Popular movements were far stronger than ever before in Brazil by the end of the 1970s. This was reflected particularly in higher rates of blue-collar unionization (and more independent unions), but also in neighbourhood associations and such new social movements as peasant unions and church-based communities. The organized working class was still a relatively small proportion of Brazil's popular sectors, even in urban areas. Despite their impressive organizational gains, popular movements were to fail in their effort to force direct presidential elections in 1984. Nevertheless, by contributing to the dramatic growth of opposition political parties, it can be argued that these social movements helped to split the ruling Democratic Social party, by revealing its bleak electoral future.

The evolution of Brazil's AR began as a shift towards a *dictablanda* after 1974. If a decline in the legitimacy of the government and its ruling party were a major factor influencing President Geisel and his close advisor General Golberry to initiate the liberalization of the regime after 1974, by a strange paradox military governments then found a certain intangible revival of their legitimacy tied to further progress toward the promised return of democracy. The continued resort to *ad hoc* manipulation of electoral and constitutional rules did, however, eventually exhaust what might be called the capital of legitimacy which the regime had held onto by never fully abolishing elections or political parties. And the steady growth of the opposition continued unabated.

Opposition strategies in Brazil were comparatively moderate. Lacking much choice, opposition parties were continually forced to accept the sudden changes of political rules imposed by successive governments, as when for example the carefully nurtured (and artificial) two-party system was abruptly dissolved from above. Eventually the main opposition group, the Party of the Brazilian Democratic Movement formed an alliance with a renegade faction of the ruling PDS known as the Liberal Front behind a veteran civilian moderate, Trancredo Neves. One of the major reasons the pro-military PDS split was that large sections of the party opposed the presidential candidate adopted for the 1985 (indirect) election, largely on the grounds that he was unpopular and thus a liability. Ten years after the liberalization had begun, Brazil's transition thus moved toward making the regime more accountable. Many in the military would have preferred a form of *democradura*, but they were forced to concede something closer to real democracy.

In Uruguay, the military's rule lacked legitimacy almost from the start, and this became particularly acute after their extraordinary defeat in the 1980 plebiscite on a proposed tough new constitution.

Trapped early on in language of democracy in order to justify their actions, the military found they had little choice but to seek a negotiated way out. In 1980 they sought to construct a *democradura*, but, unlike their Chilean counterparts, they had little active elite support – and almost no political allies – although for four years they continued to insist on certain guarantees allegedly to strengthen democracy. However, the corporate interests of the military as an institution had drifted apart from those of the Alvarez administration by early 1984. Alvarez had in fact forced his way into power in 1981 only by threats against his fellow officers. His plans for using state resources to create a new political movement were dismissed by most of his colleagues as not feasible. They also became increasingly angry at his deliberate strategy of sabotaging negotiations with the opposition, which broke down in 1983. The armed forces were nevertheless determined to block the most intransigent and probably most popular opposition leader, Wilson Ferreira of the Blanco party (Gillepsie, 1987).

By 1982, the economic disaster and fiscal crisis in Uruguay led a majority of the military to oppose any populist adventures by President Alvarez (who would have dearly liked to stay in office) and to be increasingly anxious to extricate. Nevertheless, the economic crisis, which resembled that across the River Plate, did not precipitate a transition to democracy. Uruguay's business elites were much more scared of strikes and disorder than their Brazilian counterparts, if less so than Chilean capitalists. On the other hand, rural elites were anti-military from the start, partly because they resented their exclusion from influence. Labour remained disorganized and unable to protest until 1984, while Uruguay's other popular movements were rather weak by Southern Cone standards. There were, to take a revealing example, no major strikes till 1984. In many cases, too, new social movements such as those engaged in human rights work or community organization were often largely façades for illegal left parties and thus subordinated to those parties' strategies.

Opposition strategies were ultimately to be very flexible and moderate in Uruguay. In return for their legalization, in mid-1984 the parties of the Left made the crucial decision to agree to negotiate with the military alongside the moderate Colorado party. The military in turn agreed to legalize the Left in order to help block Ferreira's ambitions, by splitting the opposition vote. They also vetoed Ferreira's candidacy by jailing him. The denouement of Uruguay's transition was thus close to O'Donnell's model for transition pacts between military softliners and opposition moderates.

According to this model, the military softliners must isolate those officers eager to block any movement toward democracy, while opposition moderates must agree to compromise (without being co-opted entirely) (O'Donnell, 1979a). Ironically, however, this pact was made possible only by shattering the unity of the opposition parties. This had the consequent danger of risking future discontent on the part of the Blanco party which opposed the terms of the transition, so long as its leader was jailed.

Of the four BA regimes, only Chile's was to survive by the mid-1980s. Rather in the manner of De Gaulle, Pinochet was able successfully to manipulate the use of plebiscites in 1978 and 1980 in order to bolster his support. In the latter year he was able to persuade a majority of the electorate to endorse a new Constitution with a built-in timetable for the eventual inauguration of a form of *democradura*. By this time he had purged his potential rivals in the other services and established a very concentrated form of personalist power. Chile's economic experiment was at once the most rigorous and the longest-lasting – even when it produced a wave of bankruptcies and a financial collapse in 1982. Over the course of the following two years Pinochet was able to buy time by naming Sergio Jarpa Prime Minister and allowing him to hold talks with moderate opposition parties over Chile's political future. While these dragged on fruitlessly, the government was able to regain control over the economy, and even manipulate the economic crisis to re-solidify wavering petit bourgeois support. By late 1984 Pinochet had regained enough strength to cancel the supposed liberalization. It was not until he lost the 1988 referendum on a further term of office that Chile's AR seemed at last to be breaking down.

EXPLAINING REGIME TRANSITIONS: FIVE PERSPECTIVES

Having reviewed the four cases, we turn now to competing available explanations of why, when and how transitions occurred – or failed to. Five theoretical frameworks seem especially relevant as we attempt to build explanations of given regime transitions.

Legitimation crises

The most fundamental approach to explaining regime (in)stability centres on the problem of political legitimacy, or its absence. Sadly, the word is used with little precision and difficulties often stem from the circularity of many accounts of legitimacy. There is an unfortunate tendency to merely assume that regimes which survive are legitimate, those which collapse are not (*ipso facto*). However, there would seem to be advantages for treating legitimacy as something other than either support or performance. The work of Juan Linz on democratic breakdowns is apposite in so far as a clear distinction is made between the legitimacy and efficacy of a regime (Linz, 1978). Effectiveness is not the only source of legitimacy, and this is particularly true of long-established and institutionalized regimes. In fact, somewhat as Dworkin has defined 'rights' as entitlements which 'trump' utilitarian calculus, we may define legitimacy as a quality which 'trumps' regime performance. Thus regimes which are performing quite poorly sometimes seem to survive for relatively long periods because they are legitimate. One can also imagine the opposite circumstance: the collapse of a regime that performs 'well' (i.e. takes effective decisions vis-à-vis 'challenges') because it is illegitimate.

The major difficulty of Latin American military ARs seeking to institutionalize is precisely the *absence* of legitimacy, particularly if we compare them to pre-war fascist regimes. Undoubtedly their weakest link is the lack of a legitimating ideology so that much of the time they more of less lamely claim to be defending democracy from 'subversion' or from 'totalitarianism'. However much national security doctrine may have influenced elites, and been inculcated in the armed forces, nowhere has it achieved mass popularity. A pretended transitory nature by definition rules out institutionalized legitimacy. So long as the military retain power, therefore, a state of exception effectively exists. This does not imply that ARs inaugurated by military intervention can nowhere achieve institutionalization and legitimacy. It does, however, mean that they cannot remain as 'Stratocracies'[5] forever. In fact, attempted institutionalization which 'gets out of hand' is a common way for transitions from ARs to begin. The reason is that institutionalization is both imperative and very difficult to achieve.

Apart from the question of the legitimacy of a given political order, there is the question of the legitimacy of the social order. Challenges to each of these structures may be quite separate. Much of the literature on legitimation crises is in fact about crises of social domination. In particular we have the mass of highly theoretical literature stimulated by Habermas. Others focus instead on empirically observed challenges, such as delegitimation of private business, educational systems, professional elites, and the patriarchal family. Though derived from advanced capitalist democracies, this list is very relevant to contemporary ARs in less developed countries; but sadly it is by no means merely destabilizing to them alone. Though often symptoms of democratizing urges, such contestations can be equally dangerous to polyarchies. In fact a crisis of social domination may have the perverse effect of strengthening an AR for a time (as seems to have been the case in Chile).

Nevertheless, there is strong evidence that the crimes committed by South American ARs stimulated the revalorization of formal democratic liberties vis-à-vis other goals (typically 'socialism', or simply social justice or equality). How far such trends are merely cyclical and/or confined to elites remains an open question. Their contribution to *transitions* may, however, be significant.[6] Although there may be little agreement as to what democracy entails, it remains a legitimizing ideology par excellence of Western civilization, with no foreseeable challengers, and a few signs of reconvergence over its definition (Barros, 1986).

Analysis of the underlying political legitimacy of regimes is clearly crucial for the purpose of predicting their stability, but legitimacy is by no means the only factor in regime change. A lack of legitimacy may help us to understand why a certain political system is unstable, but other forms of analysis seem to be needed to explain the timing of transitions, and the path that they follow.

Political economy

A notoriously different approach to explaining regime change focuses on the impact of economic processes on the state, though our discussion of the legitimacy of the social order has begun to take us in this direction. While many authors use forms of analysis derived from political economy in attempting to explain the transition from ARs, two writers who have privileged this form of analysis are Guillermo O'Donnell and Nicos Poulantzas. O'Donnell's BA model has already been sketched: its installation was made possible by an exclusionary alliance of state, national, and transnational bourgeoisies, designed to do away with the 'populist' model of development common in post-war Latin America. Yet 'transnationalization' has the effect of weakening the state, while austerity and economic stabilization early on hurts the national bourgeoisie's weakest elements. Finally, the military are both nationalist and not necessarily subject to free enterprise profit 'worship'. Together these are held to constitute a number of 'ambiguities in the system', whereas the state is no longer easily able to pose as operating for the 'general good', but is increasingly revealed as nakedly self-serving. Thus the BA is ulti-mately 'a suboptimal form of bourgeois domination' lacking in the mediations for achieving consensus. It is manifestly coercive and anti-popular, while serving a bourgeoisie that is the least national element within the societies. Finally the necessary importance of organiza-tions specialized in coercion clashes with the social elite of the state, in so far as their values and behaviour are not the same (O'Donnell, 1979b). A process of *erosion* 'results from the efforts of the dominant classes ... to satisfy their demands upon the state'. In this way democracy is revived as an alternative *faute de mieux*.

In words similar to O'Donnell's, Poulantzas argues, 'the form of regime of these military dictatorships did not permit the regulation of contradictions by the organic representation of ... diverse factions [of capital] within the state, nor, therefore, the establishment of balanced compromises without serious upsets' (Poulantzas, 1975, 32). The split in the dominant classes corresponds to the distinction between what Poulantzas calls *comprador* versus *interior* bourgeoisies.

What are the 'pros and cons' of explanations for transitions from ARs that are rooted in political economy, and especially class-centric analysis? O'Donnell's analysis is mainly directed towards explaining why the BA fails to become permanently institutionalized. It is not really relevant to explanations of the actual course (or timing) of the transition. By dint of a pronounced reductionist tendency, such analyses tend to void a great deal of what we commonly think of as 'politics' from their account. They seem most fitting for long-run analyses, and pose great difficulties when we try to use them to predict short-run political phenomena, or the actual course of events. The BAs which O'Donnell devoted many early works to describing in terms of their installation and 'necessity' did not really achieve institutionalization (with the partial exception of Brazil and Chile). In other words, structural analyses such as those rooted in political economy, with deterministic long-run implications, can hardly be the most appropriate form of analysis for transitions.

Popular movements

What role can social actors play in the demise of authoritarian regimes? Although popular movements were very much present in the rhetoric of Latin American political scientists concerned with thinking about how to promote transitions from ARs, they have hardly figured in our previous approaches to transitions. Nevertheless, Stepan has emphasized the task of 'raising the costs of repression' for the AR and thus our third approach seeks to go one step further by affording those movements a *protagonistic* role. In a sense, it is hardly surprising that the popular masses and the movements they constitute were for a time neglected, given that the modern form of exclusionary AR in Latin America is determinedly demobilizing and atomizing in its impact on both political and civil societies. In this respect these new ARs are fundamentally different from their populist and fascist predecessors. Few ARs were as successful as the Southern Cone BAs in totally disarticulating the institutions of opposition, in effect crushing or flattening civil society and 'privatizing' politics by shrinking the public sphere. Nevertheless, some autonomous institutions managed normally to survive (unions, church communities, autonomous faculties, rural organizations, etc.) while new ones were eventually nurtured into life (Stepan, 1985).

One feature of the new ARs of the Southern Cone during the 1970s was the dismantling of the populist coalition which had symbiotically existed alongside the process of import-substituting industrialization. Hence the new emphasis on re-insertion in the world market on lines of comparative advantage, privatization of public services and state industries, and the freeing of markets, whether for products, labour, or financial services. All of these were designed to promote the atomization of the popular sectors, the dissolution of alliances between the middle classes and the industrial workers, and a less crudely evident form of demobilization. In so far as success was achieved in these aims, even short-lived ARs achieved quite important changes in social structure: notably the increase in female participation in the labour force, and the growth of the informal sector. The response of opposition was to attempt to promote new social movements. If the industrial proletariat is under physical assault, and in any case never reached the proportion of the population attained in advanced capitalist democracies, there seems to be little sense in pinning hope for social transformation on it. The prototypical new movements include shanty-town dwellers, ecclesiastical base communities, women's groups, human rights committees and so on.

Only if ARs reach such an egregious state of crisis that the bourgeoisie enters a temporary alliance with the popular sectors, and the security forces collapse, can revolutionary discontinuity plausibly emerge. However, there is a path from ARs called by Stepan 'society led regime termination', in which popular movements play a major role (Stepan, 1986). This essentially consists of a violent paroxysm of social protest, such as the Argentine Cordobazo of 1969, the uprising of students in Greece in 1973, and the strikes in Peru in 1977. According to Stepan, this galvanizes the AR's decision to extricate, and initiate a transition – which may then involve some other path to democracy, including a reform pact. Alternatively, it may merely lead to a reformulation of the AR, as the protests in Chile did. In fact, the 'popular moment' is more likely to come *after* liberalization in many cases (as in Brazil). In this case, as before, it may promote a deepening of democratization, or it might fuel an authoritarian regression.

Ultimately, however, the rhetoric of popular movements is in tension with the practical fact that ARs are almost never liable to defeat by *frontal* assault. In negotiated transitions the organized masses are required to play a subordinate political role: they must glare fiercely at the repressive apparatuses of the AR, and if necessary flex their muscles with the occasional general strike or pot-banging protest, but then they must sit in the back seat, so to speak, while political elites demobilize them and adopt a strategy of negotiation with the AR, consociation amongst themselves, and even concertation with the representatives of capital.

Corporate interests of power-holding institutions

Our fourth approach to explaining transitions stems from a very simple axiom at the beginning of Dahl's *Polyarchy*: power-holders such as the military will opt for liberalization when the costs of repression exceed the costs of toleration. This states the conditions under which one might predict an AR would tolerate more opposition. It does not say anything about the other dimension of polyarchy, namely, making the regime more accountable. Furthermore, such analysis is carried out without reference to resources. Presumably, there may be times when an AR simply lacks the coercive resources for repression. Nevertheless, regarding the 'costs' of rule, Stepan has laid emphasis on the military's 'bottom line' commitment to surviving as a hierarchical institution, which can require a retreat to the barracks if factional disputes lead to irreconcilable conflicts. Here the feared symptoms are a subversion of the top-down command structure (which happened in Portugal after 1974) or even armed combat (which pitted 'blues' against 'reds' in Argentina in the early 1960s). Stepan has fruitfully distinguished 'transition initiated by the military as government' from 'extrication by the military as institution'. By distinguishing these two paths, Stepan is also implying the possibility of dyarchic situations under military ARs where the Commanders-in-Chief of the different services remain distinct from the general(s) in control of the government. Stepan maintains that institutional extrication is by far the more common, as the relative autonomy of military governments *vis-à-vis* the armed forces is closely circumscribed. Indeed, he can think of only one concrete example apart from Brazil of transition initiated by the military as government.[7] The problem with such 'voluntaristic' liberalizations according to Stepan, is that the military may block them where the pressures from civil society for change are too weak. This brings us to the calculus of interests rooted in the balance of forces between military and opposition, where each is trying to raise the costs for the other.

Opposition alliances and strategies

Our fifth and final approach to regime transitions privileges the analysis of coalition-formation, negotiation and pacts. Leaving aside insurrectionary strategies, these alliances are aimed at strengthening the negotiating position of the opposition. On the one hand, a pact within the opposition will raise the prestige of parties and other opposition movements relative to the military. Mutual criticism can otherwise have an overall debilitating effect on the credibility and reputation of the opposition. In terms of altering objective conditions, the achievement of a pact will greatly raise the level of domestic challenge to the AR, as divide and rule is the central strategy by which ARs dominate civil society. Military dispositions are favourably affected by the possibility of a pact between themselves and the opposition – clearly the key to protecting military interests, and providing 'guarantees'. Finally, pacts can improve the military's perception of a fitting civilian organization to hand over power to.

For this reason, a great deal of writing has been done on the importance of the 'Consociational' model of democracy, often detected in the politics of Colombia and Venezuela. Ultimately, however, there would seem to be value in paying greater attention to investigating the conditions under which pacts are or are not possible.

This is precisely the intention of a stimulating and fascinating essay by Angel Flisfisch. Flisfisch classifies opposition systems as a bloc according to their dominant strategies along two dimensions: (a) their *flexibility*, or willingness to negotiate and compromise with the AR to secure the transition; and (b) the *breadth*, or inclusiveness of their alliances (Flisfisch, 1984). For Flisfisch, the 1983–84 stalemate in Chile was caused by the fact the opposition split into narrow (competing) alliances, and was inflexibly insistent on an immediate democratic rupture, rather than an incremental evolution of the AR.

How may we explain the emergence of different patterns? First of all, the flexibility or willingness to negotiate of the opposition will depend on the existence of a generalized perception that the regime is not on the verge of collapse. As in Argentina following the South Atlantic war, oppositions otherwise will insist on unconditional surrender. Second, flexibility requires its counterpart – if not a sense of trust in the power-holders who are willing to negotiate, at least a sense that they may really mean business (rather than be playing for time, as Pinochet was clearly doing when he appointed Jarpa as Prime Minister). Together, these conditions constitute grounds on which moderates on both sides may be able to find a tactical common interest. On the other hand, the breadth of the alliances within the opposition (the second level of pact) also depends on a similar tactical convergence for the purposes of achieving a 'way out' from the AR. This tactical convergence may be complicated by several factors, including past rivalries. In the second place, the breadth of opposition alliances depends on the degree to which the ideologies and political projects of rival components of civil society are mutually exclusive. This is *not* to say that all parties must converge on an utterly bland form of social democracy – but that they translate their global designs into the future, where these mean radical departures from the existing social and economic order.[8]

There exists even a third level of possible pacts or stabilizing alliances: that between parties and interest associations, especially unions. Normally, these are more relevant in the wake of transition during the phase of democratic consolidation, but no logical reason exists why the two might not be telescoped. Although 'concertation' at the level of civil society does seem far harder to achieve than 'consociation' at the level of political society, it can be a very powerful 'multiplier' of the level of challenge to the AR, just as it can hold out the prospect of a transition within stable parameters.

FROM COMPARATIVE PERSPECTIVES TO COMPARATIVE TRANSITIONS

It would be naive to believe that the examination of four cases can validate a particular theory of transitions from ARs. All we shall attempt to do in this conclusion is to compare the five approaches to what happened in the Southern Cone countries. In this way, we hope to move towards a framework for the comparative analysis of transitions which provides the key to explaining the divergent paths they followed.

What role did *legitimation* crises play in the breakdown of our four ARs? In Argentina, there is little doubt that military rule was at first greeted with widespread acquiescence in 1976 and outright support from social elites.[9] The claim that Argentine society was 'diseased' and the catastrophic failure of the previous Peronist government gave the first Junta a certain political capital. However, this did not amount to 'legitimacy' in the real sense of the word. The fickleness of the Argentines meant that the armed forces were obliged to search for rapid solutions to the country's economic problems, and appeal to the artificial boom they created as a surrogate for legitimacy. Once the economic model produced a disastrous collapse in 1981, their lack of legitimacy quickly became apparent. A good indicator of this long term, underlying isolation was the repeated failure of attempts to launch credible pro-military parties in the decades after 1955 when Peron was ousted. Hence, the military were forced to resort to desperate measures to try and save their position. When President Galtieri's attempts to use public barbecues to test the mood of support for his government failed to produce encouraging signs, he turned instead to whipping up nationalist fervour (Rock, 1987, 375). Patriotism may have been, as Doctor Johnson once said, 'the last refuge' but when the war with Britain was lost, it proved an inadequate one.

By contrast, the Brazilian military regime's initial legitimacy was greater and its subsequent erosion far more gradual.[10] Unlike any of the other three ARs we have examined, it was able to mount a credible party to support military tutelage. Even then, however, the most enlightened generals began to fear their increasing isolation from society by 1974, and therefore launched the decade-long liberalization which was to culminate in the inauguration of a civilian president. Paradoxically, however, the project for eventual transition became a principle source of legitimacy for the liberalizing administrations after 1974. The growth of opposition movements and parties revealed that authoritarianism was an increasingly non-viable ideology in the fast-growing and urbanizing centre–south of the country (see Lamounier, 1980).

In Uruguay, opinion data and the language the military were forced to adopt, as well as the result of the 1980 plebiscite, all point in the same direction. The AR was chronically low in legitimacy, perhaps more so than any of the other three ARs we have examined (see Gonzalez, 1983; Gillepsie, 1986). Liberal democracy remained ingrained in Uruguay's political culture, and this was a constant constraint on the military in a way which was not, for example, the case in Argentina. Furthermore, the legitimacy of the traditional parties, however besmirched by the crises of 1958–73, prevented the military from embarking on a creative project of building a pro-regime party as in Brazil. The only hope would have been somehow to co-opt the traditional parties, but they failed also to do that. Nevertheless, the path and timing of Uruguay's democratic transition remained uncertain for four years after the 1980 plebiscite.

The contrast between Uruguay and Chile is illuminating. Carlos Huneeus has emphasized the ability of General Pinochet to cloak his rule in a form of legitimacy by appealing to the past (for example by appointing former presidents as members of the Council of State) to the future (largely by promising his free market reforms would bring prosperity) and to legality (particularly by successfully ratifying a new Constitution in 1980) (Huneeus, 1987). Though there was no pro-regime party, the parties of the right had deliberately disbanded after the 1973 coup, in effect abdicating authority to the Junta. The level of support for Pinochet's new constitution and its very slow built-in timetable for return to a restricted democracy was particularly revealing. Business groups were notoriously outspoken in their calls to support the new institutions and demands that Chile never again elect a left-wing government (Stepan, 1985, 326–9). Even when General Pinochet lost the 1988 plebiscite he still obtained a far higher share of the popular vote than had the last democratic president, Salvador Allende, in 1970.

In sum, legitimation crises played an important role in preventing the institutionalization of our four ARs, but they did not determine either the path or the timing of democratic transitions. They thus constituted a form of background condition for authoritarian breakdown.

With respect to *political economy*, judgements must be

impressionistic regarding the behaviour of particular classes and their fractions. Can we identify contending sectors of the bourgeoisie (if we may be allowed to synthesize Poulantzas and O'Donnell some-what), one oriented towards the domestic market, the other towards the external market? Did BA policies hurt the latter and favour the former? And did this cleavage translate into differential support/ opposition to the regimes?

In Uruguay, the rural sector was highly critical of the government's policies. On the other hand, industry had been so scared by labour militancy, strikes and factory occupations, and had benefited from such total labour peace and massive wage compression, that it was very pro-regime until the slump became really serious. Though businessmen grumbled about imports, they had two ways of adapting to competition: shifting into non-traditional exports with the aid of subsidies (until the USA complained), and shifting into the importa-tion and distribution of foreign-made goods (World Bank, 1979). Finally, the policy of currency overvaluation to fight inflation (after 1978) hurt producers of all tradable goods, whether they were exporters or not. The same policy got practically all productive economic sectors into a swamp of debt, so that the only real fraction of capital left supporting the regime was finance (and even the banks had reservations about fiscal policy).

In Argentina, similar but more extreme economic policies pro-duced disaster even faster than in Uruguay. According to William Smith, foreign capital benefited little while 'the real beneficiaries of post-1976 policies [were] limited to a small group of large national firms' (Smith, 1985). The main opponents of overvaluation after 1978, as in Uruguay, were agro-exporters. However, domestic manu-facturers of tradables also objected as this was compounded by import liberalization. The country therefore experienced a flood of imports and underwent a rapid period of 'de-industrialization'. As capital flight and huge trade deficits mounted, and foreign loans mushroomed, the government could no longer defend the overvalued exchange rate, which was allowed to rapidly plunge from 1981. The only long-term beneficiaries of this experiment, as Sabato and Schvarzer have pointed out, were those financial interests able to take advantage of the speculative opportunities and exorbitant real interest rates which were a consequence of the accompanying finan-cial liberalization (Sabato and Schvarzer, 1985). When the entire economic model collapsed, however, the wave of industrial bank-ruptcies began to drag down the entire domestic financial system.

The most eloquent indicator of the lack of business confidence generated by the debacle was the massive rate of capital flight. Yet it was internal military feuding over economic policy, more than pressure from the business community, which paralysed the regime.

If Argentina's reckless attempt to defeat inflation by exchange rate overvaluation 1978–81 produced enormous pain and little gain, similar policies in Chile did at least succeed in dramatically reducing the rate of price increases (Ramos, 1986, 52–5). The eventual wave of industrial backruptcies and financial collapse was equally severe, but Chile's economic technocrats (unlike their Argentine counterparts) were slowly able to regain control of the situation. No doubt because of the memory of the Popular Unity government of Salvador Allende and the benefits of labour repression, business remained supportive of the Pinochet administration. It has even been argued that the government was able to exploit the economic crisis in various ways in order to strengthen its position. The great paradox was that the most sustained business opposition to military rule emerged in Brazil – the one country which was able to pursue more successful policies leading to long-term growth (Bruneau and Faucher, 1981). Between 1967 and 1974 Brazil underwent its so-called 'miracle', achieving annual rates of growth of 10 per cent (Serra, 1979, Table 2). Yet the increasing state role in the economy began to produce major pressures for political change from domestic industrialists, principally located in Sao Paulo. The so-called 'Estatizacao' debate implied not just a call for new policies but, increasingly, a demand for changes in the *regime* (Cardoso, 1986; Boschi, 1979).

To sum up, economic crisis contributed to the military's decision to withdraw in Argentina, and Uruguay, but a consistent pattern of cleavages between domestic and foreign capital did not emerge. Nor did a similar economic crisis in Chile prove sufficient to produce a transition, while (if anything) in Brazil the transition originally grew out of the regime's self-confident economic success. When Brazil did enter its own economic crisis in the 1980s many argued that this weighed against the democratization project of the military's more enlightened officers. In fact, the impact of economic crises seems to vary according to a country's specific political context. They are neither a necessary nor sufficient condition for the breakdown of authoritarian rule, though, as we shall see, they may certainly play a role in the decision of power-holders to agree to give way to elections.

The level of analysis relating to *popular movements* was very apposite to an understanding of transitions, but not in the way that some would have predicted. There is no doubt that in Brazil, particularly, they played a vital role in the rebuilding of civil society and the mobilization of opposition to military rule. Yet they were ultimately unable to force the holding of direct elections, despite the massive *Diretas Ja* campaign of 1984. Instead, the eventual path of transition was based on an elite deal in the form of the defection of a sizeable bloc of the ruling party to the presidential ticket of moderate opposition leader Tancredo Neves (Mainwaring and Share, 1987).

In Uruguay, the relative weakness of social movements and their close subordination to the parties of the Left, forced them to accept a strategy of 'mobilization, negotiation, concertation' in the words of the Left's leader.[11] The priority, however, was negotiation. At least until the new government was installed, pressure was used as potential power rather than possibly counterproductive disorder. Social mobilization was closely related to the economic crisis, and the role of 'new social movements' was on the whole marginal. By contrast, Chilean social movements and street protests were far stronger, yet they did not achieve their goal of ousting Pinochet. In fact, there is a case for arguing that they backfired, once they turned violent in 1983. Popular movements did come into their own in Argentina and contributed to the crisis of military rule, but the Peronist unions remained the most powerful social force. It was the fact that Argentina's transition was based on near unconditional surrender by the military that gave social movements more leverage.

The analysis of *interest calculus* by power-holders in authoritarian regimes is obviously appropriate to such institutions as the military. Indeed, this level of analysis is necessarily central to almost any account of transitions (or non-transitions). In Uruguay, a deep-seated belief in civilian administration; widespread demoralizing opposition; at least some minimum guarantees (and the insurance policy of re-entry if not); and a rather suitable party to form a government, were the determining factors which entered into the military's calculations. What was perhaps the most important thing, however, was the fact that the armed forces came to see their interests as not being served by their own military government. Uruguay's Naval Club Pact was negotiated by the Commanders-in-Chief of the armed forces over the scarcely concealed opposition of President Alvarez.

In Brazil, the situation was the reverse: significant opposition to the government's plans for democracy existed within the armed forces. Nevertheless, an important group within the regime had come to believe that the costs of rule were becoming unacceptable, and the military were able to retain a great deal of influence even after the inauguration of the first civilian president (Stepan, 1988). In Argentina, military hardliners were able to abort the first government attempt at liberalization under President Viola in 1981–82, presumably because they did not see it as in their interests. They thus hung on until the failure of their gamble in the South Atlantic war left them too divided and discredited to continue in office. At this point they were unable to prevent the trial of their leaders.

By contrast, in Chile the refusal to negotiate seriously with the opposition did not lead to the eventual collapse of military rule. President Pinochet combined the position of Commander-in-Chief of the Army (and thus head of the Junta) with the Presidency. The strains between the military as government and as institution were held carefully in check, as were divisive policy debates. At least until 1988, the military simply did not consider that the available alternatives to Pinochet might be more favorable to the survival of their prerogatives. In that year, Pinochet's defeat in the Plebiscite brought Chile to approximately the same position as Uruguay in 1980 or 1982: transition was now unavoidable, but the terms remained to be worked out.

Ultimately, *opposition alliance strategies* were, with military interests, the key factors which determined the path and timing of all four democratic transitions. Using the two dimensions proposed by Flisfisch, the evolution of party alliances and negotiating strategies may be illustrated thus:

	Negotiating Stances	ALLIANCES	
N E G O T I A T I N G S T A N C E		Broad	Narrow
	Rigid	**A** Multipartidaria circa November 1983 in Uruguay; Argentine Multipartidaria	**C** Uruguayan Blancos after June 1984; Chile 1983–84
	Flexible	**B** Colorados and Left after June 1984 in Uruguay; PMDB and PFL in Brazil	**D** Risk of isolation

FIGURE 2.1   *Party Alliances and Negotiating Strategies Compared*

The evolution of party alliances in Uruguay is particularly illustrative and thus the Uruguayan case is broken down into different phases and alliances. Following the collapse of the Parque Hotel talks in 1983 the Uruguayan parties were in a phase of unified confrontation with the military (A). For reasons that were discussed above, however, the Colorados and Left parties had decided within a year that their interests lay in negotiating with the military, moving to (B). The Blancos thus became isolated in their position of intransigent refusal to attend the talks (C), while the other main parties provided a broad enough alliance to avoid the danger of negotiating from a position of weakness (and risk accusation of 'sell out' that might have arisen had any party taken position (D).

In contrast to Uruguay's Colorados and Left, Argentina's main parties steadfastly refused to negotiate, and there the democratic transition came by means of a complete rupture of military rule. Brazil's parties pursued a strategy closer to that of Uruguay's Naval Club. The main opposition party, the PMDB first allied with the Workers' Party in the failed bid to force direct presidential elections in 1984. Then a section of the pro-regime PDS broke away under the banner of the Liberal Front to back a joint presidential candidate with the opposition PMDB. Once the Brazilian Democratic Movement had allied with the Liberal Front, Tancredo Neves reached a series of implicit agreements with the armed forces as the price for the defeat of the official candidate. In Chile, at least during the crucial lost opportunity of 1983–84, the opposition remained both divided and intransigent – a combination which proved particularly disadvantageous. The subsequent trend toward broader alliances and more moderate demands proved belated.

THE ROLE OF POLITICAL PARTIES IN THE COURSE OF TRANSITION

We have identified three key axes of confrontation and conflict-regulation in regime change: (a) relations among parties; (b) relations between parties and the military; and (c) relations between parties and social movements, such as trade unions. These form three convenient dimensions along which to compare the three transitions, and the Chilean case of authoritarian stalemate.

In Argentina politicians refused to deal with the military since, by the time negotiations were proposed in the wake of the South

Atlantic debacle, the armed forces were simply too discredited. Any proposal made by the military was rejected at once. Relations between the parties were cordial until the electoral campaign got underway, but subsequently Alfonsin attempted to gain political advantage by suggesting that certain Peronist labour union bosses were close to the military. Subsequently, the Radical government of President Alfonsin found perhaps its major weakness to be the failure to achieve any kind of *modus vivendi* with the Peronist-dominated labour unions. One can thus sum up the Argentine transition as one characterized by practically no concessions to the military, little consociation among the parties, and no successful corporatist pact between government and labour. The subsequent costs have been shown in serious frictions with the military over their demand for an amnesty, constant difficulties in Parliament (where the Radicals never won a majority in the Senate), and disruptive cycles of expansionary fiscal policy and austerity which produce waves of inflation and labour militancy.

In Uruguay, the transition to democracy was born of the most explicit pact between the opposition and the armed forces seen anywhere in South America. Since one major party was adamantly opposed to the negotiations, the transition was far from consociational, but certain concessions were made to the military. (There were no triumphant Nuremberg-style trials, in contrast to what was going on in Argentina). Finally, because the Left was a party to the pact with the military, and largely dominated the union movement, a breathing space was gained with regard to the pressing issue of economic policy in the era of massive foreign debt which provided strong pressures for austerity. A degree of cooperation (if not consociation) was thus belatedly achieved between the traditional parties by late 1986. On the other hand, the period of concertation with social movements and labour unions was by that time definitively dead.

In Brazil, the principle of a transition to democracy was conceded by the outgoing regime while it was still powerful, and this led to a decade of phased military withdrawal from power. The armed forces were nevertheless able to retain a significant degree of political influence, including cabinet positions. The military's position of strength guaranteed that many of their prerogatives would not even be questioned by politicians. Meanwhile, relations between the parties in Brazil's transition were characterized by alternating phases of unity and competitive struggle. Party alliances thus oscillated in a manner not unlike the Uruguayan experience. However, a major difference was the comparative weakness and fluidity of Brazilian parties. Economic and social issues were complicated by the divisions on the Left, the strength of the grass-roots in unions, and the weakness of centralized labour leadership. Brazil's proto-democracy thus faced serious labour unrest and dashed hopes regarding wage discipline. In sum, concessions were made to the military, consociation among the parties was limited, and attempts at corporatist-style economic stabilization failed.

In Chile, finally, opposition parties struggled to forge a consensus strategy regarding conditions for negotiating with the regime, but they remained ideologically polarized by the legacy of the Popular Unity years. Although they began cooperating after 1986, at the crucial moment in 1984 when negotiations were offered by Pinochet they were split into two rival alliances. This radicalized their stances and made negotiations nigh impossible. Meanwhile, the regime showed itself to be far more resilient and able to mobilize its core support than was the case, for example, in Argentina. There were, in other words, no concessions made to the armed forces, little consociation proved possible between the Left and the Centre, while corporatist labour restraint was simply not attempted.

The path and timing of transitions to democracy may best be predicted by an examination of the interaction of power-holders' interests and opposition strategies. Negotiated transitions from authoritarian rule, whether by means of explicit or implicit pacts, seem to require, on the one hand, the perception by opposition leaders that regime collapse is not imminent; that the armed forces are willing to make concessions; and that liberal democracy is the most important immediate political goal. On the other hand, regime power-holders must feel sure that elections will not lead to victory for their most radical enemies; that revenge trials will not be held; and that to hold on to power will be more damaging to their long-run interests than to give it up. If these evaluations and preferences are missing on either side, then successful negotiations are blocked, as in Argentina and Chile. That can mean the collapse of the AR, or its prolongation.

Notes

1. Linz terms the negotiated transition path a 'Reforma Pactada'. Juan J. Linz, 'The Transition from Authoritarian Regimes to Democratic Political Systems and the Problems of Consolidation of Political Democracy', paper presented to the Tokyo Roundtable of the IPSA, 29 March–1 April, 1982.
2. Here for convenience taken to include Brazil and exclude Paraguay.
3. Upwards of 10000 Argentines 'disappeared' as a result of the so-called
    'dirty war' against terrorism in the mid-1970s. Similar numbers of Chileans were rounded up and executed in a shorter space of time after the 1973 coup. In Uruguay, there was comparatively little assassination, but about 60000 people were arrested out of a population of less than three million. All of these countries generated a mass wave of political exiles. Brazil's armed forces were able effectively to achieve similar levels of repression more 'economically'.
4. O'Donnell has tended to refer to BAs as 'states'; many authors would prefer to use the term *regimes*, however.
5. Samuel Finer coined the phrase Stratocracy in *The Man on Horseback*, revised edition (Harmondsworth: Penguin, 1976).
6. See the Argentine journal, *Critica y utopia*, especially no. 9.
7. This was Aramburu's decision to allow the election of Frondizi, which the Navy and Air Force opposed. Argentina probably also provides a second example, this time frustrated, in the short-lived presidency of General Viola, who was ousted by Galtieri. See Andres Fontana, *Fuerzas armadas, partidos políticos y transición a la democracia en Argentina* (Estudios CEDES, 1984); and a similar essay of the same title in Augusto Varas (ed.), *Transición a la democracia* (Santiago: ACHIP-Ainavillo, 1984).
8. Heraldo Munoz, "Ideologías y redemocratización", *Alternativas* 1; Manuel Antonio Garreton, *Dictaduras y democratización* (Santiago: FLASCO Chile, 1984); and (for an author who emphasizes the 'generation of a common political interest') the introductory essay by Augusto Varas in *Transición a la democracia*.
9. In a survey of business executives and landowners carried out in 1973, interviewees were asked what social groups they agreed with most or felt best represented them. Businessmen on the whole did not identify much with the military, but landowners (Argentina's traditional elite) felt closer to the armed forces' way of thinking than to students, labour union leaders and even politicians. See Frederick Turner, *Entrepreneurs and Estancieros in Peron's Argentina* (Pittsburgh: University of Pittsburgh Press, 1983).
10. Alfred Stepan's pathbreaking analysis of newspaper editorials prior to the 1964 (and four previous) coups demonstrates the high level of legitimacy accorded to the armed forces by elite opinion leaders. See Stepam, 1971, pp. 93–121.
11. Quoted in Charles Gillespie, 'Uruguay's Transition from Collegial Military-Technocratic Rule', in Guillermo O'Donnell *et al.* (1986, p. 189).

References

Barros, R. (1986) 'The Left and Democracy: Recent Debates in Latin America', *Telos*, no. 68, Summer.
Boschi, R. (1979) *Elites industriais e democracia* (Rio de Janeiro: Graal).
Bruneau, T. and Faucher, P. (1981) *Authoritarian Capitalism* (Boulder: Westview Press).
Cardoso, F. H. (1986) 'Entrepreneurs in the Brazilian Transition Process' in: G. O'Donnell *et al.*, vol. III, pp. 137–54.
Dahl, R. (1971) *Polyarchy* (New Haven: Yale University Press).
Flisfisch, A. (1984) *Partidos y dualismo en la transición*, paper presented to the Conference on 'Procesos de democratizión y consolidación de la democracia', Santiago, April 9–12.
Foxley, A. (1983) *Latin American Experiments in Neo-Conservative Economics* (Berkeley: University of California Press).
Gillespie, C. (1984) 'The Breakdown of Democracy in Uruguay', Washington D.C., *Wilson Center Latin American Program Working Paper* no. 143. A revised Spanish version appeared in: C. Gillespie *et al.* (eds), *Uruguay y la democracia*. vol. 1 (Montevideo: Banda Oriental), 1984.
Gillespie, C. (1986) 'Activists and the Floating Voter: The Hidden Lessons of Uruguay's 1982 Primaries' in: P. Drake and E. Silva (eds), *Elections and Democratization in South America 1980–1985* (San Diego: CILAS).
Gillespie, C. (1987) *Party Strategies and Redemocratization: Theoretical and Comparative Perspective on the Uruguayan Case*, PhD thesis, Yale University.
Gillespie, C. (1989) 'Argentine Authors on Authoritarianism in Argentina', *Journal of Inter-American Studies and World Affairs*, Spring.
Gonzalez, L. E. (1983) 'Uruguay 1980–81: An Unexpected Opening', *Latin American Research Review*, vol. 18, no. 3.
Hartlyn, J. and Morley S. A. (eds) (1986) *Latin American Political Economy* (Boulder: Westview Press).
Huneeus, C. (1987) 'From Diarchy to Polyarchy: Prospects for Democracy in Chile' in: E. Baloyra (ed.), *Comparing New Democracies* (Boulder: Westview Press).
Lamounier, B. (ed.) (1980) *Voto de desconfiança: eleiçoes e mudança política no Brasil* (Petropolis: Vozes).
Linz, J. (1975) 'Totalitarian and Authoritarian Regimes' in: F. I. Greenstein and N. Polsby (eds), *Handbook of Political Science*, vol. 3, Addison-Wesley.
Linz, J. (1978) *The Breakdown of Democratic Regimes*, vol. 1: *Crisis, Breakdown and Re-equilibration* (Baltimore: Johns Hopkins University Press).
Mainwaring, S. and Share, D. (1987) 'Transitions Through Transaction' in: W. Selcher (ed), *Political Liberalization in Brazil* (Boulder: Westview Press).
Navarro, M. (1989) 'The Personal is Political' in: S. Ecktein *Power and Popular Protest in Latin America* (Berkeley: University of California Press).
O'Donnell, G. (1979a) 'Notas para el estudio de los procesos de democratización a partir del Estado burocrático-autoritario', *Estudios CEDES*, vol. 2, no. 5.

O'Donnell, G. (1979b) 'Tensions in the Bureaucratic-Authoritarian State and the Question of Democracy' in: D. Collier (ed.), *The New Authorianism in Latin America* (Princeton: Princeton University Press).

O'Donnell, G., Schmitter, P. and Whitehead, L. (eds) (1986) *Transitions from Authoritarian Rule: Prospects for Democracy* (Baltimore: Johns Hopkins University Press). Four vols. (in paperback): I Southern Europe, II Latin America, III Comparative Perspectives, IV Tentative Conclusions about Uncertain Democracies.

O'Donnell, G. (1988) *Bureaucratic Authoritarianism* (Berkeley: University of California Press).

Poulantzas, N. (1975) *La crise des dictatures* (Paris: Seuil).

Ramos, J. (1986) *Neoconservative Economics in the Southern Cone of Latin America 1973–1983* (Baltimore: Johns Hopkins University Press).

Rock, D. (1987) *Argentina 1516–1987* (Berkeley: University of California Press).

Sabato, J. and Schvarzer, J. (1985) 'Funcionamento da economia e poder político na Argentina' in: A. Rouquié *et al.* (eds), *Como renascem as democracia* (São Paulo: Editora Brasiliense).

Schmitter, P. (n.d.) *The Transition from Authoritarian Rule to Democracy in Modernizing Societies: Can Germani's Proposition (and Pessimism) be Reversed?*, manuscript.

Serra, J. (1979) *Three Mistaken Theses Regarding the Connection between Industrialization and Authoritarianism in Latin America* (Princeton: Princeton University Press).

Smith, W. (1985) 'Reflections on the Political Economy of Authoritarian Rule and Capitalist Reorganization in Contemporary Argentina'; in: P. O'Brien and P. Cammack (eds), *Generals in Retreat* (Manchester: Manchester University Press).

Stepan, A. (1971) *The Military in Politics* (Princeton: Princeton University Press).

Stepan, A. (1973) 'The New Professionalism of Internal Warfare and Military Role-Expansion' in: A. Stepan (ed.), *Authoritarian Brazil* (New Haven: Yale University Press).

Stepan, A. (1985) 'State Power and the Strength of Civil Society in the Southern Cone of Latin America' in: P. Evans *et al.* (eds), *Bringing the State Back In* (Cambridge: Cambridge University Press).

Stepan, A. (1986), 'Paths Toward Redemocratization' in: G. O'Donnell, *et al.*, vol. III, pp. 64–85.

Stepan, A. (1988) *Rethinking Military Politics* (Princeton: Princeton University Press).

Stepan, A. (1989) *Democratizing Brazil* (Oxford: Oxford University Press).

Valenzuela, A (1978) *The Breakdown of Democratic Regimes: Chile* (Baltimore: Johns Hopkins University Press).

World Bank (1979) *Uruguay Economic Memorandum*, Washington DC.

3 Retreat to Democracy: Business and Political Transition in Bolivia and Ecuador

Catherine M. Conaghan

Historians of the nineteenth and twentieth centuries provide us with a mixed picture of the role that business elites have played in the development and rupture of democracy. Their heroic moments are often followed by conservative retreats – and they have used democratic rhetoric to cloak a fear of the masses and popular participation.[1] Barrington Moore's analysis of the American Civil War (1966, 11–155) depicts Northern industrialists and Western farmers in political coalition that had democratizing effects, namely, the termination of slavery. But by the end of the nineteenth century, as Walter Dean Burnham (1965) and Samuel Hays (1980) argue, business elites in the United States were partners in a 'reform' movement which restricted lower class political participation. In Europe, business behaviour also varied. The Liberal party in Britain forged a coalition in the nineteenth century around free trade and gradual democratization that included industrialists and segments of the working class (Gourevitch, 1986, 76–83). But later, as illustrated in the debates between David Abraham (1981) and Henry Turner (1985), business played a murky role in the development of the fascist coalition in Germany.

What can be concluded from comparative national histories is that business elites have followed a variety of strategies in reference to political democratization. They might champion the cause of free labour, but oppose universal suffrage. They can become partners in a Keynesian class compromise (Przeworski, 1985; 1986) or be key players in social coalitions that support authoritarian regimes (O'Donnell, 1973; 1978). The political behaviour of business elites is conditioned by a range of historically specific factors – their material interests, their ideological proclivities, the behaviour of other social groups, the available alliance options, and cues emanating from the international system. The historical evidence demonstrates that the decision of business elites to support or retard democratization processes has much to do with their confidence in their own ability to control the processes, the character of contending groups in society, and the viability of other non-democratic political formulas.

This essay focuses on two recent South American cases in which business organizations have played critical roles in the transition from authoritarian rule to elected civilian governments – Bolivia and Ecuador. In both countries, business interest groups supported a democratization of the political system because it constituted a relatively safe retreat from the political uncertainty and unpredictable economic policy-making that prevailed under authoritarianism.[2] In the wake of the failures of military regimes in the 1970s, political democracy resurfaced as a political formula acceptable to conservative business elites. They believed that they would occupy a 'privileged position' in the system, monopolizing influence and access (Lindblom, 1977, 170–200). The transition process and the new democratic regime, however, did not prove as malleable as business had hoped. As such, business interest groups turned to extra-institutional pressure tactics to influence policy even as they took advantage of the standard practices of democratic politics.

The following essay examines the conditions that created a consensus on democracy inside the Bolivian and Ecuadorean business communities that led their interest groups to take a central role in the process of political transition. It also discusses the 'dual' political play of business in the post-transition period. Studying the role of business in political transitions is crucial to our understanding of the character of the new civilian regimes in Latin America. Because business played a central role and a conservative ethos permeated these political transitions, the prospects for socio-economic reforms and further political democratization were seriously undermined.

SLOUCHING TOWARD TRANSITION: THE ANTI-STATIST REVIVAL

The decision by Bolivian and Ecuadorean business leaders to support a return to civilian rule reflected their growing disillusionment with the military regimes of the 1970s. There was no small irony in the estrangement between the armed forces and the private sector. In each country, the business community originally supported the instalment of the military regime and largely benefited from the economic growth and modernization it sponsored. But the combination of economic growth and authoritarian decision-making structures in the 1970s produced a more politically conscious and organized bourgeoisie – one that came to resent what seemed like a sometimes irrational and overbearing state. In both countries, the movement toward political democracy on the part of business was closely intertwined with a resurgence of anti-statist sentiments.

In Ecuador, the rift between the military and business surfaced rapidly after the 1972 coup that deposed the civilian dictatorship of Jose Maria Velasco Ibarra and brought General Guillermo Rodriguez Lara to power. The coup itself was pre-emptive; it was staged to prevent a sure victory by Assad Bucaram, the populist mayor of Guayaquil, in the upcoming presidential election. Business interest groups supported the intervention; they, like the military, feared the idea of Bucaram managing Ecuador's booming oil revenues (Fitch, 1977). But almost immediately, the original coup coalition disintegrated as military reformists and civilian technocrats banded together in a progressive alliance. General Rodriguez Lara defined the new government as 'antifeudal, antioligarchic, popular, and nationalist', evoking comparisons with Peru's reformist experiment under General Velasco Alvarado. By the end of 1972, the government issued a plan setting forth its commitment to a limited agrarian reform, increased regulation of foreign capital, an expansion of the internal market, and a more dynamic role for the state as an investor and promoter of industrialization.

Once the administration laid out its mildly reformist intentions, a succession of conflicts broke out between the government and major business interest groups (Conaghan 1988). The private sector's attacks were led by the Chambers of Production. Organized in the 1930s, the Chambers grouped together Ecuador's commercial, industrial, and agricultural elites along sectoral and regional lines. The most powerful were the Chambers of Industry, Commerce, and Agriculture in the cities of Quito and Guayaquil. Separately and together, these business associations mobilized against the regime's intended reforms. They used a variety of tactics, most notably the press and public forums. In the course of these conflicts, the private sector honed its lobbying capabilities. New business associations proliferated, the regional chambers came together in national federations, and the organizations began to man technical staffs.

It is important to note that although business organizations engaged in stormy battles with the government over the reform proposals, the conflict was tempered by the substantial subsidies that flowed from the state to the private sector during the period. Businessmen enjoyed tax relief, tariff breaks, overvalued exchange rates, and cheap credit throughout the 1970s. Financial and industrial enterprises were the chief beneficiaries of this economic expansion underwritten by Ecuador's petroleum exports.

Thus, while the conflict between business and the Rodriguez Lara administration did involve some substantive disagreements, the *content* of economic policy was not the sole source of friction. Capitalists were financially strengthened and organizationally invigorated during the Rodriguez Lara period. Rather, procedural issues and the question of representation were pivotal to the deterioration in the relations between business and the military government. In a country with long-standing corporatist traditions, the Rodriguez Lara government suspended the Chambers' traditional voting rights in the government's Monetary Board and other public institutions. With the shutdown of Congress and the appointment of military officers and career civil servants to the cabinet, business organizations were marginalized from economic policy-making. Although the Chambers were invited episodically to consult with policy-makers, the suspension of regularized representation by the military government created a political limbo for all groups in society, including business. What the reformist regime discovered as opposition grew was that economic good times were not enough to secure the cooperation of business in a reformist nationalist project. Instead, what dominant class groups represented in the Chambers of Production demanded was participation in economic decision-making *and* a cooling of the reformist rhetoric that threatened the ideological status quo of Ecuadorean society.

In 1971, a new military regime was installed in Bolivia under the direction of General Hugo Banzer. Unlike the Rodriguez Lara government, it was not a reformist regime. Some analysts have argued that the labour-repressive policies of the Banzer regime mimicked those of the bureaucratic-authoritarian regimes of the Southern Cone (Dunkerley, 1984). Banzer's relationship with Bolivia's business community was not openly conflictual. Yet, Banzer's economic policies coupled with the de-institutionalizing effects of his administration restructured dominant class economic interests and altered their political perspectives by the end of the 1970s.

To understand the political behaviour of business elites in Bolivia one must take into account the relative impoverishment and under-development of Bolivia's dominant economic groups. The 1952 Revolution had a profound effect on the economic composition of dominant groups and their political power. The Revolution dispossessed the twin pillars of the Bolivian oligarchy – traditional landholding elites and the mine-owners who controlled Bolivia's tin exports. With the government's takeover of most of the mining industry and the absence of a modern manufacturing sector, the state emerged as the major employer, financier, and prime mover of the Bolivian economy in the post-1952 period (Eckstein and Hagopian, 1983).

Banzer's economic policies did not stray from the state-centric model adopted by the populist governments of the 1950s and continued by the military governments of the 1960s. He created more state-run corporations, expanded public employment, and was a ferocious public spender. The easy flow of international credit in the 1970s facilitated these policies. The result was economic expansion marked by several peculiarities. Agro-industrial enterprises in the eastern department of Santa Cruz were built with injections of state credit and enjoyed buoyant prices in the commodities markets of the early 1970s. The region also benefited from earmarked funds generated by gas and petroleum exports. Real-estate dealers and the construction industry prospered with state spending in La Paz. The purchasing power of middle-class groups expanded with increasing employment in the public sector. New consumer demand fuelled imports. Increasing consumption, rather than production was the pivot of Banzer's economic boom (Grebe Lopez, 1988).

While business and the middle class fed at the trough of the Banzer government, some discomfort over the direction of economic policy began to emerge among some business leaders. There was concern over the superfluous use of public revenues and international credit and the official tolerance of the growing business in drug-trafficking.

As in Ecuador, the authoritarian character of the regime made it difficult for business organizations to articulate these concerns and influence policy in a systematic way. Bolivian business did have the advantage of being organized into a single peak association, the Confederacion de Empresarios Privados de Bolivia (CEPB). Founded in 1958, the CEPB grouped together regional and sectoral business associations. But, the weakness of the Bolivian private sector was reflected in its organization. The CEPB was still skeletal during the

Banzerato and its political weight was limited. Banzer was not averse to threatening CEPB leaders with exile when they publicly criticized his policies.

As Malloy and Gamarra (1988) argue, the essence of the Banzer administration was its neopatrimonialism. It linked individuals and cliques to itself through clientelistic networks. Banzer integrated individuals from the business community into his government, but the ties were based on personal loyalties and opportunism. *Banzerista* businessmen in the government did not function as reliable representatives of their economic sectors. For example, despite the presence of important mine-owners in the cabinet, the Asociacion de Mineros Medianos was constantly frustrated in its campaign to rescind the high taxes on private mining companies imposed by Banzer.

In both cases, these 'representation' bottlenecks aggravated the substantive conflicts over economic policy and added to feelings of political uncertainty. In Bolivia, the uncertainty grew after Banzer botched his plan to legitimize the government through elections in 1978. That triggered a succession of inept interim governments under military and civilian direction and aborted elections culminating in the degenerate and highly repressive government of General Luis Garcia Meza in 1980–81.

Military rule in the 1970s produced inquietudes in the private sector in Bolivia and Ecuador; but these worries did not translate into unequivocal calls for political democracy. Opposition first crystallized around an anti-statist discourse. In their public pronouncements and publications, the leaders of business organizations portrayed the state as rapacious and inefficient. The private sector was depicted as the generator of economic growth and the protector of individual liberties. The ideological concerns of business were not initially focused on reconstituting political participation for the masses, but on beating back what they saw as a self-aggrandizing state. What they called for was a 'subsidiary' state, one that bankrolled private sector investment and maintained a stable investment climate. In Ecuador, the attacks by the Chambers on the state converged with pressures from right-wing political parties, producing an unsuccessful coup attempt against General Rodriguez Lara in August 1975. The right-wing mobilization against the administration was critical to the military's decision to quietly depose Rodriguez Lara in January 1976 and announce its commitment to a *retorno constitucional* (return to the constitution).

Anti-statism was the backbone of business's opposition to the military governments. Their unhappiness was important in creating a climate favourable to regime change; but it was the exhaustion of authoritarian formulas and the development of a pro-democratic consensus among other key actors, especially the military, that put business squarely on the side of transition. From the perspective of business, the military had proved to be unreliable guardians of the economy and social order. With military authoritarianism discredited, business elites joined others in pressuring for a return to civilian government. The concept of democracy could be integrated into the anti-statist discourse of businessmen because their notion of democracy was itself quite restricted. In Ecuador, the notion of *retorno constitucional* was inherently conservative; a constitutional restoration implied the resuscitation of a system that had traditionally included corporatist representation in the legislature and a restricted franchise. The advocacy of democracy by business in Ecuador was a look towards the past – a conjuring up of the 1948–64 'democratic parenthesis' when traditional party politics produced a safe rotation of conservative presidents. Bolivia's more radical past (the experience of *cogobierno* in the 1950s and the *Asamblea Popular* of 1970) made 'democracy' a riskier word in the political lexicon. And as such, Bolivian business leaders constantly qualified their use of it (Confederacion de Empresarios Privados de Bolivia, 1981). Business elites did join in the pressure for democratization, but they anxiously sought to control its scope and limit the prospective range of policy choices.

DEFEATS AND RISKS: PLAYS IN THE TRANSITION

The capacity of business groups to dominate the debates on the legal framework of the transition was constrained by their own limited political imagination, the power of contending actors and the immediate political conjuncture that effectively ruled out certain options. A critical difference between the Ecuadorean and Bolivian transitions lies in the role played by the armed forces. In Ecuador, the armed forces were able to maintain internal unity and a high degree of control over the design and execution of the *retorno constitucional*. As such, they were able to prevent any single interest group or party from dominating the designs to change the constitutional and electoral laws. Instead, the transition seesawed from 1976 through to 1979 as the military tried to mollify the right while retaining the collaboration of the centre-left. In contrast, the Bolivian military had been deprofessionalized during their exercise of political power under leaders like Garcia Meza and were overwhelmed by a society-wide rejection of its rule. Bolivian officers were unable to dictate the terms of their retreat in 1982 and the plan fell to groups in civil society, including the CEPB.

In Ecuador, the military rejected the transition formula put forth by the right to convoke a constituent assembly. Traditional parties of the right believed that they could dominate such proceedings. Instead, after public 'dialogues' with interest groups and parties, the military opted for a plebiscite in which the electorate chose between a revamped version of Ecuador's 1945 constitution and a completely new one. The two constitutional options were formulated by civilian commissions appointed by the military government. At the same time, another civilian commission was formed to devise a political parties law and supervise the electoral process. Much to the dissatisfaction of the business chambers, leaders of reformist parties (most notably Jaime Roldos of the Concentracion de Fuerzas Populares and Osvaldo Hurtado of Democracia Popular) were able to dominate the commissions. The new constitution, in contrast to the revised 1945 version, fundamentally challenged the old oligarchic style of politics. It extended the franchise to illiterates, eliminated functional representation in the legislature, established a unicameral Congress, and endorsed the development of a 'communitarian' sector of the economy to complement public, private and mixed investment.[3]

The business chambers blanched at the reform proposals and were quick to malign the work of the commissions. In Guayaquil, the Chamber of Industry denounced the constitutional plebiscite and organized a campaign urging voters to cast null ballots in protest. But the new constitution was the clear favourite in the plebiscite of January 1978. It won 43 per cent of the vote while the null ballot option garnered only 23 per cent of the vote.

Despite this defeat, the Chambers continued their opposition to the reforms. Leon Febres-Cordero, president of the Guayaquil Chamber of Industry, belittled the results and called the validity of the plebiscite into question (Camara de Industrias de Guayaquil, 1978). The Chamber of Industry of Quito demanded a sober rethinking of the constitution's principles by the incoming civilian government (Camara de Industriales de Pinchincha 1978). In short, there were different responses by business organizations to defeat in the electoral sphere. One response was to raise questions about the legitimacy of the process, thus providing ideological ammunition for a possible abrogation of the process; the other response was to suggest continued politicking and pressure to defuse reformism via the new democratic channels. These two responses became a well-worn part of business's political repertoire – and they were emblematic of the approach of business to the new political arrangements. On one hand, business organizations seemed prepared to engage in pressure politics within the confines of the new democratic arrangements. Yet, along with this play, there was a parallel tendency to undermine the game when it resulted in undesirable 'outputs'. As we shall see in the following section, this dynamic became engrained in post-transition politics and continues to wear away at the prospects of sustained democratic development in Ecuador.

By 1982, the mechanics of the transition itself were not the subject of an extended dispute in Bolivia. In the wake of the prolonged political and economic crisis, a broad consensus developed on the desirability of a quick restoration of a popularly based civilian government; but the sticking point was how to avoid the attendant problems of calling new elections. The apparent *salida* (exit) was to convoke the Congress-elect of 1980, which had the constitutional power to select a president. This solution received widespread support from all sectors, including the CEPB and Bolivia's trade union confederation, the Central Obrera Boliviana (COB).

Why did the CEPB become an ardent advocate of the recall of the 1980 Congress as the means to re-install civilian rule? The answer is not immediately obvious since the recall was sure to result in the selection of Hernan Siles as President and Jaime Paz Zamora as Vice-President. Siles headed the coalition Union Democratica Popular (UDP). The UDP included Siles' own MNRI (a fragment of the original populist MNR), the social democratic Movimiento Izquierda Revolucionario (MIR), and the Bolivian Communist Party (PCB). While no one could predict the exact course that Siles would eventually take, it was clear that his government would be highly sympathetic to the pent-up demands of the trade union movement. Nonetheless, the CEPB wholeheartedly supported the 1980 recall.

The decision of the CEPB leaders was based on their cunning (and probably correct) evaluation of the options available to them in the immediate political context. Siles had been denied the presidency twice. In the July 1979 election, he won a slim plurality of the popular vote but the Congress deadlocked and eventually endorsed Walter Guevera Arce of the MNR as an interim civilian president pending new elections. Siles went on to win the June 1980 election, but was again prevented from taking office by the Garcia Meza coup of July 1980. Thus, Siles and the UDP had a legitimate claim to executive power. Moreover, the years of right-wing military rule had discredited the right as a whole, making the imposition or election of any conservative civilian government impossible. CEPB leaders recognized that they would have to accept some veer toward the left by an incoming government as part of the package of political transition. Two assumptions made the Siles option tolerable from their perspective: (1) The Siles government would be operating under great constraints and given its 'artificial' origins could be pressured into early elections if necessary; (2) Politico-economic management by the Siles government would prove unsatisfactory, discredit the left, and create conditions for an electoral victory of conservative forces. A high-ranking leader of the CEPB described the Machiavellian reasoning:

> Well, I don't want to be cynical about this, but I think we all realized that after the military government we were going to have a very difficult time. I was willing to see whether the left could do it ... I wasn't surprised to see them fail ... Unless the left tried it, we would never have peace in this country. They had to try it. They were sure they had the majority; they had won democratically. Anything we would have done to change that and bring a government of the center or center-right would have been like snatching the government from their hands. We couldn't run that risk. We had to let them govern although we knew they couldn't do it ... Now, our questions and frustrations were two: 1) How much of a mess were they going to make? 2) How long will they resist? But we knew that after this, we had to have a chance, which is exactly what happened.[4]

In both cases, business organizations were unable to oversee a transition completely to their liking. They were important actors, but their influence was always constrained by other players in civil society and the state. Cross-cutting pressures exerted by trade unions, popular organizations, and political parties did not permit a unilateral direction of the transition by any single actor. From the perspective of business organizations, the specific unfolding of the transition was less than optimal, at least in the short run. Both transitions put in place governments with reformist intentions. But business organizations were far from defeated – instead, they were invigorated by the skirmishes with the new reformist governments and the conflicts laid the foundation for a political resuscitation of the right. This resurgence culminated in the election of subsequent governments that replaced reformism with neoliberal economics.

NORMALITY AND CRISIS IN THE POST-TRANSITION

Once civilians took over, politics was played at two levels in Ecuador and Bolivia. Formally, the new rules of 'polyarchal' play were in place (Dahl, 1971). Societal demands were to be freely expressed and channelled through the multiple access points (executive, legislature, courts) that democracy provides. But, as might be expected, ironing out the authority relationships among the new institutions and societal groups was conflictual, especially as the debt crisis of the 1980s made economic management more difficult. Struggles among branches of government and between government and interest groups became part of a chronic 'crisis production' scenario in the post-transition. Moreover, the persistence of non-polyarchal politics continually undermined 'normal' play under polyarchal rules. Frustrations or defeats inside the domain of 'normal' politics led groups to engage in other forms of pressure ranging from open threats of coups to destabilizing behaviour in the market.

Business organizations operated on both levels of politics. Sometimes, they engaged in mundane democratic politics; they lobbied quietly and called for restraint and compromise. Yet, at other times, their ferocious attacks on the new governments seemed periously close to undermining them altogether. But business groups were not alone in this dangerous play. In Ecuador, party leaders also engaged in debilitating attacks and internecine conflicts that heightened the crisis atmosphere and eroded the government's capacity to act. In Bolivia, a tripartite conflict emerged among the COB, the CEPB, and the Siles administration. The net result, in either case, was to defuse each government's capacity to engage in anything but crisis management. Out of this process, reformism was stilled and the conditions for a conservative renaissance were born.

As my earlier discussion indicates, business efforts to squelch reformist discourse in Ecuador surfaced early in the transition in their opposition to the constitutional referendum. The push to remove reform from the terms of political debate continued during the transitional presidential election of 1979. Right-wing leaders repeatedly depicted the centrist ticket of Jaime Roldos and Osvaldo Hurtado as communist sympathizers who would replay the Allende experience in Ecuador. As in the conflict over the constitution, business lost the immediate battle. The conservative candidate, Sixto Duran Ballen, was overwhelmingly defeated and Jaime Roldos of the populist Concentracion de Fuerzas Populares assumed the presidency on 10 August 1979.

Nevertheless, early business attacks on Roldos did produce some pay-offs. On the ideological level, the accusations hurled at Roldos and Hurtado forced the candidates into proving their moderation. Their platform of '21 Points' was mild, vague, and decidedly on the side of a market model of the economy. Once elected, Roldos bolstered private sector confidence by appointing businessmen to his economic team. Despite these signals, business organizations remained uneasy during Roldos' term in office. The businessmen in the Roldos cabinet were not drawn from the inner circles of the Chambers; therefore, they were generally not perceived as reliable representatives of the most developed fractions of Ecuadorean capital.[5]

Furthermore, Roldos' populist roots and mass-based support remained worrisome to business organizations. However, this anxiety did not translate into any overt business mobilization against the Roldos administration. Events *elsewhere* in the system were effectively undercutting the Roldos government and rendered any direct action by business unnecessary. The fragmentation of Roldos' CFP created an executive-legislative stalemate that paralyzed the government in its first year. The impasse was resolved but was followed by the first signs of the economic crisis in 1981 that weakened the fiscal position of the government, limiting its capacity to engage in new initiatives.

Roldos' death in a May 1981 plane crash and Osvaldo Hurtado's succession to the presidency altered the political dynamics. Business (especially the Chamber of Industry of Guayaquil) shifted to frontal attacks on the Hurtado administration, even calling for breaches in constitutional procedure to remove him. The massive anti-government campaign that involved all major business groups came in response to Hurtado's attempts to revive some of the government's reformist agenda in the areas of tax, labour, and consumer protection laws. (Mills, 1984, 83–126). Inflammatory rhetoric by business leaders raised the stakes of the conflict. Romulo Lopez, leader of the Guayaquil Chamber of Industry, called for military intervention. Leon Febres-Cordero, ex-president of the same organization and congressman from the Social Christian party, called for Hurtado's resignation. He suggested that the president of Congress replace Hurtado, a move that would have violated the succession procedure laid out in the constitution. In March 1983, the Chamber of Commerce of Guayaquil led a 48-hour merchants' strike to protest against the import restrictions which were part of Hurtado's austerity package.

The attacks on the Hurtado administration aptly illustrate how political and ideological considerations can take primacy over economic motives in shaping the strategies of business organizations, especially in the fluid circumstances prevailing in a post-transitional situation. Objectively speaking, the bulk of Hurtado's economic measures were highly favourable to the private sector. The battle between the Chambers and Hurtado was for politico-ideological ground (Handelman, 1985). Business sought to sharply limit the scope of the new political debate, enshrine pro-business values in public discourse, and ensure their influence over economic policy-making. Hurtado's public derision of the Chambers and his conscious efforts to insulate his economic team from external interference threatened to undermine the position of the Chambers as the legitimate interlocutors of the private sector. These attacks by business groups and by conservative political parties (under the emerging leadership of businessman Leon Febres-Cordero) laid the groundwork for a successful electoral challenge by the Right in 1984. The Right, by virtue of this partisan and corporate mobilization, was able to monopolize the 'oppositional space' in the political arena, a space crucial to winning elections in the context of a deteriorating economic situation. They were able to blame Hurtado for economic crisis and portray themselves as the alternative.

In Bolivia, any semblance of 'normal' politics virtually disappeared by 1983, less than a year after Siles' assumption of the presidency. Instead, nearly all of the relevant actors on the scene (parties, regional civic committees, the COB, and the CEPB) utilized highly charged pressure tactics – general strikes, business lock-outs, regional *paros civicos* (civic strikes). Intimidations and threats defined the dominant mode of political behaviour. In Bolivia, as in Ecuador, business was but one of several actors that engaged in this confrontational style of politics. The aggregate effect of this behaviour was to strain democratic arrangements to their very limits.

The threats to the Siles government were even greater than those suffered by Hurtado because of the intensity of class conflict in

Bolivia and the way in which the struggle was transposed onto the state. The main contenders in this conflict were the CEPB and the COB. The CEPB faced a formidable foe in the COB. Some leaders of the COB saw the period as a time to press for basic wage demands while others believed it was the moment to push for a socialist transformation of Bolivia. In other words, both reform and revolution became part of the stakes of the struggle (Lazarte, n.d.; Malloy and Gamarra, 1988).

The conflict between the two was expressed in direct confrontations and in clashes with the Siles government over at least five economic stabilization programs (*paquetes economicos*). Caught between such powerful societal actors and stripped of a party base with the disintegration of the UDP alliance, the Siles government slipped back and forth between attempts to appease the COB and the CEPB. In the process, it lost its capacity to initiate policy, implement it, or even keep the public order. The cost of policy incoherence was high; a catastrophic hyper-inflation further eroded the government's legitimacy (Morales, 1987; Nunez del Prado 1986).

The deepening economic crisis and the almost complete isolation of the government led parties and groups to contemplate ways of removing Siles. The options sounded out ranged from attempts to interest the military in intervention to a *golpe constitucional* suggested by the congressional opposition. The 'constitutional coup' idea involved the impeachment of Siles and his replacement by Vice-President Jaime Paz Zamora.

The ultimate *salida* was the product of a consensus among political parties and the CEPB. It was formulated in emergency meeting convoked by the Catholic Church in November 1984 (Muller and Machicado, 1986). The formula involved an early scheduling of presidential elections in July 1985. The acceptance of this scheme signalled the eclipse of the COB's power. It adamantly rejected the idea, knowing that the prospects for a conservative victory were good. Despite COB attempts to block the electoral process, the plan proceeded.

As in Ecuador, the destabilizing behaviour of business organizations quickly receded as the prospects for an electoral victory by the right grew palpable. In each country, the Right could pose as the opposition to failing heterodox economic policies. Business's decision to cling to democracy was closely tied to their hopes for electoral success and a repenetration of the policy-making process.

FROM MILITARY AUTHORITARIANISM TO UNCERTAIN DEMOCRACY

So far, business's gamble on democracy in Bolivia and Ecuador has yielded some returns. While risks and dangers have permeated transition and post-transition stages, business manoeuvred to fend off threats from labour and reform-minded governments. This success, however, hinged on the willingness of business to swing out of mundane polyarchal play and engage in more provocative methods that, at times, have threatened the durability of the new institutional arrangements. Business interest group leaders were not the only practitioners of this incendiary style of politics. Parties and other organizations joined in the fray.

The struggles of the private sector for political security culminated in the installation of conservative governments. In 1984, Leon Febres-Cordero, Ecuador's most flamboyant spokesperson for the private sector, won the presidency in a narrow election. In Bolivia, the 1985 presidential election was thrown into Congress after no candidate received a majority. Victor Paz Estensorro of the MNR emerged as the winner, striking an alliance with Banzer's right-wing Accion Democrata Nacional (ADN) and securing their support for a draconian neoliberal economic programme.

Despite the commitment of these conservative governments to orthodox economics,[6] it would be a mistake to see these electoral victories as constituting a direct re-occupation of the state by business interest groups. Rather, important groups within the private sector discovered that orthodox economic technocrats could be as uncontrollable as any reformist politician or general. Tough fights over the content of economic policy occurred even in these pro-business governments. Yet, the tone of the conflict was different; gentlemanly rules of conduct prevailed and the legitimacy of the regime was not publicly questioned by business groups.

The types of regimes that have emerged out of these processes defy simplistic classification. O'Donnell and Schmitter (1986) refer to them as 'uncertain democracies'. Power has rotated among civilian politicians through elections, but severe problems of accountability continue to wrack institutional life. The executive defies the legislature at will, economic technocrats have a stranglehold over policy, and the military still remains as an autonomous entity. Moreover, judging from pronouncements and behaviour, the commitment of relevant political actors to maintain democratic arrangements still appears to be highly contingent – that is to say, dependent on their ability to extract favourable 'outputs' from the system, either in terms of concrete policies or in ideological/symbolic pay-offs. This conditional acceptance of democracy by business and other actors injects a chronic volatility into the political environment. Under these conditions, substantive conflicts over policy can easily degenerate into crises that threaten the viability of the system as a whole. In other words, 'normal' politics remains easily and frequently disrupted.

The narrative of recent democracy in Bolivia and Ecuador is neither dull nor happy. In several instances, the crisis situations have been played out in ways reminiscent of Juan Linz's breakdown scenario (1978). The key factor preventing a breakdown so far has been the military's reticence to intervene and act as crisis manager. Meanwhile, business's ambivalence toward the regimes continues and democracy retains an uncertain quality.

Notes

This chapter is based on an ongoing research project dealing with the private sector and economic policy-making in Bolivia, Peru and Ecuador being undertaken by the author in collaboration with James Malloy (University of Pittsburgh) and Luis Abugattas (Universidad del Pacífico, Lima). To assure the anonymity of our informants, the material taken from personal interviews conducted by the author is cited only by date, location, and institutional affiliation.

1. For a discussion of business's political behaviour in the case of the United States, see the works by Kirkland (1956), McCloskey (1951), Prothro (1954), and Vogel (1978).
2. In this essay, a transition is defined as the 'interval between one political regime and another'. The period is characterized by a struggle among political actors to define the new rules of the political game. The concept of democratization encompasses 'processes whereby rules and procedures of citizenship are either applied to political institutions previously governed by other principles, or expanded to include persons not previously enjoying such rights and obligations, or extended to cover issues and institutions not previously subject to citizen participation'. These are the definitions developed by O'Donnell and Schmitter (1986, 6–8).
3. The two constitutions can be found in Calle Orleans (1978).
4. Interview, CEPB, 11 February 1987, La Paz.

5. Interviews with members of the Roldos cabinet, 19 March 1986, Quito; 21 January 1987, Quito; 2 February 1987, Guayaquil.
6. In the long run, Febres-Cordero did not maintain his commitment to orthodox policies. His government was never able to reduce public expenditures and toward the end of the term turned to public works spending to offset its flagging popularity. In contrast, the Paz Estenssoro government in Bolivia implemented a tough neoliberal economic programme.

References

Abraham, D. (1981) *The Collapse of the Weimar Republic: Political Economy and Crisis* (Princeton: Princeton University Press).

Burnham, W. D. (1965) 'The Changing Shape of the American Political Universe', *American Political Science Review*, no. 59 (March), pp. 10–28

Calle Orleans, L. (1978) *La Constitución de 1978 y el proceso de reestructuración jurídica del Estado 1976–1978*, Guayaquil: Instituto de Investigaciones Jurídicas, Universidad de Guayaquil.

Camara de Industriales de Pichincha (1978) 'Reflexión política', *Carta Industrial*, no. 34 (September).

Camara de Industrias de Guayaquil (1978) 'Informe anual presentado por el Presidente de la Cámara de Industrias de Guayaquil', *Revista de la Camara de Industrias de Guayaquil*, vol. 9, no. 38.

Conaghan, C. (1988) *Restructuring Domination: Industrialists and the State in Ecuador* (Pittsburgh: University of Pittsburgh Press).

Confederación de Empresarios Privados de Bolivia (1981) *Pensamiento de la empresa privada boliviana.* (La Paz: Confederacion de Empresarios Privados de Bolivia).

Dahl, R. (1971) *Polyarchy: Participation and Opposition* (New Haven: Yale University Press).

Dunkerley, J. (1984) *Rebellion in the Veins: Political Struggle in Bolivia 1952–82* (London: Verso).

Eckstein, S. and Hagopian, F. (1983) 'The Limits of Industrialization in the Less Developed World: Bolivia', *Economic Development and Cultural Change*, vol. 32, no. 1 (October), pp. 63–95.

Fitch, S. (1977) *The Military Coup d'Etat as a Political Process: Ecuador 1948–1966* (Baltimore: Johns Hopkins University Press).

Gourevitch, E. (1986) *Politics in Hard Times: Comparative Responses to International Economic Crises* (Ithaca: Cornell University Press).

Grebe Lopez, H. (1988) 'Innovaciones de las políticas económico-social en la Bolivia postdictatorial', *Working Paper* no. 17, FLACSO-Bolivia.

Handelman, H. (1985) 'Elite Interest Groups under Military and Democratic Regimes: Ecuador, 1972–1984, paper presented at the Latin American Studies Association Congress, Albuquerque, New Mexico, April.

Hays, S. (1980) *American Political History as Social Analysis: Essays* (Knoxville: University of Tennessee Press).

Kirkland, E. (1956) *Dream and Thought in the Business Community* (Chicago: Quadrangle Books).

Lazarte, J. (n.d.) 'El moviviento obrero: Crisis y opción de futuro de la COB', In: FLACSO-ILDIS (eds), *Crisis del sindicalismo en Bolivia* (La Paz: FLACSO-ILDIS).

Lindblom, C. (1977) *Politics and Markets: The World's Political-Economic System* (New York: Basic Books).

Linz, J. (1978) 'Crisis, Breakdown, Reequilibration', in: J. Linz and A Stepan (eds), *The Breakdown of Democratic Regimes* (Baltimore: Johns Hopkins University Press).

Malloy, J. and Gamarra E. (1988) *Revolution and Reaction: Bolivia 1964–1985* (New Brunswick: Transaction Books).

McCloskey, Robert (1951) *American Conservatism in the Age of Enterprise: 1865–1910* (New York: Harper & Row).

Mills, N. D. (1984) *Crisis, conflicto y consenso: Ecuador 1979–1984* (Quito: Corporación Editora Nacional).

Moore, B., Jr. (1966) *Social Origins of Dictatorship and Democracy: Lord and Peasant in the Making of the Modern World* (Boston: Beacon Press).

Morales, J. A. (1987) *Precios, salarios y política económica durante la alta inflacion boliviana de 1982 a 1985* (La Paz: ILDIS).

Muller, H. and Machicado F. (1986) *El diálogo para la democracia* (La Paz: Muller y Machicado Asociados).

Nunez del Prado, A. (1986), 'Bolivia: inflación y democracia', *Pensamiento Ibero-americano*, no. 9 (2. semestre), pp. 249–75.

O'Donnell, G. (1973) *Modernization and Bureaucratic-Authoritarianism: Studies in South American Politics* (Berkeley: University of California Press).

O'Donnell G. (1978) 'Reflections on the Patterns of Change in the Bureaucratic Authoritarian State', *Latin American Research Review*, vol. 12, no. 1 (Winter), pp. 3–39.

O'Donnell, G. and Schmitter P. (1986) *Transitions from Authoritarian Rule: Prospects for Democracy*, vol. IV, *Tentative Conclusions about Uncertain Democracies* (Baltimore: Johns Hopkins University Press).

Przeworski, A. (1985) *Capitalism and Social Democracy* (Cambridge: Cambridge University Press).

Przeworski, A. (1986) 'Some Problems in the Study of Transition to Democracy', in: G. O'Donnell, P. Schmitter and L. Whitehead (eds), *Transitions from Authoritarian Rule: Prospects for Democracy,* vol. III, *Comparative Perspectives*, pp. 47–64 (Baltimore: Johns Hopkins University Press).

Prothro, J. (1954) *The Dollar Decade: Business Ideas in the 1920s* (Baton Rouge: Louisiana State Univesity Press).

Turner, H. (1985) *German Big Business and the Rise of Hitler* (New York: Oxford University Press).

Vogel, David (1978) 'Why Businessmen Distrust their State: The Political Consciousness of American Corporate Executives', *The British Journal of Political Science*, vol. 8 no. 1 (January), pp. 169–73.

4 Economists and Democratic Transition: The Quest for Governability in Chile[1]
Veronica Montecinos

Because the process of transition to democracy in many Latin American countries has taken place in the context of the debt crisis of the 1980s, studies in political economy have been questioning with new emphasis the old relationship between economic growth and democratic stability.[2] This chapter deals with the role of Chilean economists in politics and policy-making during the transition and beyond.[3] Government economists in Chile acquired a highly hegemonic position in the authoritarian government, becoming notorious for the radicalism of their policies and the broadness of their influence. Also within the democratic opposition economists have greatly strengthened their political role. We wonder how 'technocratic' the next democratic regime will be in facing the challenges of a difficult economy. Will the role of economists affect the governability and/or the democratic character of the new regime? Rather than simply fearing the growing influence of economists in government, Latin American democrats should give more thought to the kind of economics, ethical and political values that economists learn as well as to the institutional position they have in parties and government.

THE CHILEAN TRANSITION TO DEMOCRACY

Compared to other experiences in the region, the Chilean transition remains delayed and problematic, in spite of Chile's long democratic tradition, the vitality of the party system, and the enormous electoral enthusiasm that the Chilean people showed in the recent plebiscite.[4] After the defeat of General Pinochet in the October 1988 plebiscite (54 per cent of the electorate voted NO to the continuation of his rule) presidential elections were to be held at the end of 1989. The democratic forces have still to consolidate their unity and strive to modify some of the provisions established in the 1980 constitution.

The Chilean authoritarian regime, encouraged by some economic achievements[5] and wrongly confident in its capacity to remain in power failed to engage in *apertura*. It has been consistently reluctant to provide changes in leadership or appropriate mechanisms for legal continuity.[6] In the opposition, many of the old political leaders are still in control of the party structures but the suppression of political rights and the long years of exile have in many ways altered the composition and behaviour of the Chilean political class. Fifteen years with no parties, no Congress, no free elections, no channels of political communication between the military and the traditional representatives of the citizenry have transformed Chilean politics in ways that still have to be assessed.

Unity and pragmatism have proved necessary to defeat such a stubborn authoritarian government. In the years after the coup, political actors of the Centre and the Left, particularly intellectuals, have busily engaged in political and theoretical self-criticisms.[7] Democratic political forces have recently involved in strategies of concertation, pragmatic inter-party negotiations and political 'realism'.[8] Economists in the opposition have been among those who call for moderation. In preparing the transition in Chile, economists, more often than politicians, have created and enjoyed opportunities to discuss their agreements and differences with respect to the specific policies of a new elected government.[9]

If these conciliatory drives last, the transition process could lead to a transformation rather than a simple restoration of the traditionally praised, but highly ideological and polarized pre-coup Chilean democracy. 'Renovacion' is a word that *almost everybody* uses in present Chilean politics, meaning the renewal of political culture, political institutions and leadership, and the rejection of economic and political experimentation that could endanger democratic survival. Perhaps pragmatism and political cooperation will also prove useful in reconstructing democratic institutions within a more participatory and egalitarian model for economic development. There is a sense that political democracy, which in Chile is framed in a small and 'difficult' economy, should not bring just another of the several paradigmatic – capitalist, reformist, socialist – solutions that governments have tried in the last three decades.

THE POLITICAL ROLE OF ECONOMIC MANAGERS

Because of the serious constraints imposed by the present economic crisis, the politics of Latin American redemocratization revolves around 'economic packages' (Malloy, 1987, 256). No matter how successful the process of democratic institution-building might be, the impact of the present economic troubles on the new Latin American democracies cannot be dismissed. The chances that new democratic leadership have of consolidating democracy are, to a significant extent, tied to an effective management of the economy. The military, the international financial community, powerful and excluded groups alike are monitoring the coherence and results of economic policies. Even though re-enfranchised populations may be willing to lower their expectations in exchange for democracy, imbalances between economic and political performance could unleash non-democratic forces or disenchant those who initially support the democratic coalition. In transitions heavily associated with the quest for governability, those who supply 'technical' ideas come closer to those who are skilful in the 'art' of politics.

With the reopening of the electoral game, Latin American politicians are expected to replace the hegemonic position that technocrats had under authoritarianism. Patronage in the distribution of resources and more participatory forms of policy-making are also expected to reappear. These expectations, however, enter quickly into conflict with the calls for economic austerity. While the debt crisis and the prevailing developmental models[10] favour the compression of power[11] and the search for centralized management, democracy invites participation and the satisfaction of long-repressed demands. In the tension between crisis management and democratic restoration, economists and politicians strive to define who gets what and when, almost regardless of how much to the left or to the right their proposals are. Being at the core of the articulation of politics and the economy, economic managers have become increasingly important political actors.

The expanded power of administrators, managers and technocrats, is a trend of parties and governments in democratic and authoritarian regimes of the Left and the Right. This trend greatly affects the organizational forms of policy-making. In Latin America, the rise in technical approaches to public policy and the technocratization of state economic elites accompanied the dilemmas posed by the exhaustion of developmental models and the political incorporation of the popular sector. Although 'technocratism' was present in reformist-modernizer governments in the 1960s, it became a crucial variable in the characterization of the authoritarian regimes (O'Donnell, 1973).

Analyses of the present wave of democratic transitions have paid less attention to the technocratic syndrome. The literature on the consolidation of democracy, although recognizing the importance of economic conditions, has concentrated on the study of party systems, constitutional rules, the strategic behaviour of political actors and their loyalty to democracy as a political regime.[12] Although economists as policy-makers manage one of the most basic sources of uncertainty in the transit from authoritarianism to democracy, they have not been a focus of scholarly attention.

Are economists prepared to perform this highly political role? Are they trying to impose the 'economist's view of the world', monopolizing government policy, providing the limits of what is politically feasible? Are politicians empowering themselves to oversee the action of economic managers? Can economists and politicians collaborate in the political economy of democratic consolidation, reshaping together the old political class in the search for democratic governability?

In comparative studies of redemocratization, the political role of economic managers seems as important as the role of business, parties and the military. While it is very clear that democratic consolidation requires the depoliticization of the military, the politicization of economic managers is a more complicated matter. In fact, politicization may be healthier than allegedly scientific, classless neutrality! The active involvement of economists in party politics may enhance their awareness of the rules and constraints of electoral competition. Economists in government do their job better when they understand the 'politics' of policy-making: the dynamics of implementation, the traditional practices of clientelism, the need for compromise, strategic delay, symbolic rhetoric, bureaucratic uncertainty.

Studies of government actors in Europe and the USA have focused on the relationships between *bureaucrats* and *politicians*.[13] In Latin America, we should pay special attention to the relationship between *technocrats* and *politicians*. Latin American technocrats have challenged, enhanced, and even replaced the power of politicians as much as powerful bureaucrats do in countries in which tenure in office is associated with technical competence and bureaucratic power.

Economists, among social 'scientists', are most akin in providing routes to social change without paying tribute to 'politics as usual'. Some economists (Becker, 1976) have tried to expand their domain of expertise by arguing that the economic approach is not only useful in understanding problems within the conventional field of economics, but in *all* human behaviour. The 'economics of politics' has evolved into a major branch by developing rational models of political behaviour. In the tradition of Schumpeter, economists are puzzled by the way in which 'voters and parties make choices about public goods' (Bosanquet, 1983, 66). The logic of bureaucratic actors, and the search for a fiscal constitution to ensure balanced budgets have become central to the study of politics by economists.

Economists, claiming to have a theory for the rational allocation of resources in society, have increasingly become a key component of political power. Members of this highly internationalized profession are giving advice on crucial state matters, usually without being held accountable for the wrongdoings derived from their ideas. They generate and interpret sensitive information, moving from public to non-public arenas, providing contacts and acting as spokesmen for those who do not speak the language of economics. Is it the growing complexity of government affairs that makes it reasonable to employ more professional economists in government? Some think that economists ritually present as incomprehensible what could be done as well, or better, by common-sense laypeople.

LATIN AMERICAN ECONOMIC THINKING AND DEMOCRACY

Traditionally in Latin America, politics and policy-making have been greatly influenced by shifts in economic thinking. In fact, the short path between new ideas and their acceptance as part of government programmes was long ago characterized by A. Hirschman (1963) as a 'pseudo-creative form of solving problems' (quoted in Foxley, 1985a, 5). Latin American countries, ravaged with endemic economic illnesses receive the often contradictory advice of native and foreign economists in successive waves of enthusiasm, dogmatism and disappointment. As Fishlow (1985) notes, in the fifties and sixties the remedies were industrialization, planning, land and fiscal reform (applied in Chile by the Frei government). Then structuralism came under attack from the Left: the dependency school proposed changes in development through alterations in income distribution and the structures of production (the Allende programme). Later, the Right counter-proposed a return to free trade monetarism and export-oriented growth (the Pinochet policies). None of these proposals worked as expected.[14] All of them, at least during their honeymoon period of trial, provided great self-confidence to their proponents, who often failed to acknowledge the strong political echoes that their proposals had over state limits and power distribution.[15]

In 1986, Hirschman suggested that the new democratic governments might benefit from the *post-ideological* mood of present economic thinking in Latin America. This new approach has been characterized as a 'pragmatic neo-structuralism',[16] a combination of various theoretical perspectives, a middle ground between *laissez-faire* and *dirigisme*, resting on the cooperation of state and market, capital and labour, redistribution and productivity (Fishlow, 1985, 142). In the post-authoritarian period, democratic economists must become very innovative indeed. The issues at stake (technical and political) are extremely controversial: concertation to support moderate income gains and increase private investments; continuation of trade liberalization and export growth while improving the provision of basic needs.

That the new thinking of economists might contribute to democratic consolidation by giving politicians new grounds for negotiation and agreement may seem daring in view of how instrumental some of their colleagues were for authoritarian governments. The stubbornness with which democratic and non-democratic economists so often stick to their pet policies does not help their image of democratic heroes. In fact, the economic teams of the new democracies in Latin America have been notorious for not engaging in broad consultation to implement their policy proposals. Can we expect economists to play a positive role in the rebuilding of democracy? Let us come back to the Chilean case.

ECONOMISTS IN THE CHILEAN TRANSITION

Economic policies have had a particularly encompassing impact on Chilean politics. The last three administrations have engaged in sweeping cycles of statizations and privatizations, affecting the distribution of property and income and the power bases of social groups. In the last decade, economists of all persuasions have been actively concerned with the future of Chilean politics. The Chicago Boys economists, in their efforts to insulate economic decisions from the 'particularism' of party politics, perceived themselves as leading the 'modernization' of Chilean democracy, which they equated with the 'depoliticization' of politics. These economists turned to lawyers to sanctify constitutionally their proposals as the ideological backbone for long-term authoritarianism. The Chicago Boys borrowed heavily from the language and social philosophy of the 'New Right'. Ironically, while enjoying the advantages of dictatorial power in dismantling state interventionism, they forcefully argued that the market should replace the conspiratory drives of government and party bureaucracies. They thought a return to politicization would inevitably lead to the decline in individual liberty, the expansion of public spending and government centralization, and the reduction in the rate of growth.[17]

Economists in the opposition have championed the idea that the modernization of Chilean politics requires moderating the trends towards polarization by making politics more consensual and less ideological and confrontational than it was before the coup. They have joined those who encourage parties to develop a less 'religious' approach to politics, a more realistic political discourse based on more sophisticated theoretical bases. These calls for a redefinition of what politics is, and how democratic forces should behave in future democracy stem in part as a reaction to the neoliberal ideology. It is also related to the unfulfilled expectations of the successive 'revolutions' of the sixties and early seventies. Of course, the extent to which Chilean politics will actually change remains to be seen.

Many opposition economists are now being defined as 'politicians'. These economists-politicians have tried to introduce new categories in the political discourse. They say they favour a politics of 'solutions', a move 'from ideology to pragmatism', using a 'theory of menus [addressing discrete issues] rather than a theory of models [global societal transformations]'. A new concept of politics is needed, they say, 'a concept in which power, institutions and policy instruments are linked together, not loose as they were before'. And another economist, minister in the democratic period, adds that 'in the past, economic exigencies were ridiculed. Now, politicians have reluctantly come to accept that unsound economic management can have disastrous political consequences.' Opposition economists of the Centre, the Left, and even some in the democratic Right, I was told repeatedly in my interviews, do not think too differently. Economists can easily arrive at agreements, whereas parties, they say, do not like to recognize that they converge. Party leaderships are reluctant to follow the consensual political line of economists and, in looking for continuities with the policies implemented during the authoritarian period, it seems easier for economists than for politicians to acknowledge that some of those changes could have a potentially positive impact on future economic development.

In the struggle to bring about democratization, politicians in the opposition came to realize that economists had more chances to participate in the kind of public debate allowed by the military. Christian Democrat and Socialist economists constantly invalidated the charges of technical ineptitude that the Chicago Boys liked to direct against the democratic opposition. Leftist economists have also contributed to reinforce the image of a renovated and modern Chilean socialism. In public debates and in party negotiations, opposition economists learned to present economic problems in a political manner. Parties with able economic teams have gained strength in current Chilean politics, even when they had a small political apparatus. Conversely, parties with small economic teams now look weak and old fashioned.

Critics of the political influence of economists say economists are over-represented in the politics of transition. Although the economists' taste for political engineering has gained legitimacy, they say, in the end economists are resisted and have more adversaries than supporters within the parties. A lawyer-politician said:

> Economists look more to Washington or Paris than to Chilean provinces. Even though some of them have gone through a perfect transmutation, they have not entered into the more sacrificed dimension of politics, in which careers are built in 25 years, not in one year.

Economists' intellectualized conception of politics – a leftist politician told me – makes them biased for negotiation and compromise, without recognizing the confrontational character of the Chilean political situation. Another member of the leftist wing of the Socialist Party said: 'The traditional political leaders of the Left may not have Ph.D.s in foreign universities [referring to those who studied abroad during the years of exile] but they are closer to what is going on in this country.'

Economists have acted as inter-party interlocutors not just due to the vocation of politically talented economists. The lessons drawn from democratic failure and the impact of authoritarian rule may have provided the incentives to link political reconciliation to basic party agreements on how to manage the economy. Chilean economists in the opposition have been actively developing a post-ideological mood.

Conciliatory efforts to arrive at a minimum framework for macro-economic management materialized in a common socio-economic programme for the next democratic administration. Some of the issues on which there is agreement are (Marshall and Morande, 1988):

(a) the importance of markets in the economy,
(b) the right of the state to adjust market signals to policy goals,
(c) the importance of integration in the international economy through the development of the export sector,
(d) the importance of assuring the competitiveness of national production through efficient import substitution,
(e) that production should be mainly in the hands of the private sector, although with an active participation by the state, and
(f) a more active social policy is necessary, to overcome extreme income inequality and poverty.

Previous democratic governments in Chile painfully experienced the problematic interaction of techno-economic and political imperatives (Molina, 1972; Bitar, 1985; Montecinos, 1988). Often, government economists felt that their policies failed because of uncontrollable political conditions. During the military government, economists permeated the entire state apparatus and controlled most policy areas, in part because economic transformations were considered central to political legitimation. Economists became active opposition spokesmen because economic criticisms could be voiced earlier than political and ethical criticisms. One of the most prominent Christian Democratic economists explained to me:

> The performance of the political class was poor. Politicians were disputing spaces that did not exist, they had lost practice in the exercise of their profession. I realized it was necessary to change first the political situation in order to apply new economic ideas.

During this period, many economists actually made politics their vocation. They started writing in journals and newspapers, reading about political science and history, travelling to cities and towns around the country, occupying posts of responsibility in political parties, producing reports that took into account the view of several parties, addressing public figures through the press. In the meantime, they remained linked to the national and international community of economists. This conversion into politicians was not always successful (or welcome). Economists are often perceived as dangerous intruders in political society, who try to impose ('their') rationality on politics. Unsuccessful conversions are frequent. According to a politically active economist, 'It is not easy for economists to do what politicians do. Economists think in terms of optimization, instead of trying to understand the logic of actors to mobilize them.' The pragmatism and flexibility of economists is sometimes interpreted as a weakness in the struggle for leadership. A politically respected economist who has been mentioned as a possible presidential candidate put it this way:

> What is important is the use of symbols and language, even if professional standards are not respected. I cannot give a speech shouting, although shouting arouses applauses. Traditional politicians prefer to follow their intuitions rather than debate carefully the pros and cons of decisions, but they will be the ones to get the votes, because they are more convincing.

What matters is the kind of role, prerogatives, and influence that economists will have in the new Chilean democracy. It is not in the interest of democratic governability to promote the excessive autonomy or political isolation of economists. Economists' proposals should be subject to the control and discipline of political parties as well as to the scrutiny and sanction of representative bodies. The uneven distribution of economists among government agencies, political parties and interest-group organizations does not seem promising either. The concentration of economists in the executive branch or in the Central Bank should be avoided. The strengthening of technical economic teams in Congress, developmental agencies, parties, business and labour organizations could be a way to counteract trends towards technocratic and exclusionary policy styles within the executive branch.

GOVERNMENT REORGANIZATION AND THE ROLE OF ECONOMISTS

A better understanding of the organizational aspects of economic policy, and the place of economic managers in policy-making institutions, may be of great importance for the consolidation of new democratic regimes. The ways in which government, parties and society are organized have a very decisive influence on policy-making capabilities. After all, policies are the outcome of organizations, not only of individuals. Even if some disillusioned people come to think that 'all forms of government organization are equally bad' (Peters, 1988, 8), that only means we have to pay *more* attention to it, not less.

The process of government or institutional reorganization after transition may enhance the degree of governability of the new regime, making it either more effective or more legitimate. Or, as March and Olsen (1983) say, reorganization may serve primarily symbolic purposes. In fact, the announcement of changes by the new elected government (deprivatization, or concertation) may create more impact than the changes themselves. On the other hand, democratic reorganization may contribute to policy instability and scepticism, especially in societies like Chile that have gone through the costs and frustrations of continuous reorganization led by the right, the centre, the left, and the military.

Right-wing authoritarian regimes that usually claim to replace their predecessors because of poor effectiveness, concentrate on the control of inflation and the balancing of budgets, preaching on the reduction of the size and functions of government. Unions, parties and Congress either disappear, or are significantly weakened. State agencies (including the military) are expanded, merged, eliminated, or transferred to the private sector. In contrast, democratic governments, usually more concerned with income distribution and employment, tend to be more generous with government expenditures and interact more with organized groups and parties.

Changes in power distribution and policy priorities are very likely to stimulate some degree of government reorganization after the transition, although many of the institutional arrangements put into place by authoritarian regimes (changes in labour code, privatization of state enterprises, government centralization) become a legacy to democratic governments. Part of that legacy will be changed, but part of it will be preserved through organizational inertia, or because it fits the intentions and policies of the democratic government. Depending on the ideological preferences of the new governing coalition, more or less drastic changes will be attempted to accommodate organizational structures to the style and priorities of democracy.

Because of theoretical and practical reasons, the importance of government organization has been overlooked in the analyses of changes in political regimes.[18] On the one hand, political actors tend to become locked into the tactical problems faced during the transition. On the theoretical side, the revival of institutional analysis in political science is fairly recent (March and Olsen, 1984). It was in the 1980s that a new wave of institutionalism and organization theory was being applied to the study of political parties (Panebianco, 1988), governance (Campbell and Peters, 1988), and economic policy-making (Hall, 1986).

Government reorganization could reduce the excessive political isolation or the excessive politicization of economic managers. It would be in the interest of democratic governability to promote the emergence of a techno-political elite, capable of bridging the gap between the political and the technical dimensions of government. New organizational structures in Congress, in parties and in the state bureaucracy seem particularly important in shaping new roles for economic managers in the context of a democratic government.

The Reorganization of Congress

In the literature on administrative accountability, confidence in rational administration alternates with worries about the dangers of excessive technocratism, presidential dictatorialism and the erosion of democracy. In Chile since the 1960s, the efforts towards planning and rationalization of policy-making led to the strengthening of presidential power and its continuous confrontation with Congress (Valenzuela and Wilde, 1979). Experts had growing influence within the executive and almost none in the legislative. Although Congress retained important budgetary and wage-regulatory functions, there was no incentive for political parties to share the responsibilities of government because coalitions were formed mainly for electoral reasons (Valenzuela, 1985, 107). To what extent did the policy-making weakness of Congress contribute to the instability of democracy? And conversely, to what extent could an increased technification of Congress be beneficial to democratic governability? A technically stronger Congress could counterbalance the technification of the executive bureaucracy. It could provide resources (information, staff) for politicians to effectively oversee the actions of government agencies. Congress could be more aware of the problems of implementation, perhaps reducing the incentives for upsetting executive policies only on the basis of ideological or short-term electoral considerations. This is an important issue, particularly in view of recent propositions that suggest that parliamentarism could be a better solution to moderate Chilean politics (Valenzuela, 1985).

Political Parties

Parties are often conceived as the key to a consolidated democracy (Mainwaring, 1988). The characteristics of the party system, however important, are not the only relevant feature to study in democratic politics. As Panebianco stresses, 'most contemporary analyses resist studying parties for what they obviously are: organizations' (Panebianco, 1988, 3). The ways in which different parties are organized influence their relationships with other parties as well as with the government bureaucracy. Parties as organizations may be more or less prone to fragmentation and conflict. Parties may be more or less open to the incorporation of societal demands, more or less effective in dealing with complex public issues, may have more or less room for the opinion of economic specialists.

Political parties in Chile used to be key partners in the policy-making process. Proposals were lengthily debated within the governing party before the executive introduced new legislation. Defeat within the party usually meant either dropping or delaying policy ideas. The centrality of parties in the Chilean political system has inspired a lively debate on whether or not the party system was responsible for the breakdown of democracy. There is no agreement on how much damage or change the authoritarian regime has been able to inflict upon the Chilean party system (A. and S. Valenzuela, 1986; Garreton, 1986). We have to wait to see how Chilean parties will re-enter the political space to intervene in policy-making, because they still remain largely unrecognized by the military government.

In what ways have parties changed as a response to exile, repression and exclusion from government decisions? How differently have parties reacted to so many years of authoritarianism? How differently will small parties, old parties, catch-all parties of the Left, the Centre and the Right face the challenges of the new democratic period? How have parties changed their economic thinking in the last fifteen years? Are those changes related to new forms of integration of economists into parties? To what extent can changes in party structure affect democratic governability?

According to Panebianco (1988, 231), professionalization is 'the distinguishing feature of the organizational change political parties are currently undergoing'. Can we expect an increase in the professionalization of Chilean parties as a result of the criticisms of traditional party politics and as a result of the new stress on reducing competition and connecting ideological goals to achievable means (FLACSO, 1985)? Are economists, who control an important zone of uncertainty, likely to acquire greater control of party structures because of the search for democratic governability and democratic survival?

Perhaps stronger economic teams in party structures could make it more difficult for government managers to ignore party criticisms of policy options (a recurrent pattern in the new democratic regimes. See Conaghan, 1988). If economic debates do not simply follow ideological cleavages but provide pragmatic bases for compromise, more consensual patterns of interaction between government and opposition could emerge. A higher level of professionalization of party structures could also help to reduce strains between ideological and technical criteria in the recruitment of government officials by complementing party membership with technical competence.

Professional roles are an unstable feature of political parties, because professionals must become party bureaucrats. Staff professionals can find work in external markets and leave the party (Panebianco, 1988, 231). For this reason, it is important to understand the incentives that experts perceive for joining various types of political parties. Qualified people tend to stay out of certain parties, especially if parties do not offer incentives for career advancement based on expertise. It is important to explore further the influence that party economists and party economic thinking could have in the policy-making of new democratic regimes.

Bureaucratic Reorganization

Even agreements between parties cannot assure policy success if bureaucratic conflict and bureaucratic politics are not taken into account. It is important to remember that too often the employment of rational models in macroeconomic management does not pay enough attention to the impact of institutional factors on policy outcomes. As policy-makers painfully learn, their intentions can be systematically frustrated by factors connected to bureaucratic power.

After transition to democracy, the policy priorities of the new government may be harmed by the bureaucratic legacy of the authoritarian period. Economic policy-makers in particular may find it difficult to balance the inherited economistic bias with drives to redistribute economic and power resources. They may ask for isolation from political pressures. Or, they may facilitate more flexible relations between state and society.

The ability that state agencies have to spend and grow depends on the bureaucratic coalitions that they are able to establish as well as on the history of the agency itself. Agencies vary in their capacity for implementation depending on the more or less marginal position in the state apparatus, the level of resources they control, the level of professionalization of their staff, and so on. How deeply was the state apparatus transformed by authoritarian rule? In these fifteen years, government authorities have tried to isolate some institutions from such external influences as the Central Bank. Other agencies were severely curtailed in their functions. Some government agencies acquired power, hired more professionals, or replaced certain types of professionals by others (lawyers, used to a monopolistic position in the Labour Ministry, are now sharing power with economists). With the reopening of political practices and electoral considerations, the new democratic government will have to rearrange the institutional framework of state policy, balancing the strong preference for cost–benefit analysis with more socio-political and cultural approaches to government action. The degree of 'technocratism' of the new democratic regime will depend very much on the bureaucratic power of economic managers.

CONCLUSIONS

This chapter has argued that in the process of transition from authoritarian rule to democracy, it is important to pay attention to the role of economists in government. What they think and where they are placed may have significant impact on the policy-making style, the stability and governability of the new regime. The delay and complexities of the Chilean transition may contribute to the comparative analysis of this topic. Economists in Chile have had a prominent political role in the authoritarian government as well as in the opposition. Chilean economists are highly politicized. What we do not yet know is how technocratic the new democratic government will be.

Notes

1. A first draft of this paper was written in the Fall of 1988 while Veronica Montecinos was invited as a Fellow by the Kellogg Institute for International Studies at the University of Notre Dame, Indiana.
2. See, for instance, the recent collection edited by B. Stalling and R. Kaufman (1989).
3. A series of interviews with Chilean economists and politicians on this subject were conducted in Santiago in January and July of 1988.
4. Seven and a half million people (85 per cent of the potential electorate) registered to vote. 97 per cent of those registered voted the day of the plebiscite.
5. The rate of inflation is low and export promotion has been successful. Some sectors of the economy have been modernized, although at the cost of highly regressive income distribution.
6. Immediately after the plebiscite, the opposition made public the need for prompt constitutional changes: free election of all members of the future senate, reduction in the congressional majority required for constitutional amendment, elimination of presidential veto over constitutional amendments.
7. Among others, Moulian (1983); Foxley (1985a); Tironi (1984); Garreton (1986).
8. In 1985 a coalition of parties signed the National Accord. During the plebiscite campaign, sixteen parties united in the *Comando por el NO*; six of those parties, including the Christian Democrats and part of the Socialists, have agreed on a common government programme. The opposition has also announced the nomination of a common presidential candidate for 1989.
9. Within the Socialist party, for instance, the faction called 'the Swiss', in which economists were particularly influential, was crucial in the unification efforts that followed party fragmentation after the coup (A. and S. Valenzuela, 1986, 211). Economists in the Christian Democratic party and in small parties of the Left have also played a role in linking various political groups.
10. Kaufman (1986) argues that the formation of durable polyarchies will require, at least transitorily, an accommodation with the economic forces that supported the authoritarian regime.
11. Malloy (1987) identifies the cycle between decompression (populist, participatory policy-making) and compression of power (centralization, exclusionary policy-making) as key to the dynamics of Latin American political economy, over and above changes in political regime.
12. See for instance the collection edited by O'Donnell, Schmitter and Whitehead (1986).
13. See for instance J. Aberbach *et al.* (1981).
14. All these proposals encountered unintended consequences such as the increase in external dependency when greater autonomy was the goal, or greater state control of the private sector, when market orientation was the ideal.

15. Industrializing structuralism was more congenial to the incorporation of middle classes and industrial proletariat in democratic or populist governments. Monetarism came to be associated with exclusionary political regimes.
16. Pragmatic neo-structuralism supposedly differs and is better than the old Keynesianism which Przeworski (1986, 62) links to democratizing coalitions because of its appealing but in the end vulnerable package of income redistribution, private property and a strong state.
17. The Friedmanian advocacy for automatic rules at the expense of discretionary control of government officials was finally distilled in constitutional norms protecting the future autonomy of the Central Bank from political pressures.
18. Here, organizational variables refer to autonomy, conflicts and coalitions among bureaucratic agencies, the recruitment and career patterns of organizational elites and staff, the adaptation of organizations to changes in the environment, and so on.

References

Aberbach, J., Putnam, R. and Rockman, B. (1981) *Bureaucrats and Politicians in Western Democracies* (Cambridge, Mass.: Harvard University Press).

Becker, G. (1976) *The Economic Approach to Human Behavior* (Chicago: University of Chicago Press).

Bitar, S. (1985) *Transición, socialismo y democracia. La experienca chilena* (Mexico: Siglo XXI).

Bosanquet, N. (1983) *Economics: after the New Right* (Boston and The Hague: Kleuver-Nijhoff).

Campbell, C. and Peters, B. G. (1988) *Organizing Governance, Governing Organizations* (Pittsburgh: University of Pittsburgh Press).

Conaghan, C. (1988) 'Capitalists, Technocrats, and Politicians: Economic Policy-Making and Democracy in the Central Andes', *Working Paper* no. 109, Helen Kellogg Institute, University of Notre-Dame.

Fishlow, A. (1985) 'The State of Latin American Economics', *Economic and Social Progress in Latin America. External Debt: Crisis and Adjustment*, Washington, IDB, 1985 Report.

FLACSO (1985) *Partidos y democracia* Santiago: FLACSO.

Foxley, A. (1985a) 'After Authoritarianism: Political Alternatives', *Working Paper* no.40, Helen Kellogg Institute, University of Notre-Dame.

Foxley, A. (1985b) *Para una democracia estable* (Santiago: CIEPLAN).

Garreton, A. (1986) 'Chile in Search of Lost Democracy', in G. Hartlyn and F. Morley (eds), *Latin American Political Economy. Financial Crisis and Political Change* (Boulder: Westview).

Hall, P. (1986) *Governing the Economy. The Politics of State Intervention in Britain and France* (Cambridge: Polity).

Hirschman, A. (1963) *Journeys Toward Progress* (New York: Twentieth Century Fund).

Hirschman, A. (1986) 'The Political Economy of Latin American

Development: Seven Exercices in Retrospection', *Working Paper* no. 88 Helen Kellogg Institute, University of Notre-Dame.

Kaufman, R. (1986) 'Liberalization and Democratization in South America Perspectives from the 1970s', in: G. O'Donnell, P. Schmitter and L Whitehead (eds), vol. III, pp. 85–108.

Mainwaring, S. (1988) 'Political Parties and Democratization in Brazil and the Southern Cone – A Review Essay, *Working Paper* no. 107, Heler Kellogg Institute, University of Notre-Dame.

Malloy, J. (1987) 'The Politics of Transition in Latin America', in: J. Malloy and M. Seligson (eds), *Authoritarians and Democrats: Regime Transition in Latin America* (Pittsburgh: Pittsburgh University Press).

March, J. and Olsen, J. (1983) 'Organizing Political Life: What Administrative Reorganization Tells Us About Governing', *American Political Science Review*, no. 77, pp. 281–96.

March, J. and Olsen, J. (1984) 'The New Institutionalism: Organizational Factors in Political Life', *American Political Science Review*, no. 78, pp. 734–49.

Marshall, J. and Morande, F. (1988) 'Propuestas económicas : consensos y conflictos', Santiago, unpublished manuscript.

Molina, S. (1982) *El proceso de cambio en Chile : la experienca 1975–1979,* (Santiago: Editiorial Universitaria).

Montecinos, V. (1988) 'Economics and Power. Chilean Economists in Government: 1958–1985', University of Pittsburgh, PhD dissertation.

Moulian, T. (1983) *Democracia y socialismo en Chile* (Santiago: FLACSO).

O'Donnell, G. (1973) *Modernization and Bureaucratic-Authoritarianism. Studies in South American Politics* (Berkeley: Institute of International Studies).

O'Donnell, G., P. Schmitter and L. Whitehead (eds), (1986) *Transitions from Authoritarian Rule: Prospects for Democracy.* Four vols. (in paperback): I Southern Europe, II Latin America, III Comparative Perspectives, IV Tentative Conclusions about Uncertain Democracies. (Baltimore and London: Johns Hopkins University Press).

Panebianco, A. (1988) *Political Parties: Organization and Power* (Cambridge: Cambridge University Press).

Peters, B. G. (1988) 'Introduction' in C. Campbell and B. G. Peters *Organizing Governance, Governing Organizations* (Pittsburgh: University of Pittsburgh Press).

Przeworski, A. (1986) 'Some Problems in the Study of the Transition to Democracy', in G. O'Donnell, P. Schmitter and L. Whitehead (eds), vol. III, pp. 47–64.

Stalling, B. and R. Kaufman (eds) (1989) *Debt and Democracy in Latin America* (Boulder: Westview Press).

Tironi, E. (1984) *La Torre de Babel : Ensayos de crítica y renovación política* (Santiago: Sur).

Valenzuela, A. (1985) 'Orígenes y características del sistema de partidos en Chile: Proposiciones para un gouierno parlamentario', *Estudios Publicos* no. 18, pp. 87–154.

Valenzuela, A. and Valenzuela, S. (1986) 'Party Oppositions under the Chilean Authoritarian Regime', in: S. and A. Valenzuela (eds), *Military*

Rule in Chile: Dictatorship and Oppositions (Baltimore: Johns Hopkins University Press).
Valenzuela, A. and Wilde, A. (1979) 'Presidential Politics and the Decline of Chilean Congress', in: J. Smith and L. Musolf (eds), *Legislatures in Development: Dynamics of Change in New and Old States* (Durham: Duke University Press).

5 Transition to Political Democracy in the Philippines: 1978–88

David Wurfel

The redemocratization of the Philippine polity contains some unique elements. Many participants, in fact, even including Mrs Aquino, have regarded it as a miracle, the consequence of divine intervention (Elwood, 1986). Fortunately for the social scientist, however, the unique and miraculous characteristics are embedded in patterns that are found to be quite similar to Latin American, other Asian, and even Southern European examples.

Comparison can thrive if terms are clear. Out of the welter of terms which have become common in the discussion of transitions to democracy there are two in special need of clarification: liberalization and democratization. Though some would equate the two terms (Schmitter, 1986, 4) others, quite appropriately, I would think, have tried to make a sharp distinction (O'Donnell and Schmitter, 1986, 7; Przeworski, 1986, 56), even though there is not consensus on what the distinctions should be. Liberalization, I would argue, is a process of change which takes place within an authoritarian regime and under the control of its leaders. It may include renewed protection of at least some human rights, new offices made elective, new opportunities for opposition parties to participate in elections or policy-making, or some improvement in the degree of honesty or openness in the electoral process. The purpose is to enhance the legitimacy of the authoritarian regime, perhaps even through some sharing of power, as long as it does not jeopardize effective control by the ruling elite.

Democratization on the other hand, while including, at least, all of the elements of liberalization, has been aptly described as 'institutionalizing uncertainty' (Przeworski, 1986, 58). Though institutional arrangements may be biased to favour the protection of particular interests, the rules of the game are certain. Reforms are 'modifications of the organization of conflict that alter the prior probabilities of realizing group interest'. But in a democracy no group is able to intervene to change the rules just because their interests seem

110

threatened, unless they abide by the institutionalized procedures for rule change. Unlike 'liberalization' the ruling elite cannot always control the process of rule change. Far-sighted elites, however, if threatened with overthrow, may bargain for continued influence.

While liberalization and democratization are by definition discontinuous, historically and empirically the first may blend into the second so that it is difficult to fix the precise moment when the character of the process changes. It is nevertheless fruitful for purposes of analysis to keep the two distinct. Liberalization may or may not precede democratization (Share, 1987, 528), but usually does. Liberalization may also be halted by ruling elites if it seems to be getting out of control, as in Haiti, or El Salvador, thus preventing democratization.

Transition is an oft-used word which also needs special definition. It refers to the period which begins as liberalization ends and concludes when the new democratic rules of the game have been formally accepted, that is, the ratification of the constitution. Democratic consolidation is a longer process which, while it is working, is never finally complete. It signifies the gradual acquisition of legitimacy for the new rules. Clear evidence of progress would be electoral defeat of an incumbent chief executive and his/her smooth, legal replacement. The only well-defined conclusion of this process is its failure in a coup or revolution.

Transitions to democracy have occurred most often when authoritarian elites (or segments thereof) have felt the need to augment their legitimacy through liberalization while retaining as much power as possible (Przeworski, 1986, 50). Loss of legitimacy is an almost inevitable component of regime ageing. In other cases opposition forces have played the major role in terminating the authoritarian regime (Stepan, 1986, 65). The former initiative is, of course, more likely to be nonviolent than the latter, which may take the form of a coup or even revolutionary war. Transitions have thus been categorized in terms of the sources of initiative (Stepan, 1986, 65; Share, 1987, 529) and the means used (violent or non-violent).

Considerable attention has also been paid to the contexts which affect the character or hasten the initiation of transition: socioeconomic, cultural, institutional, elite cohesion/conflict, and international. What the literature has not done so far, however, is to look beyond an explanation of the initial transition to the impact of these various factors on the prospects of democratic consolidation. As Share notes (1987, 532), 'Legitimacy of authoritarian rule is most often undermined by a set of conditions that may also obstruct the consolidation of democratic rule.' Huntington (1984) has correctly pointed out that recent democratic break-throughs may only be a stage in a cycle that leads back to authoritarianism. And the ultimate success or failure of a transition will be determined to a considerable degree by the stage of modernization.

STEPAN'S CATEGORIES

So far the Philippines has not been treated in the academic literature on democratic transitions. As noted above, it has both unique and common characteristics. Stepan's categories of redemocratization are helpful, but do not fit neatly. It is perhaps most convincing to characterize the Philippines as a mix of his types 5, 6 and 7. The transition was 'society-led' in that it began, in some sense, with the mass, uncoordinated protests that followed Benigno Aquino's assassination. But, as Stepan suggests (1986), 'society-led upheavals by themselves are virtually incapable of leading to redemocratization'. Type 6 places the initiative in a 'grand oppositional pact'. While much organized pressure for democratization preceded it, it is true that the pact between Corazon Aquino and Salvador Laurel to run on a single ticket in December 1985 was crucial to the eventual transition. Together their followers made up almost all of the moderate opposition, that is, those willing to participate in elections at all.

Stepan (1986) contends that there are no successful examples of type 7, 'organized violent revolt coordinated by democratic reformist parties', in Asia. But the fact of some coordination between Mrs Aquino and military plotters around Secretary of Defense Enrile, which has just recently been revealed (Simons, 1987, 266–7), puts the Philippines in a category previously occupied primarily by Costa Rica. The uniqueness of the Philippine case was that the planned revolt required almost no violence from reformist-led civilian forces.

PHILIPPINE UNIQUENESS

Unique also was the role of Jaime Cardinal Sin as spokesman for the Roman Catholic Church in the reformist coalition. He was primarily responsible for the 'pact' of December 1985 and provided crucial leadership in recruiting and organizing poll-watchers as well as hundreds of thousands of protesters under non-violent leadership to deter Marcos' tanks in February 1986.

The intervention of the USA was also unique, at least in comparison with cases treated in the democratization literature of the 1970s and 1980s. Concerned about the maintenance of its huge military bases, especially in view of the need to renew the bases agreement in 1991, there was increasing fear in Washington by 1985 that the Marcos regime was so corrupt, so inept, and so hated that it might bring on a Communist alternative, or at least a radical nationalist regime. Funding of poll-watchers in 1984, support to IMF/World Bank demands for economic reform, pressure for a presidential election in 1985 and subtle encouragement to young officers plotting a coup were among the types of US intervention. The involvement of the USA was crucial for the beginning of liberalization in the late 1970s as well as for the dramatic events of February 1986 that led to democratization.

The role of both the Church and the USA were in response to the Communist-led insurgency that peaked in 1985. In fact, there is no other instance, worldwide, of a transition to democracy taking place in the midst of a widening revolutionary movement. It was fear of that movement that triggered American pressure for liberalization, that brought the elite together against Marcos, and that helped restrain the outbreak of warfare between military units. The revolutionaries, despite their successful broadening of the united front in 1984–85, marginalized themselves in February 1986 by declaring an election boycott. But while they facilitated a transition to democracy, the New People's Army's continued vigour poses both a direct and indirect (by way of military reaction) threat to democratic consolidation.

THE PHILIPPINE 'REVOLUTION': PRELUDE TO POSTLUDE

Liberalization

The regime established in September 1972 by President Marcos' declaration of martial law initially had many of the characteristics of bureaucratic authoritarianism. All opposition was crushed, thousands were imprisoned for political reasons, while economic policy clearly favoured multinational corporations, low wages, and a new emphasis on export-oriented industrialization (see Haggard, 1988; Wurfel, 1988a; Hawes, 1987). Many Filipinos were prepared to accept a temporary dose of what Marcos called 'constitutional authoritarianism' if it would bring peace and order with prosperity.

But within six years most hopeful signs had disappeared. GNP growth slowed and income inequality intensified. In the countryside a Communist-led insurgency arose stronger than ever before. This was associated with a shift in regime type away from technocratic efficiency back to a more traditional neo-patrimonialism. In the late 1970s Marcos sought to rekindle regime legitimacy not through policy but by centralizing patronage, even in the military. Over confident about his success in this endeavour and sensitive to charges that he had destroyed a half century tradition of electoral democracy, Marcos declared a policy of 'normalization' and called for legislative 'elections' in 1978. He was responding in part to questions from the Carter White House on human rights and from his creditors about regime legitimacy, and since the foreign debt was soaring, they had influence.

This first step toward liberalization gained no legitimacy, however, since election fraud was rampant and hundreds were imprisoned for post-election protest. Nevertheless, by 1980 Marcos proceeded to hold elections for mayors and governors, where money was more useful. In that year it became more obvious as to why liberalization was needed. The president's health was failing – he had systemic lupus erythematosis, which soon strikes the kidneys – and evidence of a succession struggle surfaced more frequently. Liberalization was entwined in a seesaw battle between two factions, one with 'crony capitalists' and corrupt military around Imelda Marcos, and another looser coalition with technocrats, reformist military and old economic elite supporting, but not led by, Prime Minister Virata. The latter had quiet IMF/World Bank and US government backing for the establishment of clear constitutional succession to sidetrack Imelda while the former group, closer to the President, persuaded him to 'lift' martial law and get himself re-elected (without real opposition) in 1981, keeping the line of succession uncertain. (In fact, Mrs Marcos had been named successor in a secret decree.) In 1981 fraud again robbed the electoral process of any legitimizing impact.

The return and re-entry into politics of Benigno Aquino in 1983 would have posed the greatest threat to Imelda's succession, so her military allies engineered his clumsy assassination. This produced massive capital flight, economic crisis, and a collapse of legitimacy much more severe than anything the regime had yet seen. The insurgency extended to almost every province in the country.

Liberalization and reform rose on the agenda of the Reagan White House (Maisto, 1987, 530), producing a letter from the US president strongly advising Marcos that the 1984 legislative elections should be free. The National Movement for Free Elections, monitoring the vote, received American money. Under increasing foreign pressure Marcos produced the desired results: improved standing for the opposition sufficient to create the appearance of free elections without in any way threatening presidential control. Yet the succession rules remained fuzzy and the president disappeared for days at a time, fuelling the wildest rumours about his health. The legal opposition, emboldened by its 1984 'victory', grew in strength, as did the revolutionary forces.

By 1985 Reagan sent Senator Laxalt and CIA director Casey to Manila to assess the situation. Laxalt, then or later, discussed with Marcos the possibility of an early election 'to renew his mandate', an idea which Marcos himself had already floated. Laxalt agreed and suggested that Marcos announce it over US television (Bonner, 1987, 386–8), which he did.

This was the mistake that caused the president to lose control of liberalization and began the slide to true democratization. Deluded about his own popularity, and confident that the opposition would remain divided, he forged ahead. Opinion polls had shown that the president could win an election with only a modest amount of cheating *if* there were two opposition candidates. Aware of this reality, and worried that Marcos might call a snap election, as early as 1984, opposition leaders tried to establish a procedure that, if necessary, could facilitate quick consensus on a candidate to run against the autocrat. In early 1985 a 'Convenor Group' was formed, composed of three distinguished citizens who were regarded as without political ambitions of their own: ex-Senator Lorenzo Tanada, a life-long nationalist who served as president of the leftist coalition, *Bayan*; Jaime Ongpin, a respected mining company executive and one of the most outspoken anti-Marcos businessmen; and Cory Aquino. The Convenors were representative of a wide spectrum of the opposition, but could not contain the unbridled ambition of veteran politician Salvador Laurel, president of UNIDO, the largest opposition group in the National Assembly. Unwilling to accept the Convenors' authority to speak for the whole opposition, Laurel had himself proclaimed a candidate for president in June. It appeared that the attempt to form an all-opposition 'pact' had failed.

After June 1985 Cory Aquino herself was increasingly mentioned as the one person who could unify the opposition. Her personal sincerity and lack of either ambition or political experience were recognized as attractive qualities. But Cory was reluctant. Even after the announcement of the snap election she said she would not run unless a million Filipinos signed a petition asking her to do so. This was accomplished in a few weeks. Then on 3 December, just after General Ver was acquitted of assassinating Ninoy, and upon return from a religious retreat, Cory agreed to run. 'Doy' Laurel did not back down, however, so that the scenario that Marcos had counted on seemed to be unfolding. As the Aquino and Laurel camps engaged in some hard bargaining, and after Laurel had filed his candidacy, Marcos and Tolentino were formally nominated by the government party, the New Society Movement (KBL). Finally, within hours of the deadline for filing, at the residence of Cardinal Sin, Laurel accepted the vice-presidential slot with an assurance that he would be named prime minister and foreign minister (under the French-style constitution enacted by Marcos). Sin had become impressed with the results of polls that showed Aquino could win over Marcos in a relatively free election – and earlier ones indicating that no one else could (PSSC, 1985), so he told Laurel flatly that if he did not withdraw his presidential candidacy he would be responsible for perpetuating Marcos' rule. The authority of the Cardinal's office and the force of his personality could not be resisted. *He* had forged the minimal requirements of an opposition 'pact', which helped turn liberalization into democratization.

There were two other essential ingredients in the transition, the first again involving the Catholic Church. In the 1984 election Cardinal Sin had thrown his support behind the revival of NAMFREL (National Movement for Free Elections) which had first helped insure the election of Ramon Magsaysay in the 1950s. NAMFREL represented the civilian coalition against Marcos: the Church, the middle class and the old economic elite. NAMFREL was the product not only of the Cardinal's imprimatur, but also of business backing, of the enthusiasm and commitment of tens of thousands of volunteers all over the country, and of American money both overt and covert (Wurfel, 1988a, 285). American money was not only sizeable; the psychological impact of American backing, given the survival of the neo-colonial mentality among Filipinos, was probably even more substantial. To be sure, there were some nationalists among NAMFREL volunteers who would have been horrified if they had known the extent of American involvement, but for many more

American support insured the success of any enterprise. Altogether, it was estimated by knowledgeable sources that nearly $1 million in American money was received by NAMFREL. (Bonner, 1987, 409.)

Aside from the Church and NAMFREL, the other essential ingredient of transition was a faction of the military. But its role is best analysed at a later stage in the narrative of events.

The February 1986 Elections

Marcos launched his campaign in early December, attacking Mrs Aquino's incompetence, and was soon trying to tar her with the improbable label of 'Communist'. So ill that he usually had to be carried by his aides to the podium, Marcos' crowds were much smaller than those of the opposition, even though he paid at least half a day's wage to the poor to attend. Cory quite convincingly painted herself as the very antithesis of Marcos, and the people loved it.

Before election day Marcos sought to rely on his assiduously cultivated hierarchy of patron–client networks, distributing *billions* of pesos (US $1.00 = P20) of public and private money. But as often happens when local leaders fear that their patron is about to lose power, a large portion of this amount never reached individual voters but was pocketed. Voters who were successfully bought often received more than a day's wage. While the opposition depended primarily on a sweeping popular revulsion to the regime, there were both national (most prominently Mr Laurel) and local politicians in the opposition camp who attempted to revive dormant clientages. Though they had much less to spend, they could offer hope of future reward.

A large portion of that segment of the opposition which was committed to a 'new politics' based on issues opted out of the campaign. The Communist Party and various labour unions, peasant organizations and cultural groups which it influenced chose boycott, arguing that a free election was impossible, and that, in any case, the choice was between two families of great wealth who were not devoted to the people's welfare and who toadied to the Americans. However, the non-party Left generally worked for Mrs Aquino, with reservations.

On election day Marcos revealed how deep were his fears of losing (opinion polls in the last days showed Mrs Aquino well ahead) and how confident he was that Filipinos and foreigners alike could be forced to accept a fraudulent outcome. Ballot-box snatching and intimidation of NAMFREL and opposition party poll-watchers were practised not only in outlying areas but even in Metro Manila, in front of foreign television cameras. And when the count began, one had to be impressed by how fraud had been modernized. But again Marcos miscalculated, just as he had when he called the snap election. He underestimated the support for the opposition and the sophistication of its tactics and organization; he overestimated the ability of his friend and admirer, Ronald Reagan, to control American reaction to his rigging the count; and he overestimated the cohesion of his own backing.

As voting finished and reports began to come in, it was clear that this had been a far more fraudulent election than anything in Philippine history, at the registration stage, during the voting, but most particularly in the counting. NAMFREL's separate count showed Cory having 55 per cent of the votes with one-third of the precincts reporting. But the official returns, much slower in coming in indicated a steadily rising Marcos lead. NAMFREL was not allowed to complete its count, so critical estimates can be based only on the analysis of internal discrepancies in registration and in the official returns. It seems likely that Marcos stole two to three million votes at some stage of the process (Sacerdoti, 1986; Manlapaz, 1986).

The response in the Aquino camp to the Marcos claim of victory was, of course, incredulous, but opposition protests were given additional force by reactions in two other power centres, the Church and the US government. On the day that Marcos was officially declared winner by his legislature the Catholic Bishops' Conference of the Philippines stated that 'a government that assumes or retains power through fraudulent means has no moral basis'. Bishop Francisco Claver clarified: 'The Church will not recognize President Marcos' (quoted in *FEER*, 27 Feb. 1986, 11). But the bishops called for more than non-recognition. They added, 'The way indicated to us now is the way of non-violent struggle for justice. This means active resistance of evil by peaceful means – in the manner of Christ.' Cardinal Sin at the same time called back to the Philippines non-violent activists from Europe who had held training workshops earlier. Hildegard Goss-Mayr met privately with Mrs Aquino and Cardinal Sin to plan non-violent strategies for various contingencies. Said Goss-Mayr, 'The scenario of which everybody was most afraid was that the army would split' (quoted in Rosenthal, 1986, 300).

On 16 February, acting in the framework of the bishops' mandate, Mrs Aquino appeared before a Manila crowd of more than half a million to proclaim her own victory and to launch a nationwide campaign of civil disobedience, including a boycott of Marcos-controlled newspapers as well as tax refusal by business, which would culminate in a general strike on 26 February, a plan enthusiastically supported by the left-leaning labour federation, KMU.

The US response to the Marcos 'victory' was more complex. Reagan and his White House chief-of-staff, Donald Regan, were loyal to Marcos to the last, but the State Department and the Congress reacted quite differently. The bipartisan, but decidely conservative, American election observer team was headed by Senator Richard Lugar, chairman of the Senate Foreign Relations Committee. Lugar, though regarded as loyal to President Reagan, was well briefed by the Embassy in Manila and reacted more quickly and more negatively to Marcos' fraud than the White House could have imagined (Bonner, 1987, 410). He persuaded the whole team to criticize the fraud, but was even more forceful in his own statements to the press. Lugar's stance, buttressed by State and the CIA, and reinforced by the media, helped save American policy from the White House.

The whole electoral exercise demonstrated that liberalization was not under control. The inevitable uncertainty of democratization was beginning to hold sway. One more event, however, was needed to determine that democratization, at least in the short run, was irreversible. In that event the military was added to the list of most prominent *dramatis personae*. As in the case of NAMFREL, while Filipino leadership and initiative was primary, American backing was crucial.

'People Power Revolution'

The origin of military involvement was the break-up of the Marcos ruling circle, perhaps traceable back to the naming of General Fabian Ver, an integrated reserve officer, as chief-of-staff of the Armed Forces of the Philippines (AFP) in 1981. In that choice, which showed Marcos' preference for blind loyalty over competence – symbolized by General Fidel Ramos, who had been passed over – deep cleavages were strongly reinforced. Also important was the rise to dominance in the coconut industry by Eduardo Cojuangco, pushing aside the once prominent Defense Minister, Juan Ponce-Enrile. By 1983 both Enrile and General Ramos, vice chief-of-staff, had been marginalized in the power structure of the military, with

Marcos consolidating Ver's control. Then came the Aquino assassination and the charge by the investigating board that General Ver was a conspirator, followed by his January 1985 indictment. Ramos became acting chief-of-staff. Yet Ver, still in charge of intelligence and the presidential guard, continued plotting with Imelda Marcos to control the succession to an ailing president. In fact, Enrile, who had once thought of himself as a likely successor, had to fend off an assassination plot by Ver's men as early as late 1983.

Enrile's need for protection began to bring him closer to some bright young officers, graduates of the Philippine Military Academy, who were increasingly disturbed by the corruption and paternalism of Marcos' rule, which undermined military professionalism. This convergence was formalized in early 1985 with the organization of the Reform the Armed Forces Movement (RAM), which Enrile saw both as a means for warding off threat and for exploiting opportunity, that is to say, the tribulations of Ver. He was also positioning himself for American support in the succession, since he was aware of reservations, especially in the Pentagon and White House, about Cory Aquino's anticommunism and her position on the bases (Simons, 1987, 259). As a group of disciplined reformers, RAM went public in March. But underground RAM officers were developing more serious plans. By August they had a plot to overthrow Marcos, which Enrile soon endorsed. As the plotting matured, it was decided that political power should be turned over to a junta, which would include Cory, Cardinal Sin and General Ramos, as well as a few others, but headed by Enrile. Cory was informed of the plot in general terms, and approved, though indications are that she was not in agreement with provisions for a junta (Simons, 1987, 266–7; Bonner, 1987, 434). By December the plot was finalized (Simons, 1987, 264) and by January the date set for 23 February – after the elections (see also McCoy *et al.*, 1986b, 4).

US military attachés in Manila had been in touch with RAM officers at least since 1984 (Shaplen, 1986, 46), and by 1985 let their high regard for RAM be widely known. (One author adds, RAM was 'secretly funded' by the US; see Bonner, 1987, 368.) RAM was clearly a mechanism not only to strengthen the hand of Enrile but to help the USA put pressure on Ver for reform. When and in what detail Embassy or CIA officials in Manila were informed about a planned coup is not yet clearly known. But while there is no evidence of material support until the last day or two of the 'Revolution', neither was there an unequivocal expression of official American disapproval of the plans generally known beforehand. In fact, a few days after the election a tacit go-ahead was given by a representative of the Defense Intelligence Agency (McCoy *et al.*, 1986b), a crucial psychological boost for the plotters.

In any case, plans were put to naught when Marcos caught wind of them and arrested some of the plotters who were within the presidential guard. Enrile himself was warned that he was next. So on Saturday 22 February, Enrile, General Ramos and a small contingent of RAM troops seized control of a building in AFP headquarters and declared their rebellion against Marcos, after informing the US and Japanese ambassadors. Clearly weaker than they would have been had events proceeded on their own timetable, and thus needing Cory Aquino more, they abandoned the junta concept and declared 'Mrs. Aquino the duly elected president of the Philippines' (McCoy *et al.*, 1986a, 4).

The military rebels, having neither manpower nor firepower to stand up to a concerted assault, also needed civilian support, and quickly. General Ver, uncertain about rebel sympathy within the AFP, agreed to an overnight ceasefire, which was crucial. Meanwhile Cardinal Sin appealed over the radio for the faithful to come with food to support the rebels. And come they did; by Sunday morning there were tens of thousands, clerical and lay, rich and poor, young and old. This tactic was not as spontaneous as first thought, however. For weeks RAM had been in touch with Cardinal Sin, since they knew that loyalist firepower would be superior and they thought to neutralize it by employing human shields (Simons, 1987, 269). But the dramatic impact of 'People Power' was probably greater than it would have been if the coup had gone according to plan.

As we now know, the gentle intervention of 'People Power' and the defection or inaction of key Marcos officers prevented all but sporadic violence and forced the flight of Marcos and his entourage. The American role was particularly important in the last two days. Marcos called White House confidant Paul Laxalt for advice, and was told to 'cut and cut cleanly'. Finally American helicopters plucked Marcos and his entourage from the palace, and rebel planes which landed in Clark Field were, after some hesitation, allowed to refuel and take off. In other words, after the success of the 'Revolution' was certain, the US government moved openly to support it.

Filipinos understandably remember best Reagan's reluctance to support the democratic forces. However, somewhat independently, the State Department, the Defense Intelligence Agency, and others, had provided moral and even material support to Aquino and allies. Yet it should be noted that support for NAMFREL, for the early phase of RAM, and even for the Aquino candidacy was probably conceived within the context of assistance to liberalization, rather than necessarily to democratization. Clear support for democratization came only after it was a sure thing, a new ruling force to be reckoned with. Though Mrs Aquino had a somewhat more independent position on the US bases than Washington liked, when she was about to seize power, she had to be embraced.

It should be clear from this account that while the initiative for liberalization came from the autocrat, the push for democratization originated in a coalition of forces which included the Catholic Church, moderate opposition parties and leaders, as well as a dissident faction within the military. The degree of coordination of initiatives within this coalition may not yet be fully known, but it was much greater than first imagined.

Legitimizing Democracy

The net result of this 'transition with rupture' was a government headed by a diffident housewife, who turned out to be much tougher than in the assessment of early observers – but ultimately perhaps not tough enough. President Aquino clearly saw her goals as those of restoring constitutional democracy, and of repairing the damage inflicted on the society by authoritarian rule. The damage was perceived as ranging from unjust appropriation of private property by Marcos' cronies to the imprisonment of political dissenters, and thus solutions would benefit both right and left. Mrs Aquino and her closest advisors saw themselves at the centre of the political spectrum.

In her first 18 months in office, despite the fact that she governed most of that time by decree and without benefit of legislature, or prime minister, she largely accomplished her first category of goals, and gained legitimacy from it. The second category was addressed, but the solutions proved both more difficult to achieve and more controversial in the process. A third set of goals that circumstances require any Third World government to address – those of economic growth, equity and autonomy – have been dealt with ineffectively; there is a lack of consensus on these matters within the ruling elite, yet Cory remains personally popular and her charisma lends legitimacy to her regime. As recently as June 1988 her approval rating in a national sample survey – down five points in three months – remained at 69 per cent, a level to make most Western chief executives quite envious (*Manila Chronicle*, 4 Sept. 1988).

The first set of goals was centred in the return of constitutionalism. Evidence from the 1960s already showed that constitutionalism was a value deeply embedded in Philippine political culture (see Feliciano *et al.*, 1970). In political rhetoric the constitution sometimes became almost a holy writ (see Abueva and de Guzman, 1969, 60). Quite aside from what is said, however, one is impressed by the great personal sacrifices that Filipinos have been willing to make and the risks they have taken in defence of free elections, an exercise of accountability under the constitution. A few NAMFREL workers in 1986 even lost their lives. There can be no doubt that for Filipinos in 1986 the restoration of constitutional processes had very high priority.

Mrs Aquino was confronted with a dilemma, however. The existing constitution was the creature of an autocrat, adopted in disregard of the pre-existing rules at the time. Furthermore, it protected a legislature, elected in 1984, made up mostly of Marcos' clients and cronies who would hardly have been willing instruments of constitutional reform. Yet it was also the document under whose provisions she was elected. Some wanted her to restore the constitution which was in effect in 1972, but that was tainted as a 'colonial document'. Thus by decree she rescinded most of the 1973 constitution, inserting some new clauses necessary for the transition, and retaining legislative power in the presidency until a new constitution could become operative. She then decreed the creation of a Constitutional Commission, which she appointed, to draft the new basic law. Despite considerable criticism of the appointment process, she consulted widely, and the membership of the Commission was accepted by most Filipinos as generally representative. Unlike Marcos, she did not attempt to dominate the drafting.

Speed had been the major argument of appointment as against election of constitutional commissioners, and this benefit was realized. By October 1986 the draft had been completed and in February 1987 it was ratified overwhelmingly in a nationwide plebiscite. Almost all the government institutions provided for in the 1935 constitution were revived, including a bicameral legislature. To be sure, the lower house, elected from single member districts, was to be augmented by 50 seats elected through proportional representation. But this provision, which requires Congressional enactment, may never be implemented since it threatens patronage politics and has not received presidential endorsement. Mrs Aquino was granted a full six-year term, though some provisions weakened the power of the presidency.

The legitimacy of the process by which the new constitution was adopted was largely accepted. Elections for Congress and for local officials proceeded nearly on schedule and were seen by both observers and participants as free and more honest than anything since 1971, though some legacies of the Marcos era could not be wiped out overnight. Commission on Elections (COMELEC) officials, for instance, were largely holdovers. Local elections were held in November 1987, less than two years after Aquino took office. The 'transition' was complete and 'consolidation' had begun.

Unfortunately, restoring democratic institutions turned out to be much easier than repairing the damage to the society inflicted by Marcos' rule. Recovering 'stolen wealth' was the task given to a newly created body, the Philippine Commission on Good Government (PCGG) (Aquino, 1987, 43). Trying to stop the growing insurgency that Marcos had fuelled was also clearly a major task. Cleaning up corruption in the bureaucracy and releasing political prisoners – as well as prosecuting human rights violators – were the other main tasks in this category. But each of these policy areas was laced with difficult dilemmas.

First of all, restoring constitutional government had meant restoring the rule of law and the majesty of the courts. In a nation of too many lawyers this was a change greeted with gusto. Even though the cronies were in deep political disgrace, in keeping with the rule of law they could not be denied access to courts – and they could hire the most skilled lawyers. Even though the PCGG had been given sweeping rights of sequestration of crony assets – in one of the few instances where the powers of presidential decree were used effectively – legal challenges quickly mounted. Thus in September 1988 the PCGG, under criticism from Congress, could only claim that it had recovered P1.3 billion in ill-gotten gains when estimates of Marcos' wealth alone had gone as high as P200 billion (*Manila Chronicle*, 1 Sept. 1988).

Cleaning up corruption is a daunting task for any regime, even more so when it becomes embedded in the way of life and essential for subsistence in the lower ranks, as it had under Marcos. A similar task had been confronted by Ramon Magsaysay when he defeated President Elpidio Quirino in 1953, but in 1986 the Augean stables were piled much higher. And while her personal probity was beyond assail, it is not clear that Mrs Aquino was as fully committed to making it the standard of her whole administration as had been Magsaysay. In any case, with the restoration of the rule of law, officials charged with corruption could not be removed without due process. Those removed legally were at best a handful. The military were hardly touched.

Those who regularly dealt with the bureaucracy reported only that the under-the-table price of services was no longer certain, and with the confusion of administrative reorganization the hapless citizen often did not know whom to pay. But by 1988 that problem was being solved, the 'right' recipient was increasingly the president's brother, Jose Cojuangco, or his designees. In fact, with the naming of Cojuangco's personal attorney as chairman of PCGG in 1988 the massive efforts of that agency shifted focus from recapturing Marcos and crony funds for the Filipino people to transferring them quietly to the coffers of the Cojuangco family. In September Cardinal Sin told Rotarians in a well-publicized speech that corruption was 'the biggest problem of them all'. Then in early October the President finally did what many had long been urging and issued an administrative order prohibiting members of the Aquino or Cojuangco families from receiving 'favors, concessions or privileges' from government agencies. But how it will be interpreted and whether it will be enforced remains to be seen (*Manila Chronicle*, 11 Oct. 1988).

The insurgency, which in 1986 was 18 years old, was a national tragedy. Thousands on both sides had been killed and hundreds of thousands were refugees from the fighting. When Cory Aquino promised during the campaign to seek a cease-fire, she clearly touched a national nerve. But in this effort she was caught between hard-line revolutionaries and the short-sighted intransigence of the military and its Pentagon backers. These two groups conspired together to prevent the end of what was increasingly being called civil war. The hard liners in the NPA and the AFP seemed to agree that the outbreak of peace would threaten the continued viability of both organizations. This implicit embrace of the two extremes was very hard on the middle. In fact, there was no issue that contributed more to the break-up of the original Aquino coalition and its reformation somewhat to the right.

Ironically, even unsuccessful cease-fire negotiations, which so frightened the Pentagon, contributed more to undermining the revolutionary movement than all the military efforts in the previous decade. Just as President Aquino and some of her advisors had hoped, the hard line taken in the negotiations by NPA leaders caused some of their political support to evaporate; they underestimated the longing for peace. Mrs Aquino's miscalculation came in her estimate of the reaction of the AFP. In order to pursue the negotiations she dismissed Defense Minister Enrile and disregarded military advice. While she won sympathy in the countryside, she reaped enmity among the brass. In August 1987 she was very nearly overthrown by RAM under the leadership of Colonel Honasan – in a country where before 1986 there had never been a serious coup plot. Both foreign investors and ASEAN allies were frightened.

This was indeed the supreme irony of the democratization process. The intense politicization of the military from 1985, which proved essential for toppling the autocrat, remained the primary threat to the consolidation of political democracy from 1986. The absence of another serious coup attempt since August 1987 is largely a result of the fact that President Aquino has gone a long way to accommodate military demands. She has increased the deficit to raise their pay and otherwise expand their budget to a level much higher than that in the early 1980s. Despite her earlier release of political prisoners, including leading members of the Communist Party (which initially contributed to Party disunity), she has abandoned her policy of protecting human rights, punishing no military officers for their part in torture cases under Marcos and taking no effective steps against the increasing number of assassinations by vigilante groups trained and funded by the military (as well as indirectly by the CIA). There is still no convincing evidence that she exercises the control inherent in her title of 'commander-in-chief'. She has not dared, for instance, to go after corruption in the armed forces.

The Philippine government stance in the military bases negotiations with the USA, where more than $1 billion per year in rentals was demanded, was designed to be primarily beneficial to the military. The agreement in October for less than $1 billion over two years still increased the level of payments nearly three times. What is possible in the next two years is that a treaty renewing the bases agreement (which expires in 1991) will be signed by President Aquino – but fail ratification by the Senate. At that point the close communication between RAM and the US Defense Intelligence Agency which emerged in 1985, and which many Filipinos believe still survives, could be crucial for the future of Philippine democracy.

As we have seen, little has been accomplished in the second category of tasks which Aquino set for herself and which were vital for the consolidation of democracy. One leading Catholic educator, formerly a top advisor to Aquino, has recently described the mood among business and the intelligentsia as 'disenchantment'. Admitting that 'in no way is the present situation as acute as [that] of February 1986', he adds, 'but if not arrested, it can deteriorate' (*MC*, 30 Aug. 1988).

Fortunately for President Aquino the economy has been on the rebound since 1986. A solid growth of 7 per cent was achieved in 1987. But the best evidence is that this has happened for reasons that have little to do with government economic policy. World market prices rose for sugar and coconuts. To be sure billions of pesos of public works expenditure have stimulated consumption. But a greater stimulus seems to have come from the recovery of consumer confidence after the apparent return of stability and a halt to the flight of capital. Many observers believe the 'black economy' to have been the source of sizeable unreported savings. The resumption of international credit flows in 1986 was also crucial. The increase in foreign investment since 1986 has primarily come not from the traditional sources, the USA and Japan, but from Singapore, Taiwan and Hong Kong which have grown so fast that they are soon to lose preferential treatment for their exports to developed countries guaranteed by GATT. Investors in labour-intensive industry there are thus transferring to the Philippines, which still benefits from GATT preferences. This, like the earlier mentioned factors, may not be long-term source of growth, but a short-term spurt. In the meantime foreign exchange reserves are shrinking and foreign debt service takes over 40 per cent of the export of goods and services (*FEER*, 13 Aug. 1987, 104).

Nevertheless, economic growth did seem to have political benefits. Per capita GNP, which had fallen a disastrous 15 per cent from 1983 to 1985, rose 1 per cent in 1986 and 3 per cent in 1987. The sense of economic well-being changed even more dramatically. From 1983 to 1985 the portion of the population surveyed by researchers which classified themselves as living below the poverty line had jumped by 20 per cent. But by March 1987 it *dropped* – by nearly one third – to a national figure of 43 per cent. In part such a radical shift surely reflected a change in the character of economic activity not captured in GNP calculations (Mangahas, 1988). But it probably also revealed subjective assessments based on more than economic experience. It may have measured, in part, the impact of Cory Aquino's charisma, and the hope it engendered. By the end of 1987, however, an additional 10 per cent regarded themselves as poor, even as the GNP rose, thus indicating how unstable was this indicator. The self-declared poor diminished again in 1988. President Aquino's personal appeal can overcome economic difficulties and policy failures longer than a foreign analyst might expect, but not forever – perhaps not even to the end of her term. Charisma is not impervious to declining governmental performance.

In the euphoria of at least a temporary spurt of growth it would have seemed easier to pursue policies of social equity. It is always less contentious to divide a growing pie. But agrarian reform, the progamme that all agree tops the social policy agenda, has been most disappointing. Expectations were raised so high and accomplishments have been so few that agrarian conflict has simply been heightened (see Wurfel, 1988b). President Aquino, who comes from a family of *very* large landowners, failed to use her decree powers (which ended in July 1987) to enact land reform as many had hoped. In Congress the landlord bloc was best organized (under the leadership of her brother) and prevented the passage of effective legislation. The government, therefore, can offer very little to poor peasants whom the revolutionary opposition continues to mobilize.

In sum, a government which came to power under the banner of 'People Power Revolution' is far from revolutionary. It has restored not only the institutions of constitutional democracy which it promised, but the social structure, and the elite dominance through a fractured neo-patrimonialism which characterized the 1960s, failing to launch social reform. Yet the regime has also allowed the survival of a military politicized in the 1970s and 1980s. This is a combination of factors which could plunge the Philippines into a new cycle of authoritarianism and reinvigorated insurgency.

CONCLUSION

In further assessing the prospects of democratic consolidation in the Philippines, it would be instructive to make comparisons between the present and 1985–86, as well as with an even earlier period, 1972, the year in which Philippine democracy was overthrown from within.

In the first comparison we will be looking at the contexts of the transition to democracy in 1986 and assessing their legacy for the present. Some of those legacies are positive. The commitment to democratic values and the strength of civic organizations supportive of democracy has, if anything, grown by the trauma of a struggle some call 'revolution'. The greater freedom of organization since

February 1986 has seen a proliferation of political parties and of ostensibly non-political civic groups, most with predominantly middle-class membership. Labour unions have also become more autonomous. Even on the left there was appreciation for a time of 'democratic space' for organizing, later eroded by the assassinations and other attacks of vigilante groups.

On balance, the role of the Catholic Church continues to be supportive of democracy. Recently a new departure for the Conference of Bishops has been to urge concerted action by the citizenry for protection of the environment, clearly an attempt to deflect attention from class-based issues. But since the political demise of Marcos, because the clarity of a moral stance in politics has been blurred, the prophetic role of the Church is less in demand. And whereas before, when political opposition was repressed or constrained by autocratic rule, the organizational strength of the Church filled an essential gap, the proliferation of political groups now marginalizes a clerical role and undermines Church influence. In fact, when Cardinal Sin attempted to endorse a slate of the 'ten best' senate candidates in the May 1987 election, he made more enemies than friends – in both the Church and the political parties – and was not in the end very successful. He was acting more like a patron than a prophet. The Church's role in bringing together a broad coalition in support of land reform in 1987 – posed as a moral issue – was widely appreciated (outside landlord circles), but its political success was not much greater. In time the Church may tend to be relegated more and more to its earlier role of protecting its own institutional (Church schools) or ideological (for example, opposition to birth control) interests. Under the circumstances it may be difficult for the Church to continue to be the active core of the political centre's more progressive wing. The moral stand by the Church in favour of a renewed ceasefire with the NPA has gained popular support in rural areas, but has not swayed policy-makers.

Finally, in the next several years the Philippines is likely to be spared a succession crisis to complicate the struggle to realize democratic practice. A certain stability is to be found in the prospect that Mrs Aquino could be persuaded to run for re-election – even though she has so far disclaimed any such intention – since no other candidate could unify the country. This may simply postpone the danger, but given the timetables of economic policy and military relations with the USA, President Aquino could probably justify a re-election bid in terms of 'taking the Philippines over the hump'.

Unfortunately the negative legacies of 1985–86 may be more potent. There were three major ones: a politicized military, the continuing insurgency and foreign pressures. The Armed Forces of the Philippines was gradually policitized by Ferdinand Marcos from the early 1970s, for his own purposes. Ultimately the political consciousness of a segment of the officer corps turned against him. As we learned, the schemes of RAM, and its mentor Juan Enrile, did not turn out exactly as planned; they ended up with considerably less political power than intended. They may have first imagined that Cory Aquino was weak and pliable and could be turned quickly to their own ends. But they found that she and her advisors had unacceptable ideas about the status of the military and dealing with the insurgency. This, in turn, became a new stimulus to political mobilization, alongside the inevitable resentments of the pro-Marcos elements. Even constitutionalist generals, like chief-of-staff, now defence secretary, Fidel Ramos could not concede too much to the president for fear of losing support among fellow officers. And any attempt to clean up corruption in the AFP was resolutely resisted.

President Aquino's considerable attempts to mollify the military with changes in policies and appointments have not completely quieted rumours of further coups. The charismatic Colonel Greg Honasan is still at large, and his links with now-Senator Enrile have never been broken. From 1987 to 1988 defence and internal security already increased its share of the budget by more than 2 per cent. Yet the fear of coups remains if further budget requests are not met. The Philippine military, unlike counterparts in Argentina or Brazil, have not yet been sobered by the full responsibility of governing. This is a continuing threat that no previous elected leader in the Philippines has ever faced. Her chances of surviving it depend on the other two factors.

The insurgency in a curious way contributed to a peaceful democratic transition. It catalyzed unity in the opposition élite and motivated American support for liberalization because Marcos seemed to be feeding the fires of revolution, not controlling them. Unlike Chile where the electoral power of the left inhibited democratization, the Communist Party in the Philippines conveniently declared boycott. But now the insurgency is Aquino's problem. Rather than bring unity it has been a contentious issue that deeply divided the cabinet. President Aquino's initial soft approach was spreading confusion in revolutionary ranks, by forcing them to face so many dilemmas. But in early 1987 she endorsed a return to a primarily military approach to the dissidents, the same approach that had failed Marcos. Even the local militias, which were so notorious in their abuse of human rights as to create insurgents – the abolition of which was mandated by the new constitution – were revived under a new label and continue to be the source of problems. The revolutionary movement was dealt a blow by Mrs Aquino's initial approach; it is probably weaker than in 1985. Capture of top leaders and crucial documents in 1988 has been a further blow. But a return to Marcos policies would surely bring its revival. It may not be strong enough to seize power for decades, but the regime's inability to contain it could trigger a military intervention in the meantime. The social inequality which helps fuel revolutions has not been addressed. In fact the power of wealth at the local level has been reinforced.

Foreign pressures, both economic and political, which helped weaken the autocrat in the mid-1980s (even though they had bolstered his power earlier), could also work against the consolidation of democracy in the next few years. Debt and military bases seem to be the main issues.

A foreign debt of over $26 billion was one of the most devastating legacies of the Marcos era, especially since much of the borrowing had ended up in the coffers of the Marcos family and their friends. In fact, in 1986 the Philippines debt was the fourth largest in the world as a share of the gross domestic product (Alburo *et al.*, 1986, 38). As noted above the concerns of the IMF/World Bank and the commercial creditors had considerable impact on events in the early 1980s. Even after 1986 the debt has continued to rise, and is now nearly $30 billion. The question of whether to honour it in full has become a hotly debated issue, and will become even hotter as debt service gobbles up a larger and larger percentage of the national budget – 41 per cent in FY 1987. In 1987 $1.7 billion more was paid out in debt servicing than was received in loans, grants and investments (*MC*, 10 Oct. 1988). Congress is considering legislation which would limit the size of annual debt service – and which could cut the present outflow by nearly two-thirds. This would undoubtedly bring on a crisis, which many now quite deliberately prefer to continued bleeding. If Congress does not act, or its enactment is vetoed, and if the president does not succeed in getting more favourable debt rescheduling (Mexico and Argentina have done better), the crisis is only delayed. Some IMF conditions previously agreed to have already been repudiated. The president has emboldened such resistance by strong rhetoric of her own. But the greater prospect is that the bankers in her government will prevail and she will generally conform to whatever the creditors impose. Such 'reform', based on past experience, is likely to depress the economy, reduce social services, and thus contribute to a revival of the insurgency. It is ironic that the thrust of international economic pressure to reduce the deficit, which under Marcos favored liberalization, could now undermine the fragile democratic regime, despite a conscious effort to support it.

The dynamic of foreign military relations could bring democratic collapse even more quickly. As noted, if US bases are to remain, a treaty must be negotiated and ratified before 1991, and ratification by the Philippine Senate is very much in doubt. If elements in the Pentagon which resist the transfer of present Philippine operations to other locations are politically dominant, it will become essential to American interests to remove the Senate road-block. Since there are no Senate elections before 1991, the technique used in 1946 to insure other agreements with the USA – charges of election irregularities to prevent the seating of nationalists – is not available (unless Senate ratification is delayed beyond 1991). That is why so many Filipinos fear a coup – at least against Congress – quietly backed by the USA. If military assistance which provides most of the AFP's equipment were jeopardized by nationalists in the Senate, then the Philippine military would have an institutional interest which would coincide with the concerns of the Pentagon. The Department of State apparently believes that President Aquino is deep down pro-bases – probably an accurate assessment – and that she can ultimately orchestrate the incentives and disincentives of patronage politics to keep the Senate in line, a more shaky prospect. In any case, with opinion polls in 1986–87 showing a rise in anti-base sentiment it seems entirely possible that in one way or another American military policy will become a threat to Philippine democracy. The budget crunch in Washington could, on the other hand, exercise such constraint on the Pentagon – aided by a more pragmatic foreign policy – that in the absence of funds to further augment the bases compensation package there would be Philippine–American agreement on a gradual phase out of US facilities beginning in 1991. Such a scenario would certainly bolster democratic prospects.

Chances for Philippine democracy in 1989 may also be assessed in comparison to the threats which existed in 1972, when the rule of law was ended by a palace coup. Probably the greatest advantage for the present is that both the Filipino political elite and their foreign backers are more wary today about the dangers of democratic collapse, having experienced the Marcos autocracy and the difficulties of removing it. Furthermore, there is no political leader now on the horizon who could project the image of decisive effectiveness that Marcos did in 1972. Democracy benefits both from greater vigilance on its behalf and from the lack of a credible authoritarian rival.

But some threats to democracy are greater than in 1972. The Marcos era saw the most blatant corruption in Philippine history, reaching unheard-of proportions. And Aquino has never thoroughly cleansed the bureaucracy. With the proclivities of the president's brother more and more obvious, one has to admit that the cancer of corruption on the body politic – and especially the military – may be greater today than in 1972, thereby undermining democratic legitimacy. More dangerous than its corruption, however, is the military's political ambition, now *much* greater than in 1972.

The assertiveness of the military is, of course, a reflection in part of the continued vigour of the insurgency. The latter justifies the former. And while it is true that the revolutionary movement has lost political support since 1986 – partly because vigilantes have frightened many peasants – the regular guerrilla force does not seem to have suffered much. Though experiencing fatigue, in both political and military terms, it is far stronger than in 1972.

President Aquino presides over a recently restored democracy plagued with corruption and insurgency, though currently favoured by an expanding economy. Her popularity has carried her through several crises already. In some respects she seems to have learned from adversity. But the more fundamental problems may be beyond any solutions of which she is capable. The Philippines is a society of extreme inequalities and a relatively high level of political mobilization. This threatens a status quo of which the USA is a part, along with a politicized military harbouring ambitions inhibited by the constitution. It may take a miracle greater than the one at EDSA (Epifanio de los Santos Avenue) (February 1986) to produce steady progress toward democratic consolidation in the next decade.

References

Abueva, J. and de Guzman, R. (1969) *Foundations and Dynamics of Filipino Government and Politics* (Manila: Bookmark).

Alburo, F. *et al.* (1986) *Economic Recovery and Long-Run Growth: Agenda for Reforms*, Philippine Institute for Development Studies, May, vol. I.

Aquino, B. (1987) *The Politics of Plunder: The Philippines under Marcos* Manila: College of Public Administration, University of Philippines.

Bonner, R. (1987) *Waltzing with a Dictator: The Marcoses and the Making of American Policy* New York: Random House.

Elwood, D. J. (1986) *Philippine Revolution, 1986: Model of Nonviolent Change* (Manila: New Day).

Far Eastern Economic Review (FEER), various issues.

Feliciano, G., B. Lozare and M. T. Manahan (1970) *Opinions on the Philippine Constitution of Voting Resident in the Greater Manila Area* Quezon City: University of the Philippines, Institute of Mass Communications, September.

Haggard, S. (1988) 'The Political Economy of the Philippine Debt Crisis'.

Hawes, O. (1987) *The Philippine State and the Marcos Regime: The Politics of Export* Ithaca: Cornell University Press.

Huntington, S. (1984) 'Will More Countries Become Democratic?', *Political Science Quarterly*, vol. 99, no 2, Summer, pp. 193–219.

Maisto, J. (1987) 'United States–Philippine Relations in the 1980s', in: Carl Lande (ed.), *Rebuilding a Nation: Philippine Challenges and American Policy* Washington: Washington Institute Press.

Mangahas, M. (1988) 'SWS Survey Bulletin on the 1986–87 Economic Recovery', Quezon City, February, mimeo.

Manila Chronicle (MC), various issues.

Manlapaz, R. (1986) *The Mathematics of Deception: A Study of the 1986 Presidential Election Tallies* Quezon City: Third World Studies Center, University of the Philippines, February.

McCoy, A., M. Wilkinson and G. Robinson (1986a) 'The Shadow War', *Veritas*, October (reprinted from *National Times on Sunday*, Australia).

McCoy, A. *et al.* (1986b) 'The Plot to Topple Ferdinand Marcos', *Veritas*, October (reprinted from *National Times on Sunday*, Australia).

O'Donnell, G. and P. Schmitter (1986) 'Tentative Conclusions about Uncertain Democracies' in: G. O'Donnell *et al.* (eds), *Transition from Authoritarian Rule: Prospects for Democracy*, vol. IV (Baltimore: Johns Hopkins University Press).

Philippine Social Science Council (PSSC) (1985) *National Opinion Survey of September 1985*.

Przeworski, A. (1986) 'Some Problems in the Study of the Transition to Democracy', in: O'Donnell *et al.* (eds), *Transition from Authoritarian Rule: Prospects for Democracy*, vol. III, pp. 47–63.

Rosenthal, P. (1986) 'Non-violence in the Philippines: The Precarious Road', *Commonwealth*, 20 June.

Sacerdoti, G. (1986) 'Standing Polls Apart', *Far Eastern Economic Review*, February, no. 20, pp. 10–16.

Schmitter, P. (1986) 'An Introduction to Southern European Transitions from Authoritarian Rule: Italy, Greece, Portugal, Spain and Turkey', in: G. O'Donnell *et al.* (eds), *Transitions from Authoritarian Rule: Prospects for Democracy*, vol. I, pp. 3–10.

Shaplen, R. (1986) 'From Marcos to Aquino – II', *New Yorker*, 1 September.

Share, D. (1987) 'Transitions to Democracy and Transition Through Transaction', *Comparative Political Studies*, vol. 19, no. 4, January, pp. 525–48.

Simons, L. (1987) *Worth Dying For* (New York: William Morrow).

Stepan, A. (1986) 'Paths toward Redemocratization: Theoretical and Comparative Considerations', in: G. O'Donnell *et al.* (eds), *Transitions from Authoritarian Rule: Prospects for Democracy*, vol. III, pp. 64–84.

Wurfel, D. (1988a) *Filipino Politics: Development and Decay* (Ithaca: Cornell University Press).

Wurfel, D. (1988b) 'Land Reform: Contexts, Accomplishments and Prospects under Marcos and Aquino', paper delivered at Association for Asian Studies meeting, San Francisco, California, March.

Part III
Democratic Consolidations

6 The Political Economy of Democratic Consolidation in Southern Europe

Kostas Vergopoulos[1]

Throughout the 1960s, and in the years to follow, the anti-democratic regimes of southern Europe sought to legitimize their authoritarian political forms by invoking an *historical mission*: the industrialization and forced modernization of internal social relations which together would be destined to widen the regional bases of reproduction and accumulation.

Yet today, in light of the experience of the last two decades, one is forced to give heed to a good number of *paradoxical* aspects, as unforeseen as they are puzzling, before the explicative schemes that were proposed in the past. Thus one can readily see that the destruction of the authoritarian regimes in the three countries of the south of Europe – Spain, Greece, and Portugal – from 1974 onwards has given rise neither to a durable ascension of social forces nor to an upswing of internal accumulation. On the contrary, since the downfall of the authoritarianisms in these three countries, their respective economic and social instruments have steadily manifested a growing number of malfunctions and deficiencies whereas, on the other hand, the social, political, and cultural forces also appear to be struck by a progressive demobilization, a sort of *generalized apathy*. A remarkable passivity is to be found not only in political, social, and cultural expression but also in the material conditions of the existence of the social forces.

In these conditions it appears evident that one cannot approach the question of the institutional and political democratization under way in these three countries without taking into consideration those factors which might be at the origin of today's social fragilization. Indeed there is every reason to suppose that today's democratization is not in contradiction with the other symptoms of *social anorexia* but is rather an integral part of it.[2]

Clearly, this divergent evolution between political consolidation, on the one hand, and social fragility, on the other, has already been pointed out by a number of researchers. However, their methods of approach and evaluation are in no way unanimous. To some, economic and social decline must necessarily compromise, in the long term at least, the chances of success of the new political systems. To others, the upsurge of political democracy, being by definition free from economic and social determination, can develop fully without constraint. According to others, the present-day depoliticizing of social disputes is not a novel phenomenon but corresponds to a general attitude of our times marked by an increasing distrust towards the state and politics. It should be noted in addition that some observers have gone so far as to invert the suggested order and claim that it is not to the emergence of democracy that present-day social deterioration should be imputed. (For a complete critical inventory of the diverse approaches see, in particular, Ethier, 1986.)

Yet certain authors persist in making the supposition of a profound link between the historical movement of industrialization, the emergence of new civil societies, and the consecutive crisis of authoritarian regimes. Alain Lipietz, for example, in his remarkable study of peripheral Fordisms in Southern Europe seems to admit that such a relationship was at the basis of the process of transition in the three countries which he qualifies indifferently as the 'New Industrial Countries' (Lipietz, 1985). Apparently, in this case, short of producing the promised sociological argument synchronically, a diachronical attempt is undertaken. The same is true of other examples invoked in support of this hypothesis: the Philippines, South Korea, and so forth. In all of these cases, abstracting from the antinomy pointed out between the political and economic forms one seeks to provide a sociological explanation putting stress on its historical and diachronical dimensions, as if the advent of democratic political forms, once a certain level of development was achieved, was both necessary and inevitable.

Accordingly, the rise of democratic demands in Korea and the Philippines might be thought of as having no significant relationship with the economic and financial difficulties faced by the authoritarian regimes of the 1980s and yet, despite this, as being in profound harmony with the level of development reached during the earliers prosperous phase of the *miracles*.

Nevertheless, from a methodological point of view, it is not at all certain that one can utilize the same type of approach with respect to the countries of Southern Europe as those of the Pacific zone. Beyond the formal question of classification, it is certain that the economies and societies of Southern Europe have neither the degree of vertical integration typical of the industrial, technological, and financial systems of the Pacific countries, nor their level of complementarity in relation to the large ensembles dominant in each region, while at the same time their insertion into the international division of labour has proved to be profound and organic. In contrast to this, in the three southern European countries, the productive branches are still at a rather archaic and rudimentary stage of development apart from some exceptions to be found – albeit localized – in Spain. In addition to this, the insertion of these countries into the dominant system has not been brought about through the development of specialized industries but rather by way of *association* to the European system of redistribution of certain types of revenue and rent. Consequently, in order to account for the specificity of the south European countries it is necessary to distinguish between the NIC (Newly Industrializing Countries) model and the model of *associated growth* typifying the Mediterranean countries (Vergopoulos, 1986; 1987).

Beyond the fact that the societies of the Pacific are experiencing a demographic growth rate some three to four times that of Southern Europe, the styles, orientations, and rhythms of the political, economic, social, and cultural forms and activities of these two groups of countries are manifestly profoundly divergent. The strength of the move towards industrialization and the extremely rapid integration of technological progress clearly distinguish the Pacific countries from those in the south of Europe where change is slow and often punctuated by movements in the opposite direction. Ever since the nineteenth century the modernization of the Mediterranean countries has followed largely discontinuous lines, with upswings and downswings in space as well as in time. Moreover, as we have already pointed out, the prevalent economic and social circumstances of the south of Europe are evolving in a different, if not an opposite, direction to those of the Pacific group. Since 1974–75 economic activity, in general, and industrial activity, in particular, have regressed or stagnated in the south of Europe whereas in the Pacific zone growth has been sustained at a rate of over 10 per cent per annum on average from 1974 through to 1988. While present-day capital formation is largely negative in Southern Europe as compared to the beginning of the crisis, the Pacific countries are turning in annual averages of over 10 per cent. The internal dynamism of the Pacific countries is also apparent in their export trade which represents two to three times their share of their GNP when compared to the three southern European countries.

These rapid observations lead us to conclude that today's social situation in the south of Europe can be approached neither by reference to the model of growth and prosperity that has been applied to the new industrializing countries, like those of the Pacific, nor by reference to models based on the delocalization and extension of the zones of capital accumulation. In contradiction to these models, Southern Europe has been marked by an important wave of slowdowns and contractions in its economic and social activities, both of which were significantly accentuated through the 1980s. Whatever signs of recovery there might be in Spain and elsewhere since 1987, these in no way put into doubt the conclusions drawn pertaining to the specificity attached to this region. Moreover, in what follows we will evaluate this recovery as measured against the widening of the bases of the reproduction of capital. Furthermore, in the case of Southern Europe there is no clear reason to suggest the existence of a positive correlation between the historical movement of industrialization and the process of democratization.

The principle of *asynchrony* in the evolution of the forms of social life was already utilized in a large number of investigations into Brazil, Argentina, and other Latin American societies. (On the notion of social asynchronism see Germani, 1977).[3] However, the same experiences also show that the history of authoritarian forms, even though situated outside any relation of determination, is nonetheless not dissociable from the evolution of social and economic conditions. It would probably be more judicious to agree that political forms are neither autonomous, as the political approach would have it, nor determined, as the sociological approach supposes, but are, in principle, part of a *global social contract* encompassing the ensemble of social forms. In other words, in its transversal relationships, apart from any hierarchy of forms, the political sphere can be linked to the social sphere not in the sense of a representation, but rather in the sense of a compensation: political forms do not reflect what is social, *they complete it.*[4]

Let us recall how strongly the authoritarian regimes of the Third World have remained attached to the *developmentalist* gamble. Likewise, the recent experience of the south of Europe allows one to conclude that the breakdown of the authoritarianisms from 1974 onwards does not correspond to a movement towards the maintenance of industrialization and growth, but rather to a durable decline in both. In these cases it would be more realistic to link the downfall of the authoritarian regimes to the sudden disappearance of the conditions which rendered the *miracles* of the previous period possible. One might recall, in support of this hypothesis that, today, some 12 to 14 years after the disappearance of the authoritarianisms, the democratic regimes of Southern Europe still persist, although with variable and sometimes success, in providing the political conditions of *global deflation* manifested not only on the economic plane but also on the plane of cultural forms and social relations, in the name of the re-establishment of their fundamental equilibria. As disconcerting as it might seem, it would appear that the wave of *passive democratization* and political opening in the south of Europe today corresponds more to a falling off than to an uprise of social dynamism in relation to acute social setbacks: the recoiling of growth, the demobilization of social and political movements, the downfall of traditional ideologies, the emergence of electoralist and opportunistic strategies centred more on individuals than on orientations. Moreover, it is to be recognized that the drying up of the dynamism of the miracles makes manifest the urgency with which the problems of social modernization are posed in this part of the world today.

In short, the authoritarian regimes of Southern Europe have come to an end in the recent past, not through any frontal action or slow erosion, but rather through the sudden emergence of a *crisis of legitimation* due to the sudden modification of the international as well as the internal contexts. In his already cited study, Alain Lipietz notes:

> Unfortunately, coincident to the general crisis of fordism, democratization (in the south of Europe) was to precipitate the crisis of their peripheral fordisms by depriving them of the advantages from which the Asiatic countries benefitted with regard to the exploitation to the force of labor. (Lipietz, 1985)

However, the rise in wages during the recent period in the southern European countries was achieved in a context defined by recessive policies aimed at reducing inflation and re-establishing equilibrium, all of which resulted in the numbing of the economy and the freezing of capital formation. The decline in productivity is to be imputed to decapitalization, new policies, and the general evolution of the economy, rather than to some simple modifications in the cost of labour. Nevertheless, it remains true that this cost has evolved; but starting from a particularly low level in comparison to European standards, it could only rise, relatively, by a small amount: it still remains between a third and half of Germany's. In addition, let us recall that, in a recessive context, the share of wages appears to increase because value added diminishes overall. Consequently, it would be very hard to demonstrate that the crisis of profitability and the decline in productivity have their origins in the variation of labour costs. It must be remembered that, in this context, wages always being fixed *ex ante* in relation to the cycle of production, they will inevitably appear as a factor affecting the profitability of capital even if they are decreasing. Yet, it will be agreed that democratization, in so far as it is a political event of primary importance, has not had a very encouraging impact on economic activity: today's anticipation of recovery from the crisis through the constitution of new economic systems based on the anonymous dynamism of the markets, on the integration of financial markets, on the departitioning of productive systems, and on the continuous freeing of trade barriers, linked to the hypothesis of democratization, naturally dampen the enthusiasm of Mediterranean entrepreneurs. In fact, the latter, despite their avowed attachment to liberal values, have proved, in practice, to be extremely reticent in putting the whole of their trust into the dynamics of the marketplace, thereby abandoning their traditional systems of protection. Although the state hinders their access to financial markets and imposes macroeconomic constraints, the absence of the state, by putting the traditional systems of protection into question, would be felt even more negatively by the business community.

Consequently, the new legitimacy, whose absence has made itself felt from the start of the present phase, encompasses, besides the backing of social agreements aimed at absorbing the shocks due to slow growth, the modernization of social relations, and not only of their legal and institutional framework. The emergence of new socio-political blocks marked by a populist electoralist discourse and the high degree of social incoherence is undoubtedly founded on today's *atonic mobility* in search of new forms of economic, political, social, and cultural stabilization.

Up to this point, we have come to the conclusion that the downfall of the authoritarian political regimes in the south of Europe coincided with the entry of the three Mediterranean countries into a prolonged phase of general stagnation. During the 1970s, the great upheaval of the world system should not be imputed to the oil or energy markets but much rather to the international financial shock: the emergence of international financial circuits based on an autonomous dynamism beyond any control by the nation states. This new international financial reality, with its corollary, the generalization, on a world scale, of restrictive policies aimed at controlling prices and bolstering national currencies, brutally reversed the flow of financial resources away from the countries of Southern Europe. The rapid spread of financial difficulties within the three countries, traditionally dependent upon the inflow of foreign currencies (tourist trade, invisibles, transfers of all kinds) was at the origin of the new policies in the south of Europe aimed at providing equilibrium and financial control at the price of a slowdown or even a halt in growth. The political, social, and cultural destabilization manifested in the European countries from the mid-1970s onwards, and which deepened in the 1980s, should not be disassociated from the adventures of growth in the same period.

The ostensibly *autonomous* democratization and emergence of political systems appears against a background of economic and social deterioration and weakening. In the period of prosperity, social cohesion was secured by the dynamism of growth. Today, however, the three societies of the south, quite apart from a number of technical deficiencies, are showing the alarming symptoms of the disintegration of the foundations of social relations: atomization, economic fragmentation, social incoherence, the eruption of corporatist practices in all domains. As a consequence, the former social cohesion is breaking down. Conversely, a new social cohesion is in the process of constituting itself on a political basis: democratization, alternation, consolidation of the political and institutional system. In other words, political democratization is coming about precisely at the moment when all the traditional forms of social cohesion are breaking down.

The emergence of democratic political systems is therefore neither in discontinuity with economic and social conditions, as Rousseau imagined, nor in continuity with them, as was supposed by de Tocqueville and Marx, but is quite simply a transversal compensation of them. In fact, politics is not a reflection of the social sphere, but is already part of it integrated into the global social contract. The recent irruption in the three countries of Southern Europe of the themes of *citizenry, citizenship*, and of *Etat de droit*, concomitantly implying a return to the notion of popular sovereignty, even if it is only formal, might correspond to the urgent need to construct a new vector of cohesion amongst individuals, when all others are collapsing. It should be clear that this *substitution* of the political base for the economic does not correspond to social welfare and corresponds even less to real equality amongst individuals. Rather it corresponds to a phase of persistence and aggravation of the material inequalities amongst individuals.

The economic and social crisis, the neo-liberal offensive against the social state, and the consecutive aggravation of material inequalities amongst individuals were needed so that the problem of the abstract political equality of citizen could be posed. As Alain Touraine underlines, democracy is not, and cannot be, a type of society: it constitutes only a type of political regime (Touraine, 1988). Marx, in another context, attributed Bonapartist authoritarianism to the economic and social egalitarianism reigning amongst French peasants.

More recently, Nicos Poulantzas, pursuing the line of thought contained in the critical remarks of Rosa Luxembourg on the Russian Revolution, defines the democratic social contract as a system of weights and counterweights amongst the institutions of social life. The dynamics of democracy, as a tendency towards the abstract equalization of individuals defined as citizens (compare Rousseau, Furet and others), would constitute the opposite side of the coin of persistence and, perhaps, of the accentuation of differentiations on the real social plane. Let us recall that this relation of complementarity, or of compensation, between the political and social spheres is clearly pointed out by the advocates of the sociological explanation, de Tocqueville and Marx, for example, but with the difference that it is taken to be an ideological fact, not a real one, appearing in the *sky of representation*. However, in the light of the preceding remarks, one will agree that the democratic system of the abstract equalization of individuals, be it illusory or alienating, always sees itself reinforced or weakened as a function of what is, or is not, obtained on the real social plane. Consequently, the democratic illusion has a very real existence, and takes its place beside the other really existing aspects of social life. If politics is part of ideology, according to Marx, ideology nevertheless materializes itself in the institutional and political organization of society.

All in all, the process of democratic advance in the south of Europe corresponds at present to the downfall of the previously existing foundations of social cohesion, in a context of economic and social atony. Today's democratisation is undoubtedly progressing, but in a direction which is altogether abstract and unforeseen: democracy no longer constitutes the conquest of social movements which are steadily degenerating towards the most serious point of deterioration, that is, to the point of the emergence of the new reality of atonic individualism albeit *irreducible and sovereign*. In these circumstances, this democracy is not a conquest of society, in profound metamorphosis, but it is rather the social sphere which finds itself invested, conquered, by the political sphere. The outstanding symptoms of this *fin de siècle* situation are: the disappearance of any notion of social movement on all planes, accompanied by the reconstitution of the fundamental notions of the individual, of the citizen, of systems of legal rights and abstract liberties, of rules of political and formal institutional play. This *malaise* is also present in the political forms themselves: in parties, political ideologies and intermediary political processes. The political and institutional systems are being consolidated from a formal point of view, despite the fact that they appear to be losing their content, importance and interest.

In this context, it would be useful to clarify, as has been suggested by Philippe Schmitter and Adam Przeworski, the conditions of present-day *social anorexia*, as well as the manner of consolidation of formal and abstract democratic systems put in place in the three southern European countries. Is it necessary to recall that the major institutional reforms in the course of history have always been undertaken in periods of social crisis?

A NOTE ON SPAIN

Why does Spain, especially since 1986, give the impression of finally having invented its own way of securing a flourishing economy and a consolidation of its democracy? Can the results thus achieved be considered as solid and durable?

Spain, during the last three years, has radically changed its economic policies: with the dismissal of Miguel Boyer's team, unconditional supporters of a policy of recessive adjustment, the Spanish government set out strongly expansionist economic and monetary objectives, thus diverging from those of the other European countries and from the recommendations of international financial institutions. The new policy, once again, gave priority to growth, but on the basis of the internal market. Real wages, as a matter of fact, progressed regularly, despite the plans of the government, and as a consequence consumption was stimulated as well as public deficit spending. Under these conditions, it is true that signs of recovery of production, of the activity and formation of capital have come into evidence, although the level of unemployment remains particularly high. Can this recovery be considered as original and durable? Nothing can be less certain. Today's mobilization of the Spanish economy does not constitute a counter-example of the general tendency towards a slowdown, since it is obtained on the basis of a series of artificial measures which in the end cause more problems than they were set out to resolve in the first place. Today's recovery is entirely secured on the basis of deficits and borrowing, measures which will necessarily compromise the future prospects for growth. The servicing of its public debt alone amounted to 0.6 per cent of GNP in 1982 and has now risen to 2.5 per cent of the country's GNP. The growth thus obtained in Spanish production has not been followed up by an increase in exports, while at the same time imports are rapidly multiplying. The growth differential between the Spanish and European markets is at the root of a growing foreign deficit and therefore constitutes a strong barrier to the pursuit of recovery: between 1986 and 1987, the foreign trade deficit, in absolute terms, has doubled. As the OECD has pointed out, in such a context a partner country set on relatively higher levels of growth is forced to moderate its growth and align with the other member countries before long.

Consequently, it is apparent that Spain's recent flourish of activity was not the result of the recessive evolution begun in 1975 and pursued until 1985, but is rather the offshoot of a new self-limiting short-term policy. Moreover, it is also clear that the positive effects of this new policy cannot be durable, given the recessive character of the international economy and, more particularly, the fact that Spain has not yet defined a new line of attack on the international markets. The Spanish economy is still mainly specialized in labour-intensive production, in undifferentiated products on whose price international competition weighs. Spain does not possess technologies of its own, nor adequate research facilities, all of which makes not only the development of new technological lines impossible, but also the very concept of technology itself. In like fashion, what little exists of a Spanish financial system is seriously flawed. (The destabilizing effects of new expansionist policies are currently limited by large injections of foreign autonomous capital. It is precisely because of its autonomous nature that this type of financial recourse remains aleatory and does not correspond to a new model of growth.) In these circumstances, one is led to fear that today's policies for an overall economic recovery will fare no better than other analogous experiments as in the case of Brazil, for example. If this were to occur, the Spanish dissidence will have been but short-lived, without having invented a new road to growth capable of durably countering today's international recession.

During the last 25 years, the traditional societies of Southern Europe have been shaken by a succession of waves:

- the opening up of *closed* economies from the beginning of the 1960s onwards;
- the brutal reduction of the agricultural population and the rapid urbanization of economic, social, cultural, and political life;
- the spectacular development of migratory movements towards the labour markets of West European countries;
- the building up of systems of tourist-based revenues, of services, and transfers of all kinds in foreign currencies;
- the substantial penetration of financial flows coming from the supranational market;
- the collapse of the traditional authoritarian regimes concomitantly with the cessation of strong growth rates;
- the progressive lifting of tariffs and growing deprotectionism affecting the circulation of commodities;
- adhesion to the EEC, which implies the triumph of the principle of liberalization and multiple flexibility in the restructuring of productive systems.

The three countries already appear to be set on the path governed by the dynamism of the markets, not only on the economic plane but also the social and political ones. It is easy to understand that this perspective already threatens the rigid elements historically linked to the privileges and entitlements of *closed* societies, overtaken today. The real root cause of the South European problem is finally beginning to appear on the surface in all its urgency and gravity. With the erosion and collapse of the protective shields, the grave failings of the productive systems are becoming apparent. Financial exuberance, demand-led growth policies, a strong institutional and administrative presence in the heart of the economic system: all have long contributed to the masking of the deficiencies and the survival of the outmoded systems. Today, the absence of these complementary elements reveals the fundamental problems which have been in the making over several decades. The economic and social agents, albeit impeded from opposing themselves to the processes of liberalization, are at the same time little inclined to assume their functions and responsibilities in the new framework which is in the process of constitution.

During the 1970s, one tended to confuse the end of growth with contingent causes such as the oil crisis, the measures taken against economic over-heating, the economic hiccups due to the arrival of the democratic regimes. However, inflation, that central symptom of the defective functioning of the economic process, has continually risen since 1973, and that in spite of the fact that the intermittent contingent shocks were partly absorbed.

During the 1980s, one is becoming increasingly aware of the fact that the ensemble of elements listed above are, in the end, nothing but simple detours on the way to the true structural base of the question: the economic and social systems of Southern Europe, of a weak consistency as such, can function only on the basis of a strong and organic presence of the state, the administration, and the institutional framework. The state, in this context, does not reflect the social structure, but plays an active role aimed at offsetting its weaknesses, discontinuities, and inefficiencies. The modernization of the state thus becomes the condition for the persistence of the archaisms in the domain of social relations. In other words, the state appears here as the principal contributing factor to the longevity and the endurance of backward and inefficient social structures: with its compensatory action, it does not modernize society, but allows the preservation of the social edifices of another age. Even today one can still easily verify that any hypothesis of liberalization, in the sense of a withdrawal of the state, inevitably provokes the multiplication of social pressures on that very state, with the aim of extorting new kinds of subsidies. One should not be surprised to learn that in the south of Europe, notions like *liberalization of the markets* are often understood as the need to strengthen the presence of the state in the economy, with the aim of reducing the risks of entrepreneurship.

Despite the crisis and brutal slowdown, the discourse on development has still not been entirely abandoned by the dominant ideologies in the three countries of Southern Europe, contrary to what is occurring in the Western countries, where the discourse on redeployment and new lines of technology appear, for the moment, to dominate calls for a global relaunching of economies. In Western Europe today, the hypothesis of a global recovery and of a rapid return to the objective of full employment seems to be abandoned because they appear to be not only unrealistic, but also dangerous, to the degree that they risk encouraging the reappearance of elements and factors apt to slow down the desired process of structural adjustment. The refusal of Germany to give in to the pressures inviting it to 'hike' its growth rate after the stock market crash of 1987 is particularly instructive in this regard.

Conversely, according to the south European definition of new *supply-side economics*, the central position is not directly occupied by market dynamics, but once again by a renewed role of the state meant to permit the much desired functioning of the markets.

The generalized deflationist policies of the 1980s, despite being necessary if even more dangerous disruptions are to be avoided, are doubtless incapable of attaining the objective of rapid restructuring, on the economic plane, and reshaping, on the social plane. Economy and society, for the first time in the history of Southern Europe, are beginning to escape broadly from the control of the state. The policies tightening liquidity and demand are not improving trade balances, which are continuously deteriorating. The systematic squeezing of revenues and salaries is unwittingly encouraging un-declared activities, as well as drops in productivity in official activi-ties. Excessive credit controls favour the emergence of *black market credit trading*; profit controls stimulate tax evasion and investment in undeclared activities. This situation incites us to conclude that, in the societies of the south of Europe, the classical means of intervention along Keynesian or monetarist lines are no longer capable of pro-ducing the desired results. The simple financial management of the systems can no longer have an effect on the plane of the restructuring of the economic and social ensembles. Parallel and underground economies are taking on increasing importance and defeating any hypothesis or anticipation founded on the dynamics of economic automatism.

Yet, in admitting that deflationist policies, imposed today by the adhesion to the Europe of the EEC, contribute to the weakening of the order of things traditionally founded on the complicity of the state, on easy surplus profits, on cheap labour, on dilapidated technologies, and social underdevelopment, one will recognize a certain legitimation of these policies: to the degree that they involve aspects positively encouraging to the constitution of a new authentic-ally entrepreneurial order, something which has always been absent from the south of Europe. Naturally, this new order would entail characteristics of its own: the economic autonomy of enterprises, the incorporation of new flows of technology, the modernization of social relations, the adjustment of wage costs to the social norms of Western Europe, but also of technical modernization and productivity, along with profits, innovative strategies and entrepreneurial risks.

Consequently, the true problem of southern European society cannot be summed up by the hypothesis of a simple excess of demand, it is rather related in a more complex way to the organic deficiencies of the economic and social infrastructure. In the three societies of the south, without deep restructuring and social modernization, it will be impossible to secure the right adjustment and reach new terms of reference for labour as well as for enterprises.

It should be clear that a *policy of change* of the social tissues imperatively presupposes the political and social consent of those who, by definition, are called upon not only to bear the costs of this operation, but also to put it into practice. The absence of such consent would seriously compromise, for quite a long period of time, the projects of social restructuring and renewal. If such were the case, the only choice left to the countries of the south of Europe would be between the path of authoritarian *renewal* imposed from the top and, perhaps, that of a new withdrawal within national boundaries which would imply the renunciation of all modernization.

In the course of the preceding analysis, one has had occasion to recognize that, for the three countries of Southern Europe, the same causes which had triggered the dynamics of the expansionist cycle in the 1960s, were also at the origin of its exhaustion and the transition to the present phase of decline and prolonged economic and social stagnation. These causes evidently spring from the mechanisms of the *association* of the three countries, from the 1950s onwards, to the dynamics of European integration.

In this European and world context, the evaluation of the expansionist and recessive phases allows one to pinpoint the *impressive passivity* of the south European societies, particularly since the 1950s, with respect to the problems of adjustment, change and modernization. It is altogether apparent that today one is far from the antagonisms and virulent reactions which marked the period of the great depression in the 1930s. The internationalization of economic systems after the Second World War, and the transnationalization of the financial markets have today rendered the old forms of nationalist-type stabilization largely inoperative. The necessary absorption of external shocks today takes on the new forms of stabilization, subjected to the major priorities of financial movements, and changes in the rates of exchange and interest.

During the 1930s, the stabilization of national economies giving priority to the circulation of commodities inevitably took on the form of commercial protectionism. This did not fail to motivate major structural changes. Today, however, the priority going to financial stabilization through the sliding and flexibility of exchange rates, once again puts national economies in a state of isolation in relation to the rest of the world. However, considering the organic weaknesses of the satellite economies, one will conclude that the new forms of stabilization, notably those operating by way of financial and monetary flexibility, involve not a relaunching of internal activity, but rather the *immobilization* of activity on a global scale. In this context, the policies founded on the impulse of macroeconomic variables have been progressively abandoned. In its place, one is presently examining the hypothesis of the substitutive growth of firms largely benefiting from microeconomic advantages, in a global context of slow growth. This inevitably leads to the intensification of the process of concentration. In addition, in the satellite economies, such as those of the south of Europe, where the microeconomic consistency of firms is weak by definition, even the substitutive growth of solid enterprises, technical, and social changes, as well as the processes of concentration, appear equally to be retarded or blocked because of the unfavourable influence of the macroeconomic context.

Consequently, the Southern European economies and societies are marked at present by the impossibility of conceiving and developing a dynamic and autonomous perception of the international recession. Torn between a simple alignment with the European deflationist positions and a utopian recovery deprived of any long-term prospects of success, south European society is invaded by sentiments of profound and unprecedented *malaise*. Social dynamism seems to have vanished, social movements have recoiled, political systems have lost their sense and importance, political ideologies have become cold and distant. The new atonic individualism and social anorexia today constitutes the irreducible and necessary background against which the new systems of political democracy in the south of Europe are being erected. However, the new political cohesion, albeit ideological – since it flows from the abstract notions of the legal state, of the individual, and of the citizen, apart from any other determination – may well, under certain conditions, serve as an historical opportunity and a basis for the reconstruction of new social tissues, and the modernization of *real* social systems and relations.

Notes

1. The English translation is by Robert Mandeville.
2. The notion of *social anorexia* is derived from the concept of *unappetizing choices* used by the 17th-century English philosopher Thomas Hobbes.
3. The notion of asynchrony is in fact also employed in the analyses of O. Ianni, T. di Tella, G. O'Donnell, J. Nun, A. Touraine, and others.
4. This function of compensation between the political and social spheres was already perceived by Alexis de Tocqueville in his critical passages concerning the French Revolution when he noted: 'The French deprived of true liberties, embrace abstract liberty'. However, to his eyes, this antinomy could only be illusory: the French, he noted, are orienting themselves without knowing it towards the illusions of politics. Concerning the same problem, Karl Marx adopted an altogether analogous position in admitting that in the end real society would take its revenge on the illusion of politics. On this subject one can profitably consult Furet (1978).

References

Ethier, D. (1986) *Crise et démocratisation des régimes autoritaires dans les pays semi-industriels*. Doctoral thesis, Université Paris VIII.
Furet, F. (1978) *Penser la révolution française* (Paris: Gallimard).
Germani, G. (1977) *Politica y sociedad en una epoca de transicion* (Buenos Aires: Editorial Paidos).
Lipietz, A. (1985) *Mirages et miracles. Problèmes de l'industrialisation du Tiers-Monde* (Paris: Editions la Découverte).
Touraine, A. (1988) *La parole et le sang* (Paris: Editions Odile Jacob).
Vergopoulos, K. (1986) 'Une normalisation problématique. L'Europe du Sud', in: *Pour une définition de nouveaux rapports Nord/Sud* (Paris: Editions Publisud).
Vergopoulos, K. (1987) *An Essay on the Perspectives of Stagnation in Southern Europe* (Athens: Editions Exante).

7 The Parties and the Consolidation of Democracy in Portugal: The Emergence of a Dominant Two-Party System[1]

Alex MacLeod

With the fall of the oldest dictatorship in Western Europe, Portugal is now endowed with a liberal-democratic system very similar to that of its neighbours. This evolution towards democracy is best represented by the emergence of competitive parties. In fact, political parties played a major role in the democratization process following the military *coup d'état* of 25 April 1974. Despite this involvement, during the first year of the 'Carnation Revolution', it was widely assumed that democratic parties would be relegated to playing a supporting role in a system where the military would exercise the essential elements of power. Clearly, these assumptions underestimated the ability of political parties to impose a civil form of government on a deeply divided military which was also influenced by the parties.

With the fall of the Marcello Caetano government, Portugal's parties – most of which developed only after April 1974 – began to mobilize a largely depoliticized population. During the next year, despite the formation of a multitude of parties of all political stripes, four of these parties managed to collect almost 85 per cent of the vote in the first open election in 50 years. This four-party domination of Portuguese political life continued until 1985, when the legislative elections produced a significant change in the political landscape. The four-party system which had prevailed for a decade gave way to a sort of dominant two-party system, with a party of the centre-left, the Socialist Party (PS), doing battle with a party of the centre-right, the Social Democratic Party (PSD). Of course, the Portuguese party system cannot be explained in such simple terms. First, despite the crisis the Communist Party has been going through since 1987, the PCP is not about to disappear. Second, the Democratic and Social Centre (CDS), to the right of the PSD, is still able to attract significant support. Third, because the PS and the PCP cannot work together, there is no question of symmetry between the centre-left and the centre-right. It is therefore more appropriate to talk of an 'imperfect two-party system', with the PSD – present in every government since 1980 – continuing to be the pivotal party.

The emergence of parties as the principal political actors in Portugal is due to the dual process of demilitarization of the government and the development of a parliamentary system. At the same time, the battles for political hegemony on the left and on the right have ended in success for the PS and the PSD. This chapter will analyze these three developments, allowing us to understand the directions taken by the party system after 1985. These recent changes will be discussed in the last part of this chapter. Before examining these questions, it is useful to remember the factors which led to a political system dominated by four parties.

BACKGROUND TO THE PARTY SYSTEM

The factors which contributed to the development of the party system fall into two categories. First, those which arise from the nature of Portuguese society itself, and second, those created by the parties themselves to assure their own survival.

The first category would include the ethno-linguistic homogeneity of the country, which prevents the development of true regionalist parties opposed to the central government and the parties represented in that central government. Of course, during the revolution, separatist forces appeared on the Azores and Madeira islands, but these forces were in fact only elements of the far right attempting to counter the leftist tendencies of the Lisbon government, rather than truly nationalist movements. As for the traditional rivalry between Lisbon and the countryside, it has never brought about the rise of regionalist parties.

Regional differences, exemplified best in different economic and social structures, have nevertheless had a great influence on the formation of political parties. The presence of smallholdings in the rural areas of central and northern Portugal, still strongly influenced by the Church, guaranteed strong support for the conservative parties, namely, the PSD and the CDS. In the dechristianized region of the Alentejo region, where large-scale farms dominate, the Communists can count on a stable base of support. Unlike the other parties, the PS – while well established in all regions – has no particular strong, solid, regional and social base of support, and is forced to do battle against the Right in the north, against the PCP in the south, and against both in the industrialized urban areas of Lisbon and Oporto. This lack of a clear base explains why the PS cannot count on the loyalty of its voters.

Fifty years of paternalistic dictatorship had completely deprived Portuguese citizens of any experience of political participation. While political parties were able to organize fairly quickly following 25 April, the same cannot be said for other social forces, except, perhaps, the Church. The parties took over every aspect of social and economic life. The labour unions, the media, and public corporations all became part of the battle between the parties. This situation continued after the revolution.

The four dominant parties elected to the Assembly in April 1975 took advantage of this situation by writing a constitution that assured their own domination of political life. The constitutional changes of 1982 simply consolidated this domination. The Constitution reserves for the parties the right to organize legislative elections, prevents deputies elected for one party from joining another, and forbids citizens from belonging to more than one party. The 1976 Constitution also entrenched a voting system based on proportional representation using the d'Hondt method. This system favours large parties, has encouraged the parties to seek electoral alliances, and reinforces their advantage.

DEMILITARIZATION AND THE CONSOLIDATION OF THE PARTY SYSTEM

The fight for control of the party system between the military and the parties began immediately following the coup of 25 April 1974. At first, it seemed as though the military would dominate political life, with the parties playing a secondary role. Only the Communists and the leftist groupings backed the left-wing factions within the military to lead what had become a revolutionary process. The PS and the Popular Democratic Party (later to become the PSD) could do nothing but follow the movement and wait for the election of a constituent assembly stated for 25 April 1975. The only important party of the right, the CDS, was kept out of the political game.

The attempted counter-coup of 11 March 1975 created a temporary advantage for the military left, that is, the factions close to the PCP and to the leftists, which took advantage of the failed counter-coup to radicalize the revolutionary process. In particular, they nationalized the banks, the very heart of Portuguese capitalism. They also tried to minimize the impact of the approaching legislative elections by forcing the parties to sign a pact with the Armed Forces Movement, guaranteeing that the new Constitution would assure the regime's socialist orientation and the predominant role for the military. Despite the overwhelming victory of the Socialists and the Popular Democrats at the polls, with more than 60 per cent of the vote, the military left still wanted to pursue the acceleration of the revolution and to prevent the electoral process from superseding the revolutionary process. Despite their reservations, the Communists could do nothing but follow while the PS and the PPD went into opposition.

These events provoked a deep split within the military, finally exploding on 9 August 1975 when moderate socialist elements within the military published the famous Document of the Nine, a political platform opposed to both the adventurism of the military left and the aims of the PCP. This document provided the impetus for the final phase of the revolution. On 25 November 1975, moderate military factions intervened. This counter-coup demonstrated that the military hierarchy wanted to re-establish unity within the armed forces too long divided by in-fighting. It also marked the beginning of the demilitarization of the political system.

All the necessary conditions for the end of military involvement in politics existed in Portugal.[2] The moderate faction within the army was dominant and wanted to leave the political scene as soon as possible, while those who wanted to continue the revolution had been eliminated. At the same time, the fundamental values of the revolution had been preserved in a new constitutional pact signed by the military and the parties. Finally, the existence of a large electoral majority for the PS and the PPD led to the belief that a veritable civil alternative existed. Despite these favourable conditions, it took six years before the military yielded all political power to civil authorities. The parties themselves must accept an important part of the responsibility for this delay.

The Constitution published on 2 April 1976 continued to foresee a political role for the military. It gave an important role for the Council of the Revolution, composed solely of members of the military, which, according to article 143, was to play the role of 'political and legislative body on military results, guarantor of the smooth functioning of democratic institutions, and guarantor of the respect for the Constitution and loyalty to the spirit of the Portuguese Revolution of 25 April 1974. It could authorize the President to declare war, recommend the nomination or the dismissal of the Prime Minister, and would act as a court for constitutional matters. Furthermore, the General Staff retained its autonomy, reducing the Minister of National Defence to the role of a coordinator between the military hierarchy and the civil government. Finally, the preeminence of the military was assured by the election of one of their own, General Eanes, as Head of State. He was elected with more than 60 per cent of the vote, had real autonomous political power, and kept his military post as Chief of General Staff.

Even though the Council of the Revolution exercised its powers in a relatively unobtrusive way, frictions between the military and civil authorities were inevitable. Although the military had planned to leave politics as soon as the revised constitution was adopted after 14 October 1980, the leader of the PSD, Francisco Sa Carneiro, was impatient and wanted to purge the military from politics as soon as possible. To do so, he formed a coalition with the CDS, won the interim elections of 2 December 1979[3] and consolidated this victory in the following parliamentary election of October 1980. Not having the two-thirds majority necessary to amend the Constitution, Sa Carneiro resorted to a tactic of dubious constitutional validity. He convinced another military officer, General Antonio Soares, a man of the right, to contest the presidential elections against General Eanes. If elected he promised to put constitutional changes to a nation-wide referendum, a procedure not mentioned in the Constitution. This strategy, which created even deeper divisions within the military hierarchy, failed with Eanes' easy re-election.

In January 1981, a step was taken towards demilitarization when President Eanes, as promised, resigned from his post as Chief of General Staff. The last step of this lengthy process occurred in 1982 with the adoption of a revised constitution. It replaced the Council of the Revolution with wholly civil institutions, and put the armed forces clearly under the control of civil authorities. the Assembly also passed the National Defence Act, which ended autonomy for the military high command by creating a Superior Council of National Defence, dominated by the government and ensuring that the Ministry of Defence became a real ministry with real powers over the armed forces.

These measures did not end the skirmishes between the military and civil authorities. Except for the Communists, politicians paid little respect to the officers who had overturned the old regime. In 1983, these officers repaid in kind by creating an April 25 Association despite the absolute prohibition against political activity contained in the National Defence Act. The government prudently decided to charge the military under this law for their political activity. Despite these incidents, military guardianship of the state had ended, and political life in Portugal was now solely the domain of the parties.

THE PARLIAMENTARIZATION OF THE REGIME

Parliamentary systems allow parties to exercise maximum control over political life. Multi-party systems, where no party can form a government alone, provide the parties, and particularly the small parties of the centre, with a great deal of bargaining power. On the other hand, presidential systems, because of the separation of powers, encourage institutional rivalries, which the president can exploit to limit the control parties have over the decisional process. The president also has more independence from his own party because of the existence of two majorities – one presidential and one parliamentary. What happens then when a constitution gives independent powers to a president elected by universal suffrage and forces the government (or the prime minister) to be responsible before both the parliament and the president? Some observers have been quick to call this type of system 'semi-presidential' (Duverger, 1978, 17–26; Nadais *et al.*, 1983, 231–8). The inspiration for this model is found in the Constitution of the French Fifth Republic. But as demonstrated by the period 1986–88, where the president had no parliamentary majority, the seat of power and the operation of the system depend more on the circumstances than the basic structure prescribed by the Constitution, whatever the intentions of its authors were. A president elected under such circumstances can exercise his constitutional powers only if the party system is extremely fragmented, preventing the formation of stable governments, or if the parliamentary majority accepts without question the ultimate authority of the president (Colliard, 1978, 280). The former is quite rare, and the latter is essentially circumstantial. The concept of a presidential regime with a 'parliamentary corrective', suggested by Jean-Claude Colliard (1978, 280–1) offers a better definition of this hybrid system.

The authors of the Portuguese Constitution of 1976 opted for a system similar to that of the Fifth Republic. The president had independent powers, including the right to appoint and dismiss the prime minister, the right to dissolve the Assembly of the Republic, the right to challenge the constitutionality of laws, and the right to veto any legislation. The government, whose members could not sit in parliament, was *politically* responsible to both the President and the Assembly. Moreover, the President of the Republic, in his role as President of the Council of the Revolution, exercised certain powers completely beyond the control of the other civil political institutions. The president also owed his political career to no political party. So, in theory, he had been provided with all the necessary tools to remain independent of the parties. Unlike General de Gaulle, the Portuguese president could not count on a loyal majority in parliament. Because of this, the president could not prevent a continual shift of power away from his office toward the government, parliament, and thus, the parties.

President Eanes' two terms (1976–86) were marked by conflicts between the government and the president. In 1978, President Eanes dismissed Prime Minister Mario Soares, who had led a coalition government made up of two unlikely partners, the PS and the CDS, after the CDS withdrew its support from the government. President Eanes tried to put in place three 'presidentially inspired' governments, none of which could secure a majority in the House, forcing early dissolution of the Assembly. Clearly, the president could not control the Assembly against the will of the parties. The rivalry between the two institutions reached its peak during the constitutional debates of 1982. During this period, all of the parties except the PCP tried to reduce the powers of President Eanes. This included the PS, which had signed an agreement not to do so in July 1980.

In addition to eliminating the Council of the Revolution, these debates produced a weaker presidency in three areas. First, the notion that the government was *politically* responsible to the president disappeared, replaced by the stipulation that the prime minister and his government were responsible to the Assembly. This meant that the president could dismiss a prime minister only if 'it became necessary to ensure the smooth operation of democratic institutions and only after consulting the Council of State' (article 198). Second, the president's power of veto became limited. And third, the president's power to dissolve Parliament was restricted by forbidding him from doing so in the last six months of his term. But these changes did not mean the end of presidential intervention in Portuguese political life. In the summer of 1985 President Eanes exercised his right to dissolve the Assembly to break an impasse, and President Soares did the same in the summer of 1987. However, the presidency has not become an office for completely independent political decisions.

PARTIES AND THEIR BATTLE FOR HEGEMONY

Since the Revolution, the history of Portuguese parties has been marked by battles for the leadership of the right and the left, and more recently, the centre as well. The fight for the leadership of the left has taken place principally between the PS and the PCP. The Communist Party has never been able to challenge the PS alone in elections. It has had to come up with strategies which would allow it to weaken its rival and expand its own electoral base. Beginning in 1979, the PCP has contested parliamentary elections as the leader of a coalition with smaller parties of the left. From 1979 to 1987, this coalition was known as the United People's Alliance (APU). The Portuguese Democratic Movement (MDP), a grouping to the left with shrinking popularity, supported mainly by the intellectual community, served as the PCP's main partner. In 1983, the ecologist Green Party, joined APU. Four years later, after an intense fight between factions, the MDP quit the Alliance and contested the subsequent elections on its own. The PCP maintained the façade of an electoral alliance by creating a new coalition, the United Democratic Coalition, made up of Communists, Greens, and independents. This strategy was profitable in the 1979, 1980, and 1983 elections, but failed to bring success in 1985. In that year, another party, the Democratic Renewal Party (PRD), close to President Eanes, temporarily complicated the picture by challenging the PS and the PCP for control of the left (see Table 7.1).

The PCP gave discreet yet real support to the attempts of others to form a centre-left coalition capable of taking votes away from the PS; the PRD seemed the ideal vehicle for this challenge. With the drop in popularity of the PS and steady continued support in the opinion

TABLE 7.1 *Election Results to the Assembly: 1976–87*
(in terms of percentage of votes cast)

Party	Year					
	1976	1979	1980	1983	1985	1987
Communist Party and allies	14.6	18.8	16.8	18.2	15.6	12.1
Socialist Party and allies	35.0	27.3	28.9	36.3	20.8	22.2
Democratic Renewal Party				18.0	4.4	
Social Democratic Party	24.4			27.0	29.8	50.2
Democratic and Social Centre	16.0			12.4	9.7	4.4
Democratic Alliance*		45.3	46.7			
Abstention	14.4	12.8	16.1	21.4	24.6	28.6

* This includes the vote for the PSD and CDS lists on the Azores and Madeira islands.

polls for President Eanes, the situation was ripe in 1985 for the launching of a new party backing the President. The PRD exceeded all expectations in their first contest by taking 18 per cent of all votes, reducing by almost half the vote of the PS, and, unfortunately for the PCP, attracting some traditional APU voters.[4] The PRD challenge was short-lived. In the summer of 1987, the party dropped below 5 per cent support because it had little clear direction, Eanes' leadership was weak, and the divisions caused by the 1986 presidential election disappointed most of its electorate.

The supremacy of the PS over the PCP was overwhelmingly confirmed in the 1986 presidential elections. After having declared that under no circumstances would it support Mario Soares, the PCP had to change its tune when its own candidate was defeated on the first ballot. Biting the bullet, the PCP announced that it would support Soares in the run-off election.

The degree of organization and the ability to mobilize and control the labour movement also play their part in the battle for the leadership of the left. The PCP has always had better organization than the PS, managing to establish itself in all regions and to attract five times more members than its rival. The Communist Party has always succeeded in mobilizing its members for demonstrations when necessary. However, this image of a healthy party hides a less

impressive reality. Closer examination reveals that the PCP membership has fluctuated dramatically, and that the party is suffering from a
veritable crisis of militancy which has affected its capacity to intervene on the political and social levels. The PCP has found it more and
more difficult to go on compensating for falling electoral support with
activities in other areas of society.

Until 1979, the PCP enjoyed a virtual monopoly throughout the
General Confederation of Portuguese Workers (CGTP). The PCP
controlled all the leadership positions of this, the only central union,
as well as most of the major unions in the country, with the exception
of white-collar unions (Optenhagel and Stoleroff, 1985). Since 1979,
a new union, the General Union of Labour (UGT), dominated by the
PS and the PSD, has challenged the CGTP, which has found it more
and more difficult to organize strikes on its own since the beginning of
the 1980s. Since the 1987 legislative elections the CGTP has had to
move toward some of the more moderate positions of the UGT and
has even had to accept its leadership on some questions when it
finally agreed to enter a tripartite organization, the Permanent
Council for Social Coordination, created in January 1984 to maintain
dialogue between government, business, and labour. The CGTP and
the PCP had always denounced this organization as an instrument of
class collaboration. The CGTP's dominant role in the Labour
Movement, while not destroyed, has been seriously undermined.

The history of the Portuguese right since the Revolution has been
that of the rise of the Social Democratic Party and the attempts of the
CDS to carve out a niche for itself on the right of the political
spectrum. Beyond the rivalry between the PSD and the CDS, there
are battles within both parties over strategies, ideologies, and
personal ambitions. The two parties share the same electorate, with
many voters passing easily from one party to the other. Until 1980,
the leadership of the right belonged to PSD chief Francisco Sa
Carneiro. He had developed the strategic union between the PSD
and the CDS, known as the Democratic Alliance, which won
parliamentary majorities in 1979 and 1980. With his death, and the
re-election of Eanes, the Alliance broke down. The CDS was left in
complete disarray when its leader, Freitas do Amaral, retired temporarily, whilst the PSD went through four and a half difficult years
of bitter in-fighting, only ending when Anibal Cavaco Silva, Sa
Carneiro's former Minister of Finance, surprised everyone by winning the leadership in May 1985. After Cavaco Silva won a plurality
in the October 1985 parliamentary elections, he tried to build his own

strategy of union on the right by supporting the candidate of the right in the 1986 presidential election, Freitas do Amaral. His defeat put an end to any hopes the CDS might have harboured of taking over the leadership of the right. Instead, Cavaco Silva became its uncontested head with the crushing victory of the PSD in the legislative elections of July 1987.

In fact, the CDS has never been in a position to challenge the supremacy of the PSD. Although both parties are led by members of the elite, the PSD is a mass party, even more so than the PS, and is solidly established at the local level throughout the country. Moreover, the Azores and Madeira consistently vote PSD, guaranteeing the party not only a minimum of seven seats, often more, in every national parliamentary election, but also a strong place on the Council of State and the Supreme Council of National Defence, because the heads of these regional governments, both members of the PSD, automatically sit on these two bodies. The CDS is a typical cadre party, poorly structured with few party activists.

While the PSD dominates the right, and the PS, although a little less clearly, the left, a third battle is brewing, namely, the battle for control of the centre. Whether or not a political centre really exists, most political actors and observers act as though it does, and party strategies, platforms, and rhetoric are aimed at a segment of the electorate identified with the 'centre'. For the political class, at least, the centre is a reality and has become a major issue in election campaigns (Durrao Barroso and Condamines, 1985, 36–41). Of course, the PS and the PSD have always competed for this moderate elctorate, but as the struggles for hegemony on the left and on the right have been gradually resolved in favour of these two parties, they too have intensified their fight for the votes of the centre. This is a fundamental aspect of the emergence of a dominant two-party system.

TOWARD A DOMINANT TWO-PARTY SYSTEM

Until 1985, the Portuguese party system seemed unalterably stable. Four parties dominated political life, with only two of them able to form a government. The electoral support for each party hovered within relatively fixed limits, although the PS had less loyal supporters, with its support fluctuating between 27 per cent and 36 per cent. Almost all possible government alliances had been tried, except a

PS/PCP coalition, politically impossible, and a minority PSD government. It seemed unthinkable that one party could ever hope to form a
majority government. One could imagine a relatively homogeneous
and united coalition of the right, but the experience of the Democratic Alliance after the death of Sa Carneiro demonstrated how
fragile the alliance was without the presence of a recognized and
uncontested leader. The party system was moving toward the multi-
party model suggested by Jean-Claude Colliard (1978, 80), in which
one party is the 'pivot, the necessary focus of political life; governments are formed around it, which is the general case, or as a reaction
against it'.

But as Portuguese political scientist Joaquim Aguiar (1985) has
shown, behind this apparent stability, existed a 'hidden fluidity'. On
the one hand, since 1980 the number of abstentions has continued to
rise, indicating dissatisfaction with the existing parties. And on the
other hand, from 1983 on, opinion polls have revealed that an
important segment of the electorate has said that it is ready to
support a new party.

The existence of a communist party that was not opposed to the
political system, but rather opposed to the policies undertaken by all
governments, and which refused any changes to the social and
economic model proposed in the 1976 Constitution, has prevented
the smooth functioning of the 'limited pluralism' (Sartori, 1976, 175–
80). According to the limited pluralism model, where three to five
parties are represented in parliament and no one party is strong
enough to form a stable government by itself, one should find
alternative coalitions, competition between parties at the centre, and
moderate policies. In fact, alternating right-wing and left-wing coalitions in Portugal were unthinkable, so both main parties sought votes
at the extremes rather than at the centre. On the other hand, despite
radical-sounding rhetoric, the policies pursued by successive governments were in fact very moderate. However, with the formation of a
PS/PSD government in 1983, the political game began to be transformed. The political centre became a clear battleground for the two
major parties. The parliamentary elections of 1985 opened a new
phase in the history of Portuguese political parties.

This 1985 election can be called an 'election of realignment', one
which gives rise to a clear and persistent shift in party identification
(Key, 1964, 536). Three new factors introduced during the campaign
accounted for this realignment: the arrival of a new party, the PRD,
occupying the centre-left and supported unofficially by the President;

a new leader for a now united PSD; and the absence of Mario Soares at the head of the PS. The election results turned the political landscape on its ear. The PRD dramatically changed the Portuguese left by receiving 18 per cent of the vote, with 73 per cent of its vote coming from former PS supporters, 18 per cent from the APU, and 6 per cent from the PSD.[5] The PS and the PCP experienced their worst declines ever, the former losing almost 45 per cent of its electorate compared to 1983, and the latter doing only marginally better than its worst result ever, that of 1976. The PSD succeeded in doing better than it had ever done before, winning the right for the first time ever to form a minority government. It must be noted that just over three months later the presidential elections demonstrated that the success of the PRD did not represent the birth of a new important party, but showed rather, that voters were ready to change their voting behaviour. With the inability of President Eanes to impose his own candidate, and his decision to endorse a candidate who generated little enthusiasm, Salgado Zenha, the PRD vote split, with a third going to the candidate of the right, Freitas do Amaral.[6]

If the 1985 elections surprised everyone, the size of the PSD victory in 1987 and the formation of the first majority government by a single party since 1974 was even more stunning. These elections confirmed the volatility of almost one-third of the electorate. They also underscored the electorate's shift toward the right. All parties, including the PCP, were affected by the PSD's success. 38 per cent of the PRD vote, 46 per cent of the CDS vote, 16 per cent of the PS vote, and a little more than 1 per cent of the PCP vote went to the PSD. For its part, the PS stole 17 per cent of the PRD vote and 13 per cent of the Communist vote, while the PCP took back 2 per cent of the PRD vote. The CDS made gains nowhere, and all parties except the PSD lost voters to abstentions.[7] These figures reflect circumstantial trends as a poll after the election indicated that the great majority of voters who changed parties between 1985 and 1987 did so for reasons that can best be described as pragmatic: 53 per cent said that they voted for the party that would form the 'best government', 22.4 per cent cited their desire for stability, and 14.2 per cent explained their vote by saying they desired a majority government. More than 70 per cent of these 'pragmatists' chose the PSD.[8] Elections to the European Parliament, held the same day, highlighted the fickle nature of the electorate of the right, as the PSD vote fell from 50 per cent to 37 per cent, while the CDS vote jumped from 4 per cent to 15 per cent. Part of this change was due to the popularity of the man at

TABLE 7.2   *Results of Elections to the European Parliament:*
19 July 1987
(percentages of popular vote)

PCP and allies	11.5
PS	22.5
PRD	4.4
PSD	37.5
CDS	15.4

the top of the CDS list, Lucas Pires. There were, however, no significant shifts in the vote from right to left or vice versa (see Table 7.2).

On the left, the results provided additional proof of the decline of the Communist Party, coupled with a slight increase in support for the Socialist Party. With the collapse of the PRD and the decline of the PCP, the PS consolidated its number one position on the left. The emergence of two clearly stronger political forces on the left and on the right has prepared the way for a dominant two-party system.

In a dominant two-party system, only two parties can hope to form a government, whether it be majority or minority. The Portuguese system will favour the PSD, and therefore the right, as long as the presence of a strong communist party prevents the creation of a united left-wing alternative. The PS, for its part, can hope to recapture some of its votes lost to the PRD and the PSD, and skim some votes away from the PCP and the smaller leftist parties, as happened in France and Spain. As a matter of fact, in the 1987 elections, in 11 out of the 20 national constituencies, only the PS and the PSD managed to elect candidates. The PCP and the CDS were able to save seats only in their strongholds. *De facto*, if unequal, bipolarization is beginning to take shape.

But to what extent can we speak of an actual realignment of political forces favouring the persistence of a dominant two-party system? In other words, are there profound political and socio-economic trends that favour the evolution towards a dominant two-party system?

Socially and economically, Portugal is no longer quite the same as it was in 1974. Slowly, this largely rural and agricultural country is catching up to the other countries of the EEC (see Table 7.3).

These raw numbers though, do not sufficiently reveal the changes that had taken place within the Portuguese social structure. First, the industrial working class is declining in the two urban centres, Lisbon

TABLE 7.3 *Evolution of Civilian Sectoral Employment
in Portugal, Spain, France and Greece
(percentages)*

Year	Country	Agricultural	Industrial	Other
1974	Portugal	28.2	33.6	38.2
	Spain	23.1	37.2	39.7
	France	11.6	39.2	49.2
	Greece	36.2	27.8	36.0
1986	Portugal	23.2	35.3	41.5
	Spain	15.6	32.4	52.1
	France	7.8	32.9	59.3
	Greece	28.49	27.3	43.8

SOURCE: Economic Studies of the OECD.

and Oporto, while increasing elsewhere. This new proletariat is essentially made up of workers coming from the rural exodus (Gaspar, 1985, 142). Second, the modernization of the economy is reflected in the growth of the tertiary sector and the increase in size of the new petty bourgeoisie, composed of office workers and technical workers. The traditional petty bourgeoisie of artisans and small tradesmen is becoming less and less important in the Portuguese economy. Finally, the agricultural proletariat, the base of PCP support in the south, has decreased significantly.

It is always dangerous to transpose socio-economic changes directly into votes. Voting behaviour does not change one day to the next because of relocation or change in social status, but one can detect a long-term evolution that consistently affects the balance of power between the parties. An 'election of realignment' is one step in this process. Thus, in the legislative elections of 1985, the PRD received much of its vote from the urban middle class,[9] a group which had often supported the PS in the past.[10] Much of this vote did not return to the PS in 1987, but it is too early to say whether it will remain faithful to the PSD. If we look to the experience of France and Italy, it is possible that these new middle-class voters could just as well vote for a party of the centre-left as for a party of the centre-right.

Two new political factors could modify the electoral landscape. First, with the renewal of the leadership of both major parties, a new generation of politicians is emerging. The constitutional debate of 1988 and the basic consensus between the PS and the PSD on most amendments – particularly on economic questions – shows how much the Portuguese parties are changing. As the two parties move towards each other, it will be easier for moderates to pass from one party to the other.

Second, the Communist Party has entered a period of crisis that will only accentuate its electoral decline to the benefit of the PS. This crisis is not new. Since the beginning of the 1980s the PCP has been encountering problems of recruitment which were hidden by the fact that the party was recruiting new members, but who hardly made up for those who had left. It also experienced trouble renewing its cadres and maintaining the level of militancy. Many local PCP organizations were running into difficulties, and demonstrations and strikes organized by the party or by the CGTP were not as successful as they had once been. The arrival of *perestroika* revealed the acuteness of the crisis. The lukewarm reaction of the party leadership to the new Soviet direction provoked a reaction from some of the grassroots membership. This situation forced the leadership to delay the 12th Congress for several months. This congress, finally held in December 1988, confirmed the leadership's refusal to make any changes. This ideological battle was coupled with a generational battle, as the leadership which had directed the party during the pre-revolutionary period is growing older yet is refusing to retire or update the policies and strategies of the party. The elections of 1987 demonstrated that a portion of the PCP's traditional electorate was willing to abstain or even vote for a party further to the right that had a chance to participate in the exercise of power. Unlike the French Communist Party, however, the PCP can still count on keeping a relatively strong base, although this base is gradually shrinking amongst the agricultural workers from the Alentejo.

CONCLUSION

Despite 50 years of dictatorship and two years of military rule, and despite the fact that Portugal remains one of the poorest countries in Western Europe, the Portuguese political system today is little different than that of the other European liberal democracies. Beyond differences in political institutions, what most clearly characterizes liberal democracies is the pluralism found within their party systems. We could even say that this is the essential feature of liberal democracy, the extent to which the political system allows pluralism and free competition between political parties. Portuguese political parties have not only imposed their right to exist, they have also become the principal actors on the political stage. True, they did this by challenging the military, but it must be remembered that the behaviour of the military helped the parties assert their hegemony. After all, the military assured the peaceful transition to democracy, despite a high degree of politicization within its ranks.

The most important contributions to democratization made by political parties are not to be found so much in what the regime has accomplished. On that score, their performance has not been particularly impressive. But again, in this respect, the Portuguese parties are little different from their European counterparts. What the parties have done is to legitimize democracy as a political process. They have acted as a force for political integration, including the party most hostile to the regime, the PCP. This party has become the self-proclaimed defender of the social, economic, and political gains of the revolution and the Constitution of 1976. It has resisted any modifications to this constitution, but has never withdrawn from the political system. The PCP's presence in the system has ensured the representation of social classes that could have easily acted outside the political system as they felt more and more excluded from the changes in the economy and society.

The party system seems well established, but at present there are signs of a weariness in regard to the parties. The constant increase in the number of abstentions in legislative elections, and the meteoric success, however short-lived, of the PRD suggest that Portuguese voters are not completely satisfied with the choices offered to them. The tendency toward a dominant two-party system, which reduces further the number of choices offered to the electorate, could further increase the level of dissatisfaction with the system, which is never desirable in any democratic system. On the other hand, no party opposed to the system itself seems to be on the horizon. Liberal democracy and the parties which make it work appear to be here to stay in Portugal.

Notes

1. The English translation is by Matthew Mendelsohn.
2. For more on the necessary conditions for the withdrawal of the military from political life, see Sundhausen, 1984, 549–50.
3. The Assembly elected in 1976, which had become ungovernable by 1979, could not end its mandate until October 1980 according to the

Constitution. To get around this problem, a new Assembly was elected in December 1979 to complete the mandate of the outgoing Assembly.

4. About 18 per cent of the PRD vote came from APU voters, according to Jose Antonio Lima and Luis Fraga, 'A revolução do 6 Outubro', *Expresso-Revista*, 12 October, 1985.

5. Numbers based on calculations of Jose Antonio Lima and Luis Fraga, *op. cit.*

6. See Jose Antonio Lima and Luis Fraga, 'AD regressa e renasce o PS', *Expresso-Revista*, 1 February, 1986.

7. Numbers calculated based on the analysis of Jose Antonio Lima and Luis Fraga, 'A maioria impossível', *Expresso-Revista*, 25 July, 1987.

8. See Jose Manuel Fernandes, 'O que levou a mundança de voto', *Expresso-Revista*, 1 August, 1987.

9. Jorge Gaspar, 'Permanecem as linhas da força da geografia eleitoral', *O Journal*, 11 October, 1985.

10. Mario Jose Stock and Bern Rother, 'PS: a trajectória de um partido,' *Expresso-Revista*, 14 May, 1983.

References

Aguiar, J. (1985) 'The Hidden Fluidity in an Ultra-Stable Party System', in: De Sousa Ferreira and Opello (1985) pp. 191–227.

Colliard, J-C. (1978) *Les régimes parlementaires contemporains* (Paris: Presses de la fondation nationale des sciences politiques).

De Sousa Ferreira, E. and W. C. Opello, Jr (eds) (1985) *Conflict and Change in Portugal 1974–1984* (Lisbon: Teorema).

Durrao Barroso, Jose and Jonas Condamines, (1985) 'A competição esquerda-direita entre partidos políticos na Europa do Sul (Portugal, Espanha e Grecia)', *Revista de ciencia politica*, vol. 1, no. 1, pp. 36–41.

Duverger, M. (1978) *Echec au roi* (Paris: Albin Michel).

Gaspar, J. (1985) 'Dez anos de democracia : reflexos na geografia política', in: De Sousa Ferreira and Opello (1985) pp. 135–55.

Key, V. O., Jr (1964) *Politics, Parties and Pressure Groups* (New York: Thomas C. Crowell) 5th edn.

Nadais, A., A. Vitorio and V. Canes (1983) *Constituição da republica portugesa* (Lisbon: AAFDL).

Optenhagel, U. and A. Stoleroff (1985) 'The Logics of Politically Competing Trade Union Confederations in Portugal: 1974–1984', in: De Sousa Ferreira and Opello, pp. 179–90.

Sartori, G. (1976) *Parties and Party Systems*, vol. 1 (Cambridge: Cambridge University Press).

Sundhausen, U. (1984) 'Military Withdrawal from Government Responsibility', *Armed Forces and Society*, no. 10 (Spring), pp. 543–62.

8 Constitutions and Democratic Consolidation: Brazil in Comparative Perspective

Thomas C. Bruneau

On 5 October 1988, Brazil promulgated a new constitution of 315 articles. This event was the culmination of twenty months of debate and discussion during which the 559-member Constituent Assembly was the focal point of politics in Brazil. The constitution is the eighth since Brazil became independent in 1822. Since it replaces the Constitution of 1967, amended in 1969, which was imposed by the military regime that governed between 1964 and 1985, most Brazilian political commentators consider it the keystone to the country's democratic consolidation. This conclusion is based on the open and democratic process whereby virtually all political interests had access to the Constitutent Assembly which was popularly elected on 15 November 1986, as well as the resultant document which stipulates detailed and extensive guarantees of democratic rights and processes.[1]

In this chapter I assess the prospects for democratic consolidation in terms of the 1988 Constitution, and I am unfortunately not as sanguine as most of the Brazilian political commentators. I want to convey here a sense of the context in which the Constitution is to be implemented; this will not be in terms familiar to Americans whose 200-year-old constitution is sacrosanct. Initially it is obvious that constitutions have been replaced in Brazil with a certain frequency, and the last democratically elaborated constitution, that of 1946, was overturned by the military coup in 1964. It is also relevant that the new Constitution is promulgated at a time of unprecedented economic crisis, thus creating serious political implications. The economy has been in recession for most of the decade, the country's debt has reached approximately $115 billion, and inflation in 1988 was almost 1000 per cent. There is real question whether the stabilization plan of 15 January 1989, the third since 1985, will be any more successful than the last two which failed. The presidential elections of 1989 are the first direct elections for the president since 1960. The potential for a radicalization or polarization is high if the results of the first elections held under the new Constitution are considered. In the municipal elections of 15 November 1988, the government party, the PMDB (Brazilian Democratic Movement Party) carried Salvador, Bahia, as its most important state capital. The most important capital won by the other party in government, the PFL (Liberal Front Party), was Recife, also in the Northeast. The parties most active in opposition to the federal government, the PT and PDT, carried the key capitals of Sao Paulo, Rio de Janeiro, Porto Alegre, and Curitiba. Even a splinter from the PMDB, the PSDB, won in an important capital, Belo Horizonte in Minas Gerais. The economic and political context of post-promulgation Brazil is extremely unpromising; such instability may be so perilous as to preclude the implementation of the new Constitution.

To better understand the likelihood of democratic consolidation through the Constitution, I will review the process whereby it was formulated and the roles of important political actors. This review will enable us to appreciate the interaction of political forces at this stage of Brazil's democratic transition and assess the factors which affect the implementation of the Constitution in these perilous times. It may be useful to provide first some comparative evidence on democratic consolidation in which new constitutions figured centrally in the process.[2]

COMPARATIVE CASES

The most comparable cases to Brazil's experience are the new Iberian democracies which began their transitions at roughly the same time (mid-1970s) and sought to cap the transitions with new constitutions. Despite obvious external similarities, however, the implications arising from the processes and resulting documents in the three cases are very different.

In Portugal the transition was initiated by a coup on 25 April 1974, which brought on a revolution. In accord with commitments by the Armed Forces Movement in making the coup, elections were held exactly one year later for a Constituent Assembly. In these elections the Socialist Party (PS) and the Portuguese Communist Party (PCP), both espousing Marxism at that time, together had a majority of 151 seats in the 250 member Assembly. The Assembly was constrained by the terms of a Pact with the Armed Forces Movement which guaranteed them a continuing role in politics. The deliberations of the Assembly were also influenced by the fervour of the period, when at times it appeared as though the process would be superseded by civil and military revolutionary groups. The resultant document which was promulgated on 25 April 1976 reflects these three conditioning factors. The Armed Forces Movement was given a supervisory role in government, and the document's 315 articles stipulate in extensive detail that Portuguese economy and society would continue to be transformed on the road to socialism. In sum, the Portuguese Constitution of 1976 was extremely programmatic and socialistic (Bruneau and MacLeod, 1986).

Due to external economic factors arising from Portugal's relative underdevelopment, combined with domestic political dynamics, the 1976 Constitution became a political issue soon after promulgation. It was seen by private entrepreneurs as an obstacle to development and by the political right as an impediment to their attaining power. When the right, in the form of the Social Democratic Party (PSD) and the Social Democratic Centre Party (CDS), obtained a majority in the Parliament after 1979, one of their main goals, and thus a central political theme, became revision of the constitution. This was finally achieved in September 1982. However, as the revision was made to the detriment of the powers of the incumbent President Eanes, it was destabilizing for government and the party system. And, as it required support from the Socialist Party to achieve the necessary two-thirds vote, it changed the socialistic economic and social content only slightly. The revision, like the original document, satisfied only limited sectors of the political elite. Consequently, new demands were soon made for constitutional revision and they continue to be made until the present. By elaborating such a detailed and programmatic document which can be comprehended only in the revolutionary context of the time, the Portuguese have ensured that some sections cannot be implemented, others are irrelevant, and demands for revision will continue. While maintaining the topic of the constitution in the public view, it does little for establishing the legitimacy of the document.

In Spain the situation was very different. The Constitution signed by King Juan Carlos I on 27 December 1978 finalized a transition characterized by compromise and consensus. This constitution stands in marked contrast to the Constitution of the Second Republic of

1931 which, like the Portuguese Constitution of 1976, was a document 'imposed by one political tendency upon the rest of the country'. (See Gunther and Blough, 1981, 366; 1985, 42–70; 1987, 35–65; Bonin-Blanc, 1987.) Whereas in Portugal the Socialists and Communists attempted to guarantee the revolutionary changes and momentum by enshrining them in the Constitution, in Spain the political élites sought to avoid the polarization of the Second Republic culminating in the civil war of 1936–39.

The Constitution was written by the *Cortes* between August 1977 and October 1978, and ratified in a referendum in December 1978. The Constitution represents the end of the transition led by Prime Minister Adolfo Suarez since his appointment by the King in July 1976. Due to the composition of the *Cortes* where no party or tendency held a majority, and the general agreement to avoid polarization, the defining characteristic of Spanish constitution-making was what Gunther has termed the 'politics of consensus'. More precisely, the élites engaged in consociational strategies whereby they sought compromises on potentially conflictive issues, negotiations were conducted through 'summit diplomacy' among the highest-ranking political leaders, the talks were conducted in strict secrecy, and the constraints placed on public debate over these issues in the *Cortes* were oriented towards depoliticizing them (Gunther and Blough, 1981, 402).

The challenge facing the Spanish political elites was probably more serious than that facing the Portuguese in so far as Spain has been characterized by more conflict, particularly regarding regional autonomy and Church–state relations. Because of the trauma of the civil war which ushered in forty years of rule by Francisco Franco, the élites were well aware of the need to compromise. The Constitution is composed of 169 articles; its length is due not to extensive socio-economic sections, but rather to the delimitation of political processes to mollify competing political groups. This political process has resulted in an enviable situation where no significant political groups challenge the legitimacy of the regime although the Constitution is somewhat less acceptable to the Basques. The Portuguese were less forward- (or backward-)looking: there had been no civil war and they wanted to consolidate the profound changes brought about by the demise of the Salazar–Caetano regime. Much of what they wanted to consolidate, however, was economically unrealistic and politically limited to a specific time and conjuncture. When these changed, ascendent political forces demanded that the Constitution be amended; these demands continue.[3]

BRAZIL'S NEGOTIATED TRANSITION

On first examination it appears that Brazil's experience in writing a new constitution should parallel Spain's in that the transitions from authoritarian to democratic regimes are similar.[4] The Brazilian transition was initiated from above as was Spain's, took place in a country which was transformed from the time the military took power in 1964, involved negotiations between the regime and the opposition more or less centred on the PMDB which was also something of a front like Adolfo Suarez' UCD, and included 'understandings' on the extent of tolerable change which were similar to if less formal than the Pacts of Moncloa.[5] The most obvious differences concern the decade-long span of the Brazilian transition, its escape from control of the regime in 1984, and the absence of a king.

Symptomatic of these differences is the manner in which constitutional change entered the political agenda during the transitions. In Spain, Franco had passed seven basic laws over thirty years which overlapped and never provided a coherent constitutional framework for politics.[6] A constitution was thus required to replace the personal rule of Franco and institutionalize the emerging democratic system. In Brazil it was more complicated.

In principle the constitution of 1967, substantially amended by the military in 1969 (and thus considered by most to be a new constitution), could have been exorcised of its more authoritarian elements and retained as the document for a democratic Brazil. After all, in the political transitions of Argentina and Uruguay both countries returned to their earlier constitutions which had been either amended or superseded temporarily by the military governments. It was in the context of Brazil's long drawn out political transition that the demand for a new constitution emerged; it would later re-emerge when the transition took a different turn.

The MDB first focused seriously on a new constitution in response to the April Package of 1977, although the theme had briefly emerged within the party in 1971. In the April Package, President Geisel utilized the Fifth Institutional Act to change the constitution in order to re-emphasize control over the transition in line with *his* and not the opposition's priorities and timetable. It became obvious to the opposition that the transition would at best be slow and hesitant. As a prominent leader of the MDB, Fernando Henrique Cardoso replied in 1977 in response to a question on the desirability of focusing on a constitutent assembly, 'Because the constituent assembly is the means whereby political space can be opened to improve the chances of the majority participating in Brazilian politics. This is the real reason for proposing a constituent assembly . . . It is simply an effort in the context of a very negative correlation of forces.'[7] The MDB then promoted a campaign for a constituent assembly, the first it had promoted outside of election campaigns since it was founded a decade earlier. The theme appeared in MDB (and post-1979 PMDB) documents up to and including Tancredo Neves' speech on being elected president by the electoral college on 15 January 1985. For Neves a new constitution would finalize the transition from the military to civilian regime.

In 1977, other organizations also in opposition to President Geisel and the regime promoted the theme of a new constitution. The theme became the unifying force for the opposition to demand a more rapid and profound political transition. In August 1977 the Order of Brazilian Lawyers (OAB) published a document entitled 'Carta aos Brasileiros' which advocated a return to the state of law. In the same year the National Conference of Brazilian Bishops (CNBB) published 'Exigencias Cristas de uma Ordem Politica' which advocated a similar goal. A general consensus gradually developed which focused on the need to replace the documents of the military regime with a new constitution both in order to signify a break with the military and to consolidate a democratic regime.

THE POPULAR MOVEMENTS AND THE CONSTITUENT ASSEMBLY

Following the death of Tancredo Neves in April 1985 and the inauguration of Jose Sarney, the need to make a break with the past via a new constitution seemed less imperative. A government was formed based on the PMDB and the PFL which seemed reasonably comfortable utilizing even some of the authoritarian measures of the 1967/1969 constitutions. However, in the context of the conciliated transition, the coming to power of the PMDB, and the fear that little would be changed, other opposition elements began to focus on the constituent assembly as *the* way to make the break with the past. These elements included the OAB, CNBB, the Workers' Party (PT), some unions, and a wide variety of grass roots organizations. Many of these so-called popular movements came together in the umbrella Plenario Pro-Participacão Popular na Constitutent (Plenary), which was closely linked to the Church and grassroots groups.[8] As stated by one of their proponents, 'The convocation of a Constituent Assembly is, today, a natural and necessary consequence of the campaign [in 1984] for direct elections. It is necessary to complete this campaign and, mainly, extend its goal. We want not only the direct election of the president of the Republic, but also to open spaces in order to begin a cycle of profound change in the economic and social policies of the regime, and mainly, to bring an end to the military regime itself' (Bicuco, 1985, 186).

The Plenary, and its component parts, promoted political mobilization and the development of awareness through publications, meetings, press campaigns, and pressure group techniques. They made five demands regarding a constituent assembly, whereby the prospects for making the break with the past would be maximized.

The first was a change in state representation prior to calling elections to a constituent assembly. Each state is entitled to three senators, regardless of population. In the Chamber no state can have fewer than eight deputies nor more than sixty. This means that the more industrialized, and populated, states in the South are under-represented and the underdeveloped states of the North and North-east, where clientelistic politics prevail, are over-represented. Thus a constituent assembly elected according to the actual system of representation would seriously under-represent the more modern states.[9] Also related, and criticized by some scholars as well as the popular movements, is the system of representation where the voters elect on a state-wide and not district basis. The relationship between the voters and their representatives is thus distant; this situation is aggravated by the long tenure of senators (eight years) and deputies (four). The members of the Plenary argued that without change in the system and numbers of representation the result would be a distant and unrepresentative constituent assembly.

The second point involved the elimination of the *entulho autoritario* (authoritarian rubbish) prior to calling elections. This legislation was left over from the military regime and included the Law of National Security, the Press Law, laws prohibiting strikes, and the like (see Dallari, 1986, 67, 55). The Congress had not changed any of this legislation after mid-1985, and a good deal of it was used by the Sarney government. Even though the legislation might not have been used to control the elections for the deliberations in a constituent assembly, the Plenary argued that its mere existence restricted the independence of the constituent process.

Thirdly, the Plenary argued that the constituent assembly be called exclusively to frame a new constitution and its members need not belong to political parties; they could run as independents. They assumed that the exclusive constituent assembly would be disbanded after writing the constitution, and professional politicians would avoid it. Independents would open up possibilities for broader representation. The Plenary sought to allow for the widest representation possible thereby linking the lower classes to the new constitution.

The fourth point sought to promote further popular involvement, and thus the legitimacy of the document among the public. The Plenary wanted a plebiscite – if not for separate sections of the constitution at least for the document as a whole.

And, lastly, the members of the Plenary also wanted the people to 'write their own constitution', at least to some degree. They specifically opposed the creation of a group of notables whose mandate was to prepare a draft constitution for the president. This idea had originated with Tancredo Neves and was expanded by President Sarney, who appointed a group of 51 notables from academia, the arts, and the legal profession, in mid-1985. In the view of the Plenary, this group overwhelmingly represented the élite and its very existence would stifle popular creativity.

Taken together, the implementation of these five points would, according to the Plenary, promote involvement in politics by the lower classes, encourage them to pressure the constituent assembly for a document guaranteeing their interests, and allow for an accurate representation of interests in Brazilian society.[10]

Despite a high level of mobilization and publicity, none of the demands were adopted. President Sarney proposed a project to the Congress on 28 June 1985 which would amend the constitution and call a National Constituent Assembly composed of the two houses of Congress to begin meeting on 31 January 1987. In late November, the Congress passed legislation in line with this project whereby the Congress to be elected on 15 November 1986 would also serve as the constituent assembly. The system of representation was not changed, the authoritarian legislation remained, and candidates had to be members of political parties. A proposal had been formulated in a congressional committee headed by a PMDB deputy from Sao Paulo, Flavio Bierrenbach, which would have allowed the voters to decide by plebiscite whether the constituent assembly would be in the Congress or exclusive, and provided for other plebiscites. The Plenary was very much involved in this proposal. It was, however, defeated in committee by the combination not only of the PFL and PDS, but also the PMDB. According to Bierrenbach, though he was never informed, it was understood from the beginning that the constituent assembly would be the Congress.[11]

The Commission of notables, known as the Comissao Afonso Arinos after its chairman, met between mid-1985 and late 1986. Initially rejected by the Plenary, it was later criticized by conservatives when it presented its project to President Sarney in September 1986. The project was not only incredibly detailed, with 468 articles, but also nationalistic and populistic. Among other things, the Commission recommended a parliamentary system of government and a four-year presidential tenure. President Sarney was not interested in either proposal, received the draft, and buried it.

The prospects for making a break through the constituent assembly thus appeared increasingly less promising. Virtually none of their proposals were adopted, and the overall theme of the constituent assembly received little attention in the media. In the general elections of 15 November 1986, the constituent assembly was played down and attention instead focused on the election of the state governors. In these elections the PMDB did extremely well, winning 22 of 23 governorships and receiving a majority of 302 seats in the 559-member Congress. The PFL, also involved in government, came in second with 135 seats. These results can be explained in large part by the popularity of President Sarney and the PMDB–PFL government during the Cruzado Plan which the President decreed in late February 1986. By this decree inflation was eliminated, prices were fixed, and salaries also fixed but at a relatively high level. The result was a burst of consumer spending, generalized euphoria, and great public acclaim for President Sarney and the government. The popularity was reflected in the election results. President Sarney and the government repeatedly stated their commitment to maintain the Cruzado Plan even though economists indicated it had to be modified, and goods either completely disappeared from stores or consumers had to pay a premium. Two days after the elections the Cruzado Plan was scrapped and President Sarney's popularity with it.[12] The problems of the economy were exacerbated rather than resolved by the Cruzado Plan; indeed, economic problems would serve as the ever-present backdrop for the deliberations of the constituent assembly. Not only did the assembly begin in February 1987 but Brazil also declared a moratorium on paying the interest on its huge foreign debt. It was thus in the midst of economic crisis, declining prestige of President Sarney, and a frustrated Plenary and affiliated movements that the Constituent Assembly began its work after Carnival 1987.

THE POLITICAL CONTEXT SURROUNDING DRAFTING THE CONSTITUTION

Between 1 February 1987 and October 1988, the Constituent Assembly was the focus of politics in Brazil. The final document of 245 articles plus 70 transitory articles was the result of 330 sessions, 70 000 amendments, and 14 000 speeches. The anticipated completion date was extended four times, and there were several major shifts in the orientation of various sections and finally the whole document. A brief review of some aspects will allow us to better understand the political dynamics and the resultant shifts.

The political scene was fluid, or better complicated, and would become even more so during the negotiations in the Assembly. Unlike Portugal and Spain, no formal pact existed between the regime and the opposition. Prior to his election, Tancredo Neves entered into a series of 'understandings' with key elements of the regime, including the military. These were not documented; after his death the tenor of the various understandings would be a matter for speculation and political battle – as evidenced by the fate of the Bierrenbach project.[13] The Assembly began from scratch in that Sarney chose to withhold the Comissao Afonso Arinos draft constitution, and the political parties, except for the PT, had given virtually no attention to the Assembly, and its tasks, prior to its opening in February 1987.[14]

The political scene was made even more unstable by the relationship between the executive, Sarney, and the Assembly where the PMDB had a comfortable majority. Sarney of course had been the president of the regime party, Democratic Social Party (PDS), and joined the PMDB only in 1984 when Tancredo Neves developed the strategy to win indirect election in the Electoral College through splitting the PDS. On Neves' death some wanted his contemporary, Ulysses Guimaraes, President of the PMDB to take power. This did not happen because of concern for establishing legitimacy, but Guimaraes did assume the Presidency of the Chamber of Deputies and then of the Constituent Assembly. Thus Sarney held executive power; under the 1967/69 constitutions this power was tremendous.

For example, he decreed the Cruzado Plan in February 1986, did not consult with Guimaraes in advance, and the Congress had to get around to approve it only two months later. Yet Guimaraes would hold more power than any other single individual regarding the Assembly and the new constitution. In a certain sense Brazil became a two-phased diarchy: Sarney held power in the present, while Guimaraes sought to define the nature of power in the future.

Conflicts between Sarney and Guimaraes were obvious when the Assembly was convoked; as the former attempted to limit the interim sovereignty of the Assembly, the latter sought to expand it. President Sarney was particularly concerned about his tenure which would be defined by the Assembly. According to the 1967/69 constitutions, as amended, it was six years; Neves had indicated he would govern for four as the last indirectly elected president, and Sarney initially reiterated Neves' commitment. With his popularity declining at the end of the Cruzado Plan, Sarney came out publicly on 18 May 1987 for a five-year term in order to regain his lost prestige. From then on his main goal would be to inveigle the five years from the Assembly.

In the unicameral Constituent Assembly the PMDB and the PFL totalled 436, or 78 per cent of the 559 seats.[15] The PMDB, however, had changed and expanded tremendously since entering government in March 1985. In line with the tradition of flexibility and lack of ideological and organizational coherence of Brazilian political parties, the party was wide open to new members. David Fleischer has shown that the largest political group in the Assembly was not the PMDB but, in terms of 1977 political affiliations, the ARENA (precursor to the PDS as government party) with 217 members. The more original or authentic PMDB had only 212. Of the 298 PMDB members on whom data were available in 1987, 40 were from the PDS in 1983 and another 42 were from ARENA in 1979. Thus rather than a majority of 54 per cent in the Assembly, the PMDB could count only 40 per cent once these latecomers from its right were excluded.[16] Even if Guimaraes was President of the PMDB, Chamber, and Assembly it did not mean that he, much less Sarney, could assume that the Party would vote as directed. This fact made the process much more complicated.

Other actors beyond the political parties became involved in the constituent process. Traditionally, political parties have not been the key actors of politics in Brazil. During democratic periods individual personalities have been in the forefront; during the military regime the armed forces as institution are central. Interest representation during both periods has always been less through parties and more via a limited number of organized economic interests.

Although the popular movement did not initially succeed in its goals for the Assembly, the members remained active. After the elections, the eruption of the economic crisis, the decline in Sarney's popularity, and the opening of the Assembly, the CNBB, OAB, some unions, and other movements involved in the Plenary sought to define the issues and then influence the Assembly; still to make a break via the constitution. At the minimum they promoted a momentum to focus attention on the significance of the Assembly and a new constitution. The Assembly would of necessity become the focal point for interests and pressure groups seeking to achieve their competing goals. As the popular movements wanted change, others would have to become involved to secure what they already had. All interests wanted their goals incorporated into the basic charter of the nation. This is particularly relevant as it was clear from the beginning that the new constitution would be long, detailed, and programmatic. It was expected, at the minimum, to exceed the 312 articles of the Portuguese Constitution of 1976. The deliberations of the Assembly were as long drawn out, volatile, and polemic as these initial considerations would lead one to anticipate.

PROGRESSION AND REGRESSION IN THE CONSTITUENT ASSEMBLY

In contrast to the experience in 1946 when a 'Grand Committee' drafted a document in four months and the Assembly voted it in another three, the Assembly in 1987 went into what David Fleischer terms a 'total participation mode' (Fleischer, 1989, 13). The 559 members were divided into eight large committees by content areas to take testimony and draft sections of a working document. The committees were then further divided into three sub-committees. Another committee, the twenty-fifth, was created to systematize and integrate the final reports from the eight committees. Due to the influence of progressives in the PMDB and pressure by the popular movements, the process was extremely open. The committees were open to suggestions by all associations and movements, the debates were held in public, and there was provision for 'Popular Amendments' whereby an item would have to be considered by the twenty-fifth, or Systematization Committee, if it received 30 000 signatures and was supported by three associations. There were finally 122 Popular Amendments which received twelve million signatures.[17] In June the eight committees combined their respective three sub-committee reports into their final reports which went to the 90-member Systematization Committee. The Committee was chaired by Senator Afonso Arinos, and the more powerful position of relator was held by Senator Bernardo Cabral. The Committee enjoyed considerable autonomy as it produced one working draft in July and another in September. The Committee was dominated by more liberal elements from the PMDB, aligned with Senator Covas, and other parties which had extensive contacts with the popular movements. Further, the progressives were constantly present, whereas the more conservative elements had business interests out of Brasilia and were absent most of the time. Consequently when the Systematization Committee presented the final draft of 351 articles in November there were a number of innovative elements including the following: adoption of a parliamentary system, a mixed electoral system, decentralization of taxing powers to states and municipalities, increases in the powers of Congress thereby diminishing those of the executive, guarantees of extensive labour rights and allowing for expropriation of idle land, and prohibiting public funds for private schools. Whereas future presidential terms were set at five years, Sarney's was shortened to four. The parliamentary system was to be adopted immediately on promulgation of the constitution.[18]

The economic innovations mobilized business sectors against the draft, and the change in system of government and decrease in tenure incensed Sarney. Under the rules adopted at the beginning of deliberations, voting by the full Assembly on the Committee draft would be as follows: preference would be given to their version prior to considering amendments; only if it was defeated or lacked the quorum of 280 would amendments be allowed. The opponents to the draft mobilized and formed a conservative inter-party coalition called the 'Centrao' or big centre. By bringing almost all of its members to Brasilia in December it obtained sufficient votes to change the rules governing voting procedures. From then on any amendment with more than the absolute majority of 280 signatures would take precedence in voting. Only if the amendments failed would the Committee's version stand. In late January 1988, the Assembly began voting on the draft which was completed in June. A second stage, during which articles could be eliminated but none added, took place between July and September.

The 'Centrao' included not only the PFL, PSD, and PTB but also approximately 100 members of the (expanded) PMDB.[19] Whereas the Systematization Committee was fairly cohesive and produced a final draft with innovative elements, the 'Centrao' was neither. It was generally conservative but consensus was contingent, depending on the issue at hand. This signified that virtually every article had to be negotiated, and there was no assumption of a majority. Indeed, to further complicate the process, the PMDB was coming apart during the process with the PSDB splinter with 7 senators and 38 deputies founded before the constitution was promulgated in October; in addition, the president of the PFL, Senator Marco Maciel, had already broken with Sarney in September 1987. The already fractured party system thus came apart while lobbies of all types predominated. This is relevant as it encouraged diverse political pressures from all sides on the Assembly and made for an incredible variety of at times bizarre ad hoc alliances.

THE CONSTITUTION OF 1988

The final document reflects, and as we shall see reinforces, the political process involved in its elaboration. President Sarney pulled out all stops in cajoling, threatening, and buying votes to achieve a five-year term in a presidential system. He involved the military ministers, especially the Minister of the Army General Leonidas Pires Goncalves, in publicly supporting him, distributed government funds to allies, and bought off others by assigning radio and TV licences. The two critical votes were on 22 March 1988 which was the first and only time all 559 members were present and voting in the Assembly. The presidential system passed relatively easily as the PDT and PT were in favour of it regardless of Sarney. The five-year mandate barely passed, and after that the 'Centrao' was pulled apart by different positions on most issues. The only point of unity after 22 March was in mid-May when the section on agrarian reform was defeated, thereby pushing the situation back beyond the Castello Branco government's Land Statute of 1965. Productive land, even if not fulfilling a social function, cannot be expropriated. Aside from this key area, extensive reforms were included in the Constitution.

The Constitution stipulates a fundamental redistribution of power. The executive, whose powers increased tremendously during the military regime, is weakened in relationship to Congress, and the union is diminished in relation to other levels of government. Decree laws, which became the most common form of passing legislation during the military regime, and continuing under the civilian government after 1985, must be approved by the Congress within 30 days. The Congress has extensive powers in economic areas such as changing budgetary items and overseeing the process of economic decision-making. Congress must now approve all international agreements, including those on the debt. It also has oversight of the nuclear programme. States and municipalities are to receive increased shares of tax receipts. The federal government is restricted in creating new revenue sources and in expanding the public enterprise sector. The Central Bank is prohibited from financing the public sector deficit by printing money.

The Constitution includes provisions for tremendous improvements in human rights and social guarantees with incredibly detailed sections on everything from censorship to maternity leave. Education should benefit as the federal government is obliged to increase its contribution from 13 per cent to 18 per cent of total expenditures. There are also a variety of means of popular participation which, in addition to the vote, include the initiative, plebiscite, referendum, and popular veto. Organized labour benefited with a 44-hour working week, a maximum of 6 hours per shift, and an unrestricted right to strike. The overall tone of the Constitution is nationalistic, populistic, and statist. Foreign firms are proscribed from prospecting and exploitation of the subsoil, and the foreign firms currently involved in mining have five years to cede majority control to Brazilians. The concept of a 'national company' with headquarters and directors in Brazil, or which the owners of most of the capital are Brazilian, is defined with extensive benefits in access to strictly defined markets and a variety of incentives over foreign firms. There are provisions on sports, Indians, the environment, and culture. A few stipulations appear positively weird, especially in the Brazilian context, such as setting a 12 per cent limit on real interest rates and guaranteeing parternity leave.

Because of the major social and economic reforms, and the redistribution of power and wealth between governments and within the federal government itself, Sarney went on national television in late July 1988 and described the first draft as a document that would bankrupt Brazil and make it ungovernable. He urged the Assembly to reject it which would have pushed the process back to the beginning. The day after Sarney's speech Ulysses Guimaraes called for the vote on the first draft which passed with a massive majority of 403 to 13. Voting was completed on the second round on 1 September and promulgation was on 5 October. By this time Sarney was politically isolated, his government consisting largely of the PDS and some old friends.

THE 1988 CONSTITUTION AND DEMOCRATIC CONSOLIDATION

The document produced during twenty months in the 559-member Constituent Assembly is impressive in its scope, detail, and overall orientation. It provides something for everyone in Brazil with the exception of millions of generally poverty-stricken landless peasants.[20] In order to evaluate the chances for its overall implementation we must consider a number of factors. With such a detailed document, particularly one which includes extensive sections on the economy and factors beyond the control of any country such as interest rates, it would be unrealistic to anticipate full implementation. Earlier Brazilian constitutions were not fully implemented nor, for that matter, were sections of the Portuguese Constitution of 1976.[21] In addition, it is more appropriate to think of the Brazilian process of formulating a new constitution as open-ended. The work was not completed on 5 October 1988: it is an ongoing process. Even to begin to implement this document requires the passing of 314 items of ordinary legislation and 56 of complementary legislation. This process began only in late November 47 days after the promulgation. Further, Article 2 of the transitory items provides for a plebiscite on 7 September 1993 on the form (republic or constitutional monarchy), and the system (parliamentary or presidential) of government. And, Article 3 provides for amendment after five years by an absolute majority of the Congress. In sum, the 1988 Constitution remains somewhat tentative by design of its framers; this is well within the Brazilian tradition of negotiation and conciliation.

Beyond these initial qualifications what are the relevant factors to consider in assessing likely implementation? These can be divided into two different, albeit overlapping categories. First are those emerging from the process, and verified in the document, which deal with political structures. Second are the more conjunctural factors conditioning the Constitution as it was promulgated.

In the first category are five main factors.

1. Brazil's transition from a military to civilian regime is unique in that the role of the armed forces has diminished minimally, if at all.[22] Article 142 stipulates, in part. 'Their [the armed forces] purpose is to defend the fatherland, guarantee the constitutionally established powers and – upon the initiative of any of said powers – law and order.' This is essentially the same role they have played since the founding of the Republic in 1891. It is important to note that their structures were not diminished by creating, for example, a Ministry of Defence. The National Security Council was replaced by a Council of National Defence but it is merely consultative. The armed forces came through the transition unscathed and began a modernization programme with the inception of the civilian regime. They lobbied effectively in the Constituent Assembly and their prominence and prestige increased as President Sarney, with little political base of his own, relied upon them for support. They thus remain at the centre of power in fact and in terms of the constitution.

2. The Constituent Assembly/Congress increased its powers while simultaneously reducing those of the executive. Thus even though the proposal for a parliamentary system was defeated, the constitutional powers of the Congress approximate those of some parliamentary or semi-presidential systems. The Congress now has power but lacks the tradition, means, and possibly commitment to exercise such power responsibly. This may result in the Congress impeding and not initiating necessary legislation.[23]

3. The process involved in formulating the Constitution did nothing to strengthen political parties which could conceivably increase the ability of the Congress to exercise its powers responsibly. The PMDB and the PFL, who were the main actors due to their overwhelming majority in the Assembly, were so divided in early 1989 they could not agree on presidential candidates. It is significant that there was no change in the Constitution that might strengthen political parties in the future. The earlier legislation pertaining to political parties remained, and the district system of representation was not adopted. These elements, which could result in change in the parties in the future, did not even emerge as pertinent issues in the Assembly. Even the highly unrepresentative number of deputies remained more or less intact with a minimum of eight per state and a maximum of 70.

4. There was also little change in the key area of state–labour relations though labour gained as an interest or class. Key elements from the 1930s have been retained, including the exclusive role of one

union in a locale and the obligatory collection of union dues by the state.[24] A greater percentage of the dues now go to the union which can also collect additional dues. Unions, however, are still dependent on grants of authority from the government and are thus still linked to the state but have more power in their specific locales.

5. While unions retain a close link with the state, and political parties are fragmented, there was an explosion of new actors involved in politics. The popular movement emphasized direct access to the Assembly via the Popular Amendments and a number of instruments for popular participation were included in the Constitution. It is likely that most of these movements will work at the margins of the parties, though some are affiliated with the PT. Also on the margins is the equally new phenomenon of lobbies. Lobbies of all imaginable variations, from religious associations to ecological groups to business interests worked on the Assembly. Indeed, by one estimate one-half of the members of the Assembly were themselves representatives of lobbies.[25] It is likely that lobbies will continue to proliferate now that the access points in the political and financial systems have expanded with redistribution of power from the executive and the union.

Indeed, the process and the final document have resulted in a continuing central role for the military and an almost corporatist relationship with labour and the state. The innovations are either questionable in implementation, as with Congress, or clearly centrifugal in the case of parties, popular movements, and lobbies. It thus appears that the result of the process is a weaker political framework with which to implement the very demanding constitution.

In the second category are two considerations which aggravate the above.

1. The process of writing the Constitution was so drawn out and polemic that its legitimacy may be doubted from the beginning. Sarney attacked the Assembly for more than a year and then attempted to avoid implementing the Constitution in spirit if not in letter during its first few months. Also, while most interests are guaranteed in the Constitution so are their likely opponents. By guaranteeing so much the Assembly may in fact be guaranteeing nothing.

2. The Constitution comes into effect during an unprecedented economic crisis. The crisis is due in part to the process involved in the elaboration of the Constitution. Sarney maintained the Cruzado Plan until after the 15 November 1986 elections which guaranteed the

success of the PMDB, but the economy suffered. He did not implement the Bresser Plan in the second half of 1987 because he feared the austerity measures would further harm his popularity. And he used government resources to obtain votes in the Assembly. The socio-economic orientation of the Constitution diverges from the orientation implemented by the Sarney Government since mid-1988. These grave contradictions in policy orientation do not promote dealing effectively with the problems. The Constitution may thus come to be identified by the people as not only simultaneous with the economic crisis but at least in part its cause.

CONCLUSION

The Spanish Constitution of 1978 was framed by a relatively small group of political actors in a process characterized by negotiation involving compromise and resulting in consensus. In seeking to avoid a repetition of the Civil War, they wrote a document that is realistic and legitimate for the vast majority of the population. It is not a politicized issue today and is amended in a regularized manner. The Portuguese Constitution of 1978, amended in 1982, was framed by the whole 250-member Constituent Assembly in which the left held a majority. The members sought to guarantee the revolutionary changes and continue them into the future by inclusion in the Constitution. Instead, economic realities and domestic political changes resulted in simply ignoring some sections of the document and demands for constitutional revision. Despite revision of the political sections in 1982, demands still continue for more revision.

The Brazilian experience in framing a new constitution is closer to the Portuguese, but more extreme. As the transition controlled from above went out of control, so did the Constituent Assembly. Due to the weak political base of President Sarney, the nature and com-position of the PMDB, and the pressure of the popular movements and lobbies, there was minimal coherence in the process and in the Assembly itself. The President won on the two items of most interest to him and the Right beat down agrarian reform, but the overall tenor of the 1988 Constitution is progressive, populist, statist and nationalist. This was achieved not by consensus and compromise, as with Spain, but by simply including virtually everything most groups (with the notable exception of the peasants) demanded. Thus where-as the Spanish Constitution has 169 articles, the Brazilian has 315; it can be argued that due to regional problems the former's would be longer. In contrast to Portugal, which with 312 articles is almost as long as Brazil's, there was no revolution and the Left did not have a majority. Rather, some movements wanted to make a break with the past via the Constitution and the largely conservative political actors in the Assembly lacked sufficient coherence to resist.

In Spain the Constitution itself is not a political issue, except for some of the Basques. In Portugal it continues to be, and substantial political instability continued until a majority government was elected in 1987. In Brazil there is less concern about politicization of the 1988 Constitution; rather, it may come to be considered irrelevant due to the lack of fit between its tenor and the economic and political reality of the country it purports to guide. It guarantees much but it is unlikely that the economic resources or the political structures will emerge for its implementation. Rather it is likely that its future, just as its elaboration, will be determined by short-term political goals of competing political élites.

Notes

1.   The reception of the final document was overwhelmingly positive. In its extensive review of the Constitution the liberal weekly newsmagazine *Veja*, for example, had as the lead title 'The Document of the powers of a people' followed by 'The Constitutent Assembly completes its work and creates the broadest regime of public liberties in the country's history'. Shortly after was stated: 'The fact is that the Constituent Assembly has the authority of the 69 million citizens who voted in 1986, and the new Document is a picture of their sovereignty.' (*Veja*, 7 September 1988, 32). In a recent paper an ex-Finance Minister and Professor of Economics wrote: '... Congress just finished writing a new constitution which was freely debated and approved – a constitution that is no one's dream, that is too much conservative for the left, and too much progressist for the right, but that is indeed the best compromise that Brazilian society could eventually produce today. For all these reasons we do have a democratic regime in Brazil, and a new Constitution that, in spite of the faults we may attribute to it, is a positive factor for the consolidation of democracy in Brazil.' (Luis Carlos Bresser Pereira, 'Economic Ideologies and Democracy in Brazil', paper presented to seminar on L'Internationalisation de la Démocratie Politique, Université de Montréal, September 28–October 5, 1988, 6).

        An English translation of the 1988 Constitution is available in Foreign Broadcast Information Service (FBIS-LAT-88-2336), Monday, 5 December 1988.

2. It should be emphasized that the focus here is on democratic consolidation about which little has been written. On the earlier stages of political transitions there is abundant material available. For a review of the literature and an argument on how to approach the topic see Thomas Bruneau and Philippe Faucher, 'The Analysis of Democratic Transitions', forthcoming.

3. For an eloquent appeal for revision by ex-Prime Minister Francisco Pinto Balsemao see, 'The Constitution and Politics: Options for the Future', in Kenneth Maxwell (ed.), *Portugal in the 1980's: Dilemmas of Democratic Consolidation* (New York: Greenwood Press, 1986), pp. 197–232.

4. There is a rich literature on the Brazilian transition. See for example my 'Consolidating Civilian Brazil', *Third World Quarterly* 7, no. 4, October 1985; Wayne Selcher (ed.), *Political Liberalization in Brazil* (Boulder: Westview, 1986); and Julian M. Chacel *et al.* (eds) *Brazil's Economic and Political Future* (Boulder: Westview, 1988.) Perhaps the richest documentation is found in Jose Augusto Guilhon de Albuquerque and Eunice Ribeiro Durham (eds) *Simposio: A Transicao Politica*. (Sao Paulo: Universidade de Sao Paulo, 1987).

5. The similarities in the 'transitions through transaction' are highlighted in Donald Share and Scott Mainwaring, 'Transitions Through Transaction: Democratization in Brazil and Spain', in Wayne Selcher, 1986, pp. 175–216.

6. These are discussed in Bonin-Blanc (1987), p. 19.

7. *Movimiento* August 1977.

8. In late 1985 and the first half of 1986 I researched on the Plenary and its constituent groups through their documents, interviews, and attendance at meetings. In May 1988 I returned for more interviews with these elements and other political actors.

9. According to a weighting scheme developed by Raymundo Faoro, a voter in Rio de Janeiro has a value of 1; this drops to 0.6 in Sao Paulo; in Maranhao it is 1.8 and 12.1 in Acre. Raymundo Faoro, 'Constituinte: a verdade e o sofisma', in Faoro, R. (ed.), 1985, 13. For an historical overview and analysis of the topic see Maria d'Alva Gil Kinzo, *Representação Política e Sistema Eleitoral no Brasil* (Sao Paulo: Simbolo, 1980). A more recent analysis of this and broader themes of the parties is Glaucio Dillon Soares, *Colégio Eleitoral, Convençoes Partidarias e Eleiçoes Direitas* (Petropolis: Editora Vozes, 1984).

10. These five themes figure largely in CEDI. *Dossie Especial: Constituinte* and were dealt with in most of the newsletters in 1985–86 of the Plenary. For an historical perspective and a good summary on most of the themes see Marilia Garcia, *O que é Constituinte* (Sao Paulo: Editora Brasiliense, 1985).

11. Interview with Deputy Flavio Bierrenbach on 28 May 1986 in Brasilia. The extensive hearings of the committee are available in the *Diario do Congresso Nacional* of November–December 1985. (Comissao Mista, incubida de estudo e parecer sobre as Propostas de Emenda a Constituição nos 43, 44 e 52 de 1985, que 'convocam a Assembleia Nacional Constituinte').

12. In early November 1986 80 per cent of the respondents expressed confidence in the President. By March 1988 this figure was 33 per cent. Or, whereas in the latter month 16 per cent considered his administration 'good' or 'excellent' some 43 per cent considered it 'bad' or 'lousy'. Cited in Orjan Olsen and Silvia Cervellini, 'Transition to Democracy in Brazil: The Search for Leadership and Principles', a report from the Instituto Brasileiro de Opiniao Publica e Estatistica Ltda, presented to the WAPOR/AAPOR Conference, Toronto, May 18–22, 1988.

13. On Neves' understanding with the military and the PFL see the report on a speech by Senator Fernando Henrique Cardoso in *Folha de Sao Paulo* 19 May 1986 and David Fleischer, 'From Non-Competitive to Competitive Elections to the 1987/88 Constituent Assembly: Brazil's Attempt to Finalize the Political Transition', a paper for the Academia de Humanismo Cristiano, Santiago, Chile, 23 March 1988, p. 36.

14. The draft prepared for the PT was a contribution to encourage discussion of the new constitution, but by representing a major break with the past was not a document on which any initial consensus could be built. See Fabio Konder Comparato, *Muda Brasil: Uma Constituição para o Desenvolvimento Democrático* (Sao Paulo: Editora Brasiliense, 1986).

15. The numbers for the other parties are as follows: PDS – 40, PDT – 25, PTB – 18, PT – 16, and seven minor parties, including two communist parties, 24.

16. David Fleischer, 'From Non-Competitive to Competitive Elections . . .', p. 39. Fleischer provides in this paper extensive details on the background on the members of the assembly. On the flexibility of the parties see Bolivar Lamounier and Rachel Meneguello, 'Partidos politicos e consolidacao democratica: O caso Brasileiro' (mimeo), IDESP, 1986. On the background of the PMDB see Maria d'Alva Gil Kinzo, 'An Opposition Party in an Authoritarian Regime: The Case of the MDB (Movimento Democratico Brasileiro) in Brazil, 1966–1979' DPhil thesis, Oxford, 1985.

17. On the overall process involved see the description by ex-deputy Joao Gilberto Lucas Coelho, 'O Processo Constituinte de 1987', in Vania Lomonaco Bastos and Tania Moreira da Costa (eds), *Constituinte: Questões Polêmicas* (Brasilia: Caderno CEAC/UNB, 1988), pp. 9–17. The documentation on the popular amendments is found in Comissao de Sistematização, *Emendas Populares* in two volumes (Brasilia: Assembleia Nacional Constituinte, 1987).
   David Fleischer, 'From Non-Competitive to Competitive Elections . . .,' pp. 58–9. *Veja* and *Folha de Sao Paulo* were also used to follow the overall process.

18. One analyst gave the following composition for the Centrão: PMDB – 141, PFL – 117, PDS – 27, PTB – 16, PDT – 5, PS – 5, and PDC – 4. Benicio Viero Schmidt, 'Transição Política e Crise de Governabilidade no Brasil', in Vania Lomonaco Bastos and Tania Moreira da Costa, p. 40.

19. It may be worth noting that one of the Popular Amendments for

agrarian reform received more signatures than all the other 121 amendments: 1 200 000.

20. On different levels of implementation of the Portuguese Constitution see Jorge Miranda, *Manual de direito constitucional*, vol. I (Coimbra: Coimbra Editora, 1982), pp. 330–1 and on the non-implementation of sections of Brazilian constitutions see Tercio Sampaio Ferraz Junior, *Constituinte: Assembleia, Processo, Poder* (Sao Paulo: Editora Revista dos Tribunais, 1985).

21. The lack of complementary legislation was given for the manner in which the armed forces put down the strike in mid-November at the National Steel Company. Without such legislation the armed forces acted in line with 'already proven means'. See *Folha de Sao Paulo*, 27 November 1988.

22. For an excellent comparative analysis see Alfred Stepan, *Rethinking Military Politics: Brazil and the Southern Cone* (Princeton: Princeton University Press, 1988) and specifically on Brazil one of the best articles is Walder de Goes, 'Militares e Política. Uma Estrategia para a Democracia', in Fabio W. Reis and Guillermo O'Donnell (eds), *A Democracia no Brasil: Dilemas e Perspectivas* (Sao Paulo: Editora Vertice, 1988), pp. 229–55.

23. The unwillingness of the Congress to support some of the key proposals of the executive for the new economic plan in January 1989 can be seen as evidence of this. They rejected the proposal for privatizing state-owned enterprises and another proposal concerning abolishing some of the ministries was not approved due to lack of a quorum. FBIS-LAT, 16 February 1989, p. 31. It should be noted, however, that the President may have been acting unconstitutionally in declaring the plan under Article 62 on provisional acts when much of the plan was clearly intended to be permanent.

24. On the close links between the state and unions see Amaury de Souza and Bolivar Lamounier, 'Governo e Sindicatos no Brasil: A Perspectiva dos Anos 80,' *Dados* 24, no. 2, pp. 139–59.

25. Interview with a consultant to lobbies in Brasilia on 16 May 1988. *Veja* gave coverage to some action by business lobbies. See for example 27 July 1988, p. 35 on the involvement by different types of business groups.

References

Bicuco, H. (1985) 'O Verdadeiro Caminho da democracia', in: R. Faodo *et al.*, *Constituente e democracia no Brasil hoye* (Sao Paulo: Brasiliense).

Bonin-Blanc, A. (1987) *Spain's Transition to Democracy: The Politics of Constitution-Making* (Boulder: Westview Press).

Bruneau, T. and A. MacLeod (1986) *Politics in Contemporary Portugal: Parties and the Consolidation of Democracy* (Boulder: Lynne Rienner).

Dallari, D. (1986) 'Entulho Autoritario: Como nos Velhos Tempos', in: B. Freitag *et al. Nova República : Um Balanço* (São Paulo: L. and PM).

Fleischer, D. (1989) *The Impact of the 1988 Municipal Elections on Brazil's*

1989 Presidential Election, Mimeo. A paper for the Institute of Inter-American Studies, University of Miami, February.

Gunther, R. and R. Blough (1981) 'Religious Conflict and Consensus in Spain: A Tale of Two Constitutions', *World Affairs*, 143, no. 4, Spring.

Gunther, R. and R. Blough (1985) 'Constitutional Change in Contemporary Spain', in: R. Banting and R. Simeon (eds), *Redesigning the State: The Politics of Constitutional Change* (Toronto: University of Toronto Press).

Gunther, R. and R. Blough (1987) 'Democratization and Party Building: The Role of Party Elites in the Spanish Transition', in: R. Clark and M. Hatzel (eds), *Spain in the 1980's: The Democratic Transition and a New International Role* (Cambridge: Ballinger).

9 Economic Ideologies and the Consolidation of Democracy in Brazil
Luis Carlos Bresser Pereira

The transition to democracy was a long process in Brazil. It started in the mid-1970s and just came to an end at the beginning of 1985. Three years later, however, most people in Brazil believe that the democratization process in Brazil is unfinished. Raymundo Faoro said recently (1988, 7) that the transition to democracy in Brazil is taking so long that it will end being longer than the authoritarian regime. I understand very well this view but I do not accept it. The transition to democracy finished three years ago. But the resulting democracy, as it was not able to solve the economic and social problems the country faces, is disappointing. In other words, the political regime in Brazil is democratic, but it is far from being consolidated. Actually, as the new democratic government is unable to overcome the existing economic and social problems, a new political crisis emerged.

In a recent paper (1988a) I analyzed the political crisis existing today in Brazil – a crisis of legitimacy and governability – and related it to the inability of the Sarney government to be faithful to the modern and democratic political pact that united workers, salaried middle class and industrialists to defeat the military authoritarian regime. This was a pact of modern, industrial capital – the dominant type of capital existing in Brazil – but the Sarney government, particularly since 1987, was taken over by representatives of an archaic, mercantilistic type of capital, formed by politicians and businessmen dependent on the favours of the state. The inconsistency between the central government and the hegemonic economic and ideological forces in Brazil and also the inability of the government to face the deep economic crisis prevailing today in Brazil produced a crisis of legitimacy that endangers the new Brazilian democracy.

In this paper I will take a complementary approach, as I will try to analyse some political or ideological obstacles for the consolidation of democracy in Brazil. I will argue that the democratization process of the country was based on solid economic and social realities, it was a conquest of civil society rather than a gift of the military regime, but I will also try to demonstrate that the democratization process did not tackle some basic ideologies and political practices typical of middle-income industrialized underdeveloped countries like Brazil – some anachronistic nationalist beliefs of the left, unrealistic demands by the workers, populism and clientelism of the politicians, conservatism, short-sightedness and subordination to external interests of the élites – problems that represent serious obstacles to sound and progressive economic policies, that are required for the resumption of growth and the achievement of price stability.

The economic crisis in Brazil – defined by per capita income stagnation since 1980 and by extraordinarily high inflation rates – was in the beginning of the 1980s a basic cause of the authoritarian regime's defeat, but now, as it remains without solution, this same economic crisis is threatening the new democratic regime. Some analysts have been arguing that there is no contradiction between democracy and economic instability, using as examples the cases of Spain, Brazil and Argentina, where the democratization process took place in the middle of severe economic crisis. Actually they are adopting a static approach to the problem. Recession and high rates of inflation will be unstabilizing factors for the regime that happens to be in power, be it authoritarian or democratic. At the end of the 1980s, as most of Latin America political regimes are democratic, it is democracy that is being threatened by the economic crisis.

In this paper I will not discuss the economic crisis, but the political problems that make it more difficult to solve this crisis. It is common to hear that the present Brazilian economic crisis has political origins and should be solved in the political arena. I do not agree with this proposition. I believe that the economic and the political crises existing today in Brazil are autonomous although interacting, mutually influencing each other. The economic crisis is older; its origins are to be found at the end of the 1970s. The political crisis, in its present form, is a phenomenon of the second part of the 1980s; it is defined by the inability of the Sarney government and, more broadly, of the Brazilian élite to face the challenge of establishing in Brazil political practices and ideologies consistent with a modern and democratic capitalism.

To say that economic problems have political origins or that their solutions depend just on political will is to reduce economic policy to an all-powerful social engineering device. The original and more correct name of economics – political economy – underlined the political and social character of the economic process. But this does not justify a transformation of real economic problems into political problems, or saying that the economic crisis that Brazil faces today will be overcome provided the political obstacles find an adequate solution. There is here a curious contradiction, because the conservative economists who defend the political and ideological neutrality of 'positive economics' are precisely the ones who say that economic problems can be easily solved by political means. The political obstacles to sound economic policies have a paramount importance, but their solution is no guarantee that the economic problems will be successfully solved.

The consolidation of democracy in Brazil depends both on overcoming the present economic and political crisis. Simon Schwartzman observed (1988, 4) that it is a 'political myth' to believe that democratic regimes are more efficient than authoritarian regimes in producing social and economic benefits. That is true. Democracy should not be considered as a means but as an end in itself. But it is also true that the democratization process gave rise to great expectations due to this myth. Now, the inability of the new democratic regime to manage Brazil's economic and social problem is a source of disappointment, representing a major threat to the consolidation of democracy. In this chapter I will try to understand why this is happening, looking for the political and ideological obstacles to a sound and reformist economic policy – an essential factor for the consolidation of democracy in Brazil.

REDEMOCRATIZATION PROCESS

The redemocratization process that occurred in Brazil between the mid-1970s and 1984 was the result of a deep political process. The resulting democracy was not a gift or a concession of the military, but a civil society conquest. It was based on the consolidation of a modern type of capitalism, that dispenses the use of direct violence for surplus appropriation.

There are actually two opposite interpretations of the redemocratization process in Brazil. One says that first, Geisel's 'distensao', and, second, Figueiredo's 'abertura' demonstrate that the redemocratization process was an initiative of the military; civil society may have had some role in protesting or pressing for democracy, but the redemocratization process was essentially the result of a political strategy of the authoritarian regime (see Martins, 1983; Diniz, 1985). My interpretation goes in the opposite direction (1978, 1985). What indeed happened in Brazil was a dialectical process between the 'redemocratization' demanded by civil society and the delaying strategy of 'abertura' conducted by the military. The redemocratization process, beginning from the coup of 1964 with the support of workers and of the intellectualized middle class (democratic technobureaucracy), received the decisive adhesion of the bourgeoisie (more specifically of the leading industrialists) around 1977. It was this support that gave strength to the redemocratization process, but it was also the factor which, leading to a 'conservative transition' (see Weffort, 1984), made some analysts say that the transition effectively did not take place (Fernandes, 1985).

These analysts are wrong. They are victims of their natural disappointment with the new democratic regime. Actually the redemocratization process did take place. The fact that the new president was not directly elected by the people is important, but it is not essential. The facts are that we had free elections in 1986, that the press and the formation of political parties are free, that the judiciary power is working with independence, that the Congress has just finished writing a new constitution which was freely debated and approved – a constitution that is no one's dream, that is much too conservative for the left, and too much progressive for the right, but which is indeed the best compromise that Brazilian society could eventually produce today. For all these reasons we do have a democratic regime in Brazil, and a new Constitution which, in spite of the faults that we may attribute to it, is a positive factor for the consolidation of democracy in Brazil.

I know very well that this new democracy did not bring either economic development or social justice to the country. But it is important not to amplify the concept of democracy, not to try to include in it all our objectives. Democracy is a type of political regime, not a utopia. Democracy is not necessarily a means for economic development and social justice. Historically, 'democracy came as a late addition to the competitive market society and the liberal state. . . it was an attempt by the lower class to take their fully and fairly competitive place within those institutions and that system of society' (Macpherson, 1966, 10–11).

We may have authoritarian regimes that are very successful in promoting economic development (it was the case of Brazil during a large part of the authoritarian period) and in producing a more equal distribution of income (see, for example, the contemporary statist formations that have the Soviet Union as prototype). Democracy, economic growth and a more equal distribution of income should be final objectives of every society. And certainly we can consider each one of these objectives as related to the others. It is, for instance, easier to maintain democracy when the country is growing, and I hope that the reverse is also true. Growth, price stability and income distribution are major factors in consolidating democracy. But it makes no sense to confuse democracy with economic development or with a more equal distribution of income.

MODERATE LEFT IDEOLOGIES

Democracy in Brazil is more solid, more entrenched in the economic and social system than is usually thought. The reasons behind this proposition could be summarized in this way: (1) modern industrial capitalism is able to appropriate economic surplus through the market, dispensing the use of direct force necessary in pre-capitalist and mercantilist societies; (2) the bourgeoisie does not feel threatened by the left; (3) the revolutionary left is in crisis all over the world and particularly in Latin America, and so it does not have a revolutionary project that would threaten the hegemony of the bourgeoisie; (4) the same can be said of the military and, more broadly, of the authoritarians: they do not have an alternative project for Brazil, they are as perplexed about the economic and political crisis as the bourgeoisie.

But it is not possible to say that democracy is consolidated. Guillermo O'Donnell (1988, 85) underlined that if a military coup is not likely, the 'slow death' of democracy – that is, a process of continuous loss of effectiveness and credibility of the political institutions due to the government's failure in facing the economic and social problems – is another possibility.

Government failure in facing these problems cannot be attributed exclusively to its personal limitations, nor to the sheer size of the economic obstacles. It is also clearly related to the political practices and ideologies that are not conducive to the adoption of the bold, coherent and firm economic policies that are needed.

Let us examine these ideologies and political practices. I will classify them according to their origin: (1) in the moderate left, (2) the opportunistic right, (3) in the ideological right.

I will start with the moderate left. Although I personally feel myself identified with this group, I have been convinced for a long time that an essential task today is to criticize the anachronism of some ideas of the left. In the 1950s I was engaged in the fight for industrialization through import substitutions and state intervention, but already in the 1960s I was pointing out new historical facts tied with the modernization of Brazilian capitalism that required a new interpretation of Brazil (see Bresser Pereira, 1983, 1984). This moderate left criticized severely the orthodox economic policies of the authoritarian regime. Sometimes they did it correctly, but on other occasions they were just repeating old-fashioned slogans, that could have made sense in the 1950s, but did not do so any more in the 1980s. Let us review these ideas:

Old fashioned nationalism

In the 1940s and 1950s the left developed the thesis that imperialism was allied to agro-mercantile capital in order to prevent industrialization. The large investments of the multinationals in manufacturing industry since the mid-50s proved that, if their thesis was correct in the past, it has ceased to be true since then. The new dependency theory acknowledged this fact (Cardoso and Faletto, 1969). But even today we have nationalists thinking in terms of the 1950s. They do not understand that to be nationalist today is rather to fight the irrational attempt of fully paying the external debt, or to strive for the development of autonomous scientific and technological progress within the country, than to oppose the multinationals which make an effective contribution to economic growth.

Orientation to internal market

In the mid-1960s the authoritarian regime decided on an export-led strategy of development. It was a correct decision, although it had the perverse short-term consequence of making compatible sustained rates of internal demand growth with income concentration. The moderate left opposed this orientation from the beginning, not acknowledging that the alternative growth pattern, based on highly capital-intensive import substitution projects, besides having exhausted its virtues as a growth model in the early 1960s, is much more income-concentrating in the long run than a growth strategy based on exports of labour-intensive manufactured goods. In the 1970s the left used to criticize Korea and Taiwan as 'export platforms'. Today we know that these countries, besides having taken advantage of the international competitiveness embodied in export-led development, present a much more even distribution of income than Brazil. The agrarian reform that was undertaken in these countries just after the Second World War is one cause of that; the other is export-led growth.

Refusal to adjust attitude

That is a consequence of an entrenched – and not dutifully revised later on – 'developmentism' that characterized the Latin American structuralists, including myself, in the 1950s. The adjustment of the 1960s was severely criticized by them. The fact that the adjustment was based almost exclusively on the reduction of wages (see Lara Rezende, 1982) was indeed a good reason for criticism, but the left based its disagreement almost only on a 'no-to-recession' slogan. In 1979, when adjustment was absolutely necessary, the irresponsible developmentist economic policy of the Planning Minister of the authoritarian regime was supported by economists of the structuralist moderate left. When adjustment finally began in 1981, the basic idea of the left was that the adjustment was not necessary, when, indeed, it was. Actually at that moment it was just impossible – besides being undesirable – to try to maintain the large trade and current account deficits. The only innovative and serious criticism to the orthodox adjustment policies originated in the moderate left came from the economists who developed the theory of inertial inflation (see Bresser Pereira and Nakano, 1987, chapter 1, for a survey of this theory).

Wage distribution

Income concentration is recognizedly a major problem in Brazil. We have one of the most uneven and unjust patterns of income distribution in the world. But this fact does not legitimate unrealistic wage distribution. A progressive economic policy in Brazil will necessarily have as a major objective the achievement of a less uneven income distribution, but it will have to be very careful about increasing real wages above productivity levels. Whenever this is tried, profits are threatened and acceleration of the inflation rate is unavoidable. Actually wage policy should be limited to three objectives: to protect real wages from inflation, to assure that productivity increases are transferred to the workers, and to reduce wage differences through the gradual increase of the minimum wage. Otherwise, agrarian reform, progressive tax reform and the orientation of public expenditures to the poor are safer and much more efficient distributive strategies.

These ideas, however, are not usually accepted among the moderate left. A slogan is often used: 'wage increases are not a cause of inflation'. For a long time, during the authoritarian regime, this phrase corresponded to reality, since real wages either increased less than productivity or were reduced in absolute terms. But, at the end of the 1970s we began to see a different picture. And after the defeat of the authoritarian regime, in 1984, unrealistic demands by the workers, particularly the salaried middle class employed in the public sector, increased sharply, provoking inflation directly (cost inflation) and through the increase of the public deficit. Given the acceleration of inflation, however, the gains in real terms tended to have a short life, and the only lasting result was a higher rate of inflation.

In conclusion, some ideas and political practices of the moderate left – old-fashioned nationalism, the ideology of the internal market, the refusal to adjust attitudes and wage distribution – are no more consistent with rational, coherent economic policies. They represent an obstacle to growth and price stability, and, as a result, to the consolidation of democracy in Brazil.

OPPORTUNIST RIGHT IDEOLOGIES

Different, but in the end leading to the same results, are the ideologies and political practices of the opportunistic moderate right and of the ideological moderate right. The moderate ideological right in Brazil calls itself 'centre', but the concept of centre makes no sense in political science. It is only a disguise for the conservatives, who, in Brazil do not like to be called right or conservative. On the other hand, the opportunistic right is part of the right for the simple reason that Brazil is a capitalist country. Actually, an opportunist is by definition a politician without firm ideological convictions. In a capitalist country, even if he pretends to belong to the left, he will in the last analysis be a conservative, because he will make all the required compromises with the ruling class.

Let us start with the political practices of the opportunists that influence economic policy:

Economic populism

This is a basic political disease in Brazil. I am aware that the word 'populism' has several meanings. That is why I qualify populism with the adjective 'economic' in order to distinguish it from other meanings, as, for instance, the 'populist pact' of the 1950s. One who spoke very precisely about economic populism in a few pages was Carlos Diaz Alejandro (1981), describing the causes of the economic crisis that used to precede the stabilization policies in the countries of the Southern Cone. In one phrase, economic populism is the political practices of saying 'yes' to the demands of all sectors of society at the expense of the public sector. Populistic economic policies lead directly or indirectly to public deficits and to balance of payments problems. Increase in wages and salaries for public workers and officials, increase in the purchases from the private sector, increase in subsidies to consumption and in subsidies and incentives (tax renunciations) to the private sector, artificial valorization of the local currency, increase in subsidized credit given by official banks are among the more common populist practices.

The result of populism is the 'populist cycle'. At first, as the government increases wages and raises public expenditures, while holding down the exchange rate, the internal interest rate and the prices of the public sector, the economy undergoes high rates of consumption and investment, growth and low rates of inflation. But soon the distortions provoked by these practices appear – balance of payment problems and inflation – and the cycle ends in a radical change in economic policy and/or in a big crisis. The expansionist policies of 1979–80 (probably the worst mistake in the history of economic policy in Brazil) and of the Cruzado Plan (an excellent plan, a lost opportunity due to incompetent management) are typical examples of the populist cycle in Brazil, the first coming from the right under Delfim Netto, the second, from an alliance of the left with President Sarney.

Clientelism

This is a political practice in the middle of the road between populism and sheer corruption. The three practices imply the use of public funds: in the case of populism they are used in an impersonal form, to assure the goodwill of the groups or communities which benefit by the public expenditure; in the case of corruption, in a very personal form, to become rich; while in the case of clientelism, they are used in a semi-personal form, benefiting persons or groups who are potential voters. Brazil has invented a new and very expressive word to mean clientelism: 'physiologism'. The politician 'fisiologico' is an opportunist by definition. He is a person who transforms politics into a special kind of business – a business where he uses his political power to give and receive favours. He is physiological because he puts material, personal interests above ideas, above political and moral principles.

These two opportunist political practices are deeply embedded in the Brazilian political system, as a consequence of the low level of citizenship of the people. Lack of information, poor political education, mistrust in relation to the élites, a favourable attitude in relation to 'popular' candidates are typical characteristics of the average Brazilian voter. Thus, in the words of Wanderley Reis (1988a, 24), 'given the characteristics of the Brazilian electorate, it is not realistic to expect that the stabilization of the democratic game take place around parties defined in ideological terms; it is more likely that the process of formation of the political parties will continue to be based on traditional clientelism with an electoral appeal of populist tonalities'.

CONSERVATIVE RIGHT IDEOLOGIES

The ideological right is also a major source of irrational economic policy. The bulk of the business élite in Brazil should be included in this category. They are not opportunists, but conservative, and conservatism in developing countries – besides putting order above social justice, besides resisting change – means ideological subordination to the value and belief system of the business élites in the developed, central countries.

They are truly convinced that their views on economic policy are intrinsically rational. The logic of capitalism and their own logic would both be pure rationality – a rationality that they confront with the irrationality of the left and of the opportunistic politicians. Given their control of the means of communication, they are usually able to pass along these ideas to the people, thus reinforcing their ideological hegemony.

Actually, their ideas are very far from being pure rationality, and represent a major obstacle to the adoption of a consistent economic policy in Brazil, especially at a moment when bold, far-reaching economic decisions must be taken. Let us see these ideologies and political practices of the ideological right:

Social conservatism

This is an obvious problem in a country where income concentration is amazingly high. The tax burden is relatively low and very regressive in Brazil, and so a progressive tax reform is an obvious tool for reducing the public deficit and improving income distribution. The ideological right systematically opposes tax reforms that increase the tax burden. On the other hand, state subsidies and incentives to business enterprises are a major source of budget imbalance, and although most of them lost their *raison d'être* long ago, the elimination of these tax renunciations is also opposed by their beneficiaries. The ideological right is formally concerned with income concentration in Brazil, but does nothing to solve the problem; it knows that a social pact, which would be essential to control wages and curb inflation, cannot be implemented without concessions to the workers in terms of social reforms, but as a rule they tend to oppose social reforms.

Monetarism

This is the conservative counter-revolution against Keynesianism; it may appear in its original Friedman version or in the rational expectations approach called 'neo-classical' by Sargent, Lucas and others; it is founded on a basic contradiction: it is a macroeconomic theory oriented (as the original Keynesian macroeconomic theory was) to economic policy, but professes a radical abstinence of state intervention – an abstinence that actually is not put into practice, given the fact that economic policy must be very active to impose the stabilization policies that their followers advocate.

At present, monetarism is the economic religion of the developed capitalist countries; it is therefore adopted almost without restrictions by the ideological right. Inflation in Brazil has structural origins and an inertial character, but they believe that it can be controlled just by the adoption of monetary and fiscal policies. Economic imbalances in an underdeveloped economy like the Brazilian are very deep, but they believe that the market forces will be able to solve all problems.

The successive failures of this approach to solve the economic crises in Argentina, Brazil and Chile led monetarism to a certain degree of discredit in the early 1980s, but after the failure of the heterodox Austral and Cruzado plans, monetarism regained part of its prestige. Suddenly, as a result of a very interesting ideological *manoeuvre* of the ideological right, conventional stabilization policies and coherent and rational economic policies were equated to 'orthodox' monetarism and opposed to Keynesian and to structuralist 'heterodoxy', when, in fact, a large part of these policies is shared by competent economists of all schools. Actually, the economic policies recommended by monetarists proper, given their ideological and dogmatic character, given the fact that they do not take in account the specific characteristics of the Brazilian economy, and, more broadly, given their theoretical shortcomings, are often inadequate or simply irrational.

Crude liberalism

This is the complement of monetarism. The ideological right knows or should know that the state played a major role in Brazilian industrialization, but now the state is bankrupt in Brazil (see Rogerio Werneck, 1987; Bresser Pereira, 1987), making the possibilities for industrial policy very limited. The business élite has very little to gain additionally from the state. On the other hand, the conservative, neo-liberal creed is today dominant in the central industrialized countries, and it is not difficult to understand why the neo-liberal slogans against state intervention turned dominant also in Brazil.

The country is today undergoing the worst crisis in its economic history. Income per capita has stagnated for the last eight years. The major cause of this situation is the fiscal crisis of the state. Very strong measures are therefore needed to solve this structural financial imbalance of the public sector that turned the savings of the public sector into negative savings, reducing dramatically its investment capacity. The ideological right, however, minimizes the problem, speaking of public deficit when we have a fiscal crisis, and proposing to dismiss some public officials, when what is needed are much more drastic fiscal policies and decisions. They speak also against 'statization', against state intervention in general, when the problem is to rescue the public sector which was led to bankruptcy partly by the big subsidies it granted to the private sector.

Subordinated internationalism

A greater internationalization of the Brazilian economy is a natural aspiration of the local business élite. Actually what they want is a stronger integration of Brazil's economic and social system into the First World, of which they wish to be part. They understand that this integration, or, rather, this association will make Brazilian capitalism economically and ideologically less vulnerable. I will not argue about these objectives. I believe that they are quite consistent. If there exists – as I believe it does – a clear economic and ideological hegemony of the bourgeoisie, if capitalism is well established in Brazil, this desire of a greater integration with the developed world is quite natural. The problem, however, is that this internationalism takes very often the form of a uncritical subordination to the interests of the developed countries. This attitude, which I propose to call subordinated internationalism, is a phenomenon of everyday life in Brazil. It is a consequence of the economic and cultural domination that the central developed world exerts over its periphery. But in the case of the ideological right, this subordination takes a militant character, as inconsistent with the national interests as the old nationalism of the left.

The more dramatic example of this subordinated internationalism is the view adopted by the ideological right in relation to the external debt. The external debt is the single major cause of stagnation and inflation in Brazil since early 1980s: it reduced the saving capacity of the country; it increased the public deficit given the fact that more than 80 per cent of the external debt is public; it accelerated inflation due to an increase in public deficit and to the devaluation of the local currency; it reduced investments due to the reduction of savings and also due to the increase in the interest rate it provoked. Clearly the Brazilian external debt is too high and cannot be paid. A reduction of the debt is a necessary condition for overcoming stagnation and inflation in Brazil. The alternative would be an enormous reduction of internal consumption that is neither feasible nor desirable (see Bresser Pereira, 1988b). The ideological right, however, does not acknowledge these facts. Given that its major objective is to make Brazil a part of the First World, it rejects any type of confrontation with the bankers, fearing that the unilateral measures that Brazil must take in order to negotiate a reduction in its external debt – a reduction based on the discount existing in the secondary financial market – will endanger the desired integration in the First World. What they do not understand is that this integration will not be achieved unless growth is resumed and price stability achieved. At this moment there is a basic inconsistency between the full payment of the interests on the debt and growth and price stability. Thus, a certain degree of confrontation with the banks is a necessary condition for a further integration of the Brazilian economy with international capitalist economic system.

ECONOMIC POLICIES FOR THE CONSOLIDATION OF DEMOCRACY

Authoritarians and conservatives in Latin America are today presenting Chile as an example of sound, rational economic policy. They have as arguments the very low levels of inflation and the positive growth rates since 1985. They do not mention that income per capita in Chile in the end of 1987 was 2.5 per cent below the 1980 level, that wages in 1987 were 6 per cent below the 1980 level (Piedra, 1988), they do not say that income concentration and poverty increased, they forget that the Chilean economy is being thoroughly denationalized as the local assets are being swapped by the external debt on unfavourable terms. In the words of Miguel Urbano Rodrigues (1988, 3), 'in the last 15 years there was no economic progress in Chile; instead the dictatorial regime promoted a savage redistribution of GDP'. Since the beginning of the authoritarian regime, per capita wheat consumption has fallen by 8 per cent, milk by 5 per cent, meat by 15 per cent, sugar by 8.3 per cent, and rice by 14 per cent.

At any rate, it is necessary to acknowledge that the recent favourable economic results in Chile, when compared with the crises of her democratic neighbours, particularly in Brazil and in Argentina, pose a basic threat to democracy in Latin America. In the present political campaign for the referendum in Chile the military regime shows television commercials portraying the economic and social problems in Brazil and Argentina, and asks if it is this type of democracy that the Chilean people desires.

John Sheahan (1986, 161) says that the distinctive economic policies of the authoritarian regimes in Latin America are reduced price controls, lower protection, serious efforts to limit budget deficits, strict wage controls and highly favourable conditions for foreign investors. Sheahan is mixing discourse with effective action. Actually authoritarian regimes in Latin America do not adopt necessarily orthodox economic policies but certainly show a conservative rhetoric. Their discourse is invariably against state intervention and for fiscal austerity, but they are not always faithful to what they say. The excessive external indebtedness and the corresponding public deficits of the 1970s were the responsibility of authoritarian regimes in Brazil, Argentina, Chile and Peru. But Sheahan is correct when he worries about the survival of non-authoritarian governments in Latin America on account of irresponsible increases in the wage rate above the growth of per capita income, excessive protectionism, and an unduly restricted attitude to foreign investment.

Actually what is needed in Brazil or in Latin America for the consolidation of the democratic regime are economic policies conducive to growth, price stability and income distribution. What we are having today in Brazil, after democratization, is just the opposite: economic stagnation, very high rates of inflation and income concentration. In the first six months of the Sarney government we had a conservative economic policy; it did not work. Then, for almost two years, a moderate left economic policy which, after a correct diagnosis of inflation, led the country to a deep financial and economic crisis with the loss of control over the Cruzado Plan. Now, after the seven months and a half during which I was in charge of economic policy, we have had again, for the last nine months (I am writing in September 1988), conservative policies in action, in accordance with the ideologies and political practices of the moderate right; but the rate of inflation continues to rise, the rate of investment is very low, the economy remains stagnated, real wages are again being reduced.

The economic policies that are required in Brazil are not orthodox or heterodox, from the left or the right. These distinctions are of minor significance, given the seriousness of the present economic crisis. The fiscal crisis of the state, the external debt, inflation, the reduction of the rate of investment are problems of such dimension today in Brazil that it is not enough to criticize nationalism, protectionism, the refusal to adjust attitudes and the distributivism of the left, the populism and the clientelism of the opportunists, social conservatism, monetarism, the crude liberalism and the subordinated internationalism of the right. Besides coherent, rational and pragmatic economic policies, what is badly needed today in Brazil is

212   *Democracy in Brazil*

political courage and vision. Democracy is quite well established today in Brazil, but the continuous failure of the new democratic regime in solving some basic economic and social problems represents a political danger that should not be underestimated.

References

Alejandro, C. D. (1981) 'Southern Cone Stabilization Plans', in: W. Cline and S. Weintraub, *Economic Stabilization in Developing Countries* (Washington: The Brookings Institution).

Bresser Pereira, L. C. (1978) *O colapso de uma aliança de classes* (São Paulo: Brasiliense).

Bresser Pereira, L. C. (1983) 'Six Interpretations of the Brazilian Social Formation', *Latin American Perspectives'*, vol. II, no. 1, winter 1984. Published in Portuguese in *Dados*, vol. 25, no. 3,, 1983.

Bresser Pereira, L. C. (1984) *Development and Crisis in Brazil: 1930–1983* (Boulder, Colorado: Westview Press).

Bresser Pereira, L. C. (1985) *Pactos Políticos* (Sao Paulo: Brasiliense).

Bresser Pereira, L. C. (1987) 'Mudancas no patrão de financiamento dos investimentos no Brazil', *Revista de economica politica*, vol. 7, no. 4, October.

Bresser Pereira, L. C. and Y. Narano (1987), *The Theory* of *Inértiál Inflation* (Boulder: Lynne Rienner).

Bresser Pereira, L. C. (1988a) 'De volta ao capital mercantil: Caio Prado Jr. e a crise da nova república', mimeo paper presented to the *Jornada de Estudos Caio Prado Jr.*, UNESP, Marilia, May.

Bresser Pereira, L. C. (1988b) 'The 1987 Approach to the Negotiations of the Brazilian External Debt', paper presented to the *LASA* Meeting, New Orleans, March. To be published in *World Policy*.

Cardoso, F. H. and E. Faletto (1969) *Dependency and Development in Latin America* (Berkeley: University of California Press). Originally published in Spanish in Mexico: Siglo Veintiuno Editores.

diniz, E. (1985) 'A transição política no Brasil : uma reavaliação da dinâmica da abertura', *Dados*, vol. 28, no. 3.

Faoro, R. (1988) 'Um estado autenticamente militar desde 1930'. Interview to Lourenco Dantas Mota, in OAB – *Revista da ordem dos advogados do Brasil*, no. 43/48, Winter.

Fernandez, F. (1985) *Nova Republica?* Rio de Janeiro: Jorge Zahar Editorial.

Lara Rezende, A. (1982) 'A política brasileira de estabilização : 1963/68', *pesquisa e planejamento econômico*, vol. 12, no. 3, December.

Macpherson, C. B. (1966) *The Real World of Democracy* (New York: Oxford University Press).

Martins, L. (1983) 'Le régime autoritaire brésilien et la libéralisation politique', *Problèmes d'Amérique latine*, no. 65, third quarter. Also published in G. O'Donnell, P. Schmitter and L. Whitehead (1986a), pp. 72–95.

O'Donnell, G. (1988) 'Hiatos, Instituções e Perspectivas Democráticas', in: Wanderley Reis and G. O'Donnell (eds).

O'Donnell, G., P. Schmitter and L. Whitehead (eds) (1986a) *Transition from Authoritarian Rule: Prospects for Democracy*, vol. II *Latin America* (Baltimore: Johns Hopkins University Press).

O'Donnell, G., P. Schmitter and L. Whitehead (eds) (1986b) *Transition from Authoritarian Rules: Prospects for Democracy*, vol. III, *Comparative Perspectives* (Baltimore: Johns Hopkins University Press).

Piedra, Pinto de la M. (1988) 'El componente social del ajuste económico en América latina', mimeo. (Santiago de Chile: ILDES, NU/CEPAL Center, June).

Rodrigues, M. U. (1988) 'O cruel "milagre" chileno', *Folha de S. Paulo*, 14 September.

Sheahan, J. (1986) 'Economic Policies and the Prospects for Successful Transition from Authoritarian Rule in Latin America', in: G. O'Donnell, P. Schmitter and L. Whitehead.

Schwartzman, S. (1988) 'A situação atual da América latina : os problemas-chave da democratização', mimeo, Instituto de Estuados Avançados da Universidade de São Paulo.

Wanderley Reis, F. (1988a) 'Consolidação democrática e construção do estado', in: F. Wanderley Reis and G. O'Donnell (eds).

Wanderley Reis, F. and G. O'Donnell (1988b) *A democracia no Brasil : dilemas e perspectivas*, (São Paulo: Editora Revista dos Tribunais).

Weffort F. C. (1984), *por quê democracia?*

Werneck, R. L. F. (1987 *Empresas estatais e política macroeconomica* (Rio de Janeiro: Editora Campus).

10 Social Movements, Party System and Democratic Consolidation: Brazil, Uruguay and Argentina

Renato R. Boschi[1]

Certain attributes of civil society are generally viewed either as important preconditions for the emergence of democracy or as positive elements in breeding a favourable environment for the long-run consolidation of democratic institutions. From earlier versions dealing with social preconditions of democracy (Lipset, 1963) and classical approaches such as that of polyarchy (Dahl, 1971), going through analyses of political development and modernization (Huntington, 1968, 1984), up until more recent works on the transition of authoritarian regimes (O'Donnell and Schmitter, 1986) and cross-country studies of structural factors in democratization, some space has been given to the role of certain social sectors, groups, and movements, or structural characteristics of civil society as a whole in favouring democratization.

More specifically, in so far as analyses of democratization in the Southern Cone are concerned, there has been increasing emphasis on the relationship between civil society and democratization, both in the sense of generating opportunities for transition (O'Donnell, Schmitter, and Whitehead, 1986), and in the sense of constituting new parameters for the functioning of the political system (Santos, 1985).

As an expression of civil society, social movements were given a lot of attention due to the apparent simultaneity of their emergence and the process of transition in a number of countries. By now, a large body of literature relates different aspects of social movements to politics, especially in Brazil – where their presence has been more conspicuous (Mainwaring, 1986, 1987; Boschi, 1987, 1988) – but also in Uruguay, Filgueira, 1988), Chile, and other countries (Tironi, 1987; Campero, 1988).

The relationship between civil society and democratization,

whether as precondition or as an element of renewal and activation of the political system towards democracy is, however, far from clear. It is well known that changes in the social morphology do play a role, but what exactly is to be expected from, say, an increase in society's organizational density? Does such an increase favour a pluralistic order, or does it concur to the mainstream of state-supervised corporatism? Likewise, it is also known that social movements did have an impact in terms of cementing the liberalizing coalition that favoured transition in Brazil and have elsewhere also played an important role. But is the role of social movements merely conjunctural, strategic, and, therefore, cyclical, or can there be a more stable link between this type of mobilization and the party system?

This analysis will look into some of these questions with the purpose of specifying the relationships between civil society and the process of democratization, focusing on the cases of Brazil, Uruguay, and Argentina. While in these three countries the dilemmas facing the consolidation of democracy may be similar, their respective trajectories were quite different in terms of the nature of the process of transition, characteristics of civil society and the party system, thus making them suitable for a comparative analysis of theoretical relevance.

The discussion will proceed along two axes: on one hand, the nature and timing of structural changes, and the position of social movements within this context; on the other, the characteristics of the process of transition and the relative situation of the party system *vis-à-vis* society and the state. Each of our cases will be briefly reviewed along these dimensions before attempting some conclusions. Since the objective here is that of establishing broad generalizations on the basis of the three cases in point, a detailed account of the experiences will be avoided.

BRAZIL

Two aspects regarding recent structural changes in Brazilian society are worth mentioning. The first concerns the timing, and the second refers to the content of these changes. Not only did the major changes occur under the military regime and as a result of policies undertaken by the military, but also the pace and nature of the changes shaped a brand new society which emerged by the time the political transition towards democracy started to take place. In short, the country went, over a period of two decades, from a basically rural traditional setting to a modern industrial society, albeit characterized by profound social inequalities (Diniz and Boschi, 1987). If one can talk of anything resembling a modern industrial society with growing rates of urbanization, a relatively articulate entrepreneurial class, a combative working class, and an expanded middle class, it is in this period that such a society flourishes in Brazil.

In the wake of those deep structural transformations, the fact that society's organizational density increased mostly outside the realm of the state's regulatory spheres is quite significant (Santos, 1985). Moreover, it is also striking that the associational impetus, loosely speaking, was proportionately higher in the case of urban salaried categories, although it also occurred in rural areas and for the entrepreneurial and working classes. In other words, a new urban middle class, which proved to be politically active and organized, was shaped under the authoritarian regime. Unlike the industrial entrepreneurs and the working class, this new middle class forged its collective identity basically outside the state's tutelage which had been exercised since the 1930s through the existing corporative structure (Boschi, 1988). In this sense it is possible to talk about a society which displays some of the characteristics conducive to the establishment of a pluralist order: a network of intermediary relations and competition between organized interests as a complement to representative institutions and a functioning party system.

The associative impetus which became visible simultaneously with the so-called 'political opening' in the late 1970s was dotted with the activity of social movements organized around specific demands on the quality of living, and around sex- or race-related issues. These movements were basically of a middle-class component and encompassed from narrow to very broad activities, ranging from demonstrations and mob action to more articulate struggles involving professional associations and the trade union movement. But they also included the population of peripheral urban areas, squatter settlements, and working-class neighbourhoods. Initially turned towards the re-establishment of democratic values and practices which had been curtailed by the authoritarian regime, these movements progressively shifted from a specific and locally based action to that of supporting the anti-government coalition with the campaign for direct presidential elections (Diretas Ja).

The wave of associative activities of which social movements are but one expression thus became the landmark of a new style of making politics. This style was characterized by an emphasis on direct participation, an anti-representation rhetoric, and by friction of the new political actors with the existing party system. And while the basic organizational network persisted with the inauguration of civilian rule, the movements' activities decreased substantially under the New Republic, at least in terms of public visibility. Side by side, in a context of competition where the state had traditionally played a crucial role in supervising distributive conflicts by means of a well-devised corporatist structure, the movements soon started to lose ground in the degrees of autonomy they had achieved *vis-à-vis* the state. Progressively, the processing of demands required state intervention, therefore leading to cooptation or 'corporatization'. Finally, given the anti-party ideology and also because of aspects inherent to the very party system which will be examined next, the movements were unable to establish organic links which might serve to channel their interests and demands into the parties.

Any of the previous observations implies positive and negative aspects regarding the prospects for democratic consolidation. On one hand they suggest that structural changes pose constraints and new challenges, thus shaping the context in which politics is carried out. On the other, they also suggest that tradition and political culture are very important in determining the course of events. An objective evaluation of the social movements expressing the structural transformations that took place in Brazil would then have to take into account these two-sided aspects involved in their cyclical nature, their pattern of relationship with the state, and their links with the party system.

Regarding the cyclical nature of the movements, it must be pointed out that their genesis is intimately related to the authoritarian regime. Not that similar organizations did not exist before. The fact is, however, that associative activities were greatly activated under the authoritarian regime, whether in terms of the creation of associations of several types, the new trade unionism, and social movements in a strict sense (Boschi, 1987). Social mobilization in the form of movements is largely stimulated by conjunctural factors. In this case, such stimulus appeared in the attempt to recreate a democratic space at the level of interpersonal relations, in a struggle against the authoritarian regime, and in opening up new arenas of interest intermediation and participation. Such 'tidal' motion alternating between periods of great visibility and reflux is related to a number of factors, such as the nature of demands – which are usually punctual and short-run oriented – the difficulty of sustaining high and stable levels of participation, and the absence of horizontal links with other social segments. In addition, once the liberalizing stage of the process of transition was over, the central role the movements had played in terms of providing a sense of political identity and citizenship shifted to the constitutional sphere. In the stage of institutionalization of political democracy social movements lost their vitality as the nucleus of promotion of civic identity and citizenship rights.

Regarding the movements' relations with the state, it should be noted that, still before the New Republic, a large majority of successful demands in fact implied some type of regulation or state intervention (Boschi, 1987). Thus, if on one hand the movements tried to escape state control, on the other their demands emphasized active state regulation over conflicting interests. If this was true of the pre-transition years, it became even more so in the stage of reconstitutionalization, in which all sorts of groups brought pressure to bear in the direction of corporative protection of their interests in the new constitution. In this sense, the pattern of relationships between the movements (and by extension, of interest organizations created outside the aegis of the state) and the state apparatus is rather complicated, particularly in view of prospects for their institutionalization. The state grants these organizations the monopoly of representation and in turn renders them more vulnerable to control. On the other hand, the movements have professed an ideology of autonomy leading, in many instances, to their shying away from demanding legitimate rights. Hence the fact that different modes of relationship may result, ranging from co-option to sectoral neo-corporative arrangements in some cases. The impact of the associational wave of the late 1970s was twofold: it rendered more flexible the regulated society that had historically been shaped in Brazil through pluralization; at the same time it proved unsuccessful in institutionalizing autonomous channels *vis-à-vis* the state.

The interface between movements and the party system is still insufficiently studied (Kowarick, 1987). Some problem areas can be pointed out, however. In the first place, relationships between movements and parties are tense by definition, given the potentially divisive impact of party identification at the community level. Close ties between the latter and a given political party in electoral periods can also be complicated. In the first case, dissociation may take place between the ideology of autonomy and the political praxis committed to a given party. In the second case, although supposedly mobilized to support a party, the actual voting pattern in some communities has shown reasonable independence from pre-electoral commitments. Nonetheless, an anti-party ideology has been a common feature of the new social movements. The emphasis on participation to the detriment of representation has, on occasion, reached exaggerated levels. Such emphasis expresses itself in distrust as to the efficacy of established organic links with the parties and in favouring a pattern of topical and direct action. Again, while carrying positive implications, this pattern can also be detrimental in so far as democratic consolidation is concerned. On the positive side, the obvious enlargement of alternative political spaces should be mentioned. On the negative side, distrust and political disenchantment, so typical of some post-transitional situations (Caciagli, 1984; Maravall, 1982; Pintor, 1982), could weaken the endemically fragile position of congressional politics *vis-à-vis* the executive branch in countries like Brazil.

The previous remarks lead to the second axis of the present discussion, namely, that of the nature of the process of transition and the relative position of the party system. As is well known, the Brazilian transition from an authoritarian regime has been characterized as 'transition through transaction', that is, negotiated at the level of political élites from the top (Share and Mainwaring, 1986; O'Donnell and Schmitter, 1986). The main features of this model are the slow pace and gradualism in carrying out political reforms, the decisive role of the authoritarian élites in promoting the transition, the moderate nature of changes, and the control of the whole process from within the state apparatus. In addition, the former regime is not abruptly dismantled, the process of reconstitutionalization tends to be slow, therefore placing obstacles in the way of dealing with situations requiring new institutional mechanisms. In view of the heterogeneity and complexity of the coalition responsible for the process, a strategy of compromise at the level of the élites results in substantial institutional continuities. Such compromise is meant to isolate radical sectors both at the right and at the left of the ideological spectrum. While some consensus around a minimalist agenda of reforms may operate against regression, resistance to change on the part of conservative groups may also jeopardize the transition through widening the gap between politics and the structural transformations brought about by modernization.

Over time, the net result of what is probably the longest process of transition in the recent wave of transitions was the filtering of the coalition in a progressively conservative direction. While in the crucial moments during the replacement of the military, the progressive forces enjoyed a central role galvanizing both popular and élite support, they were gradually displaced in the aftermath of each successive political crisis involving the balance of power between the executive and legislative branches. Thus, starting with the project of political opening down to the approval of the new constitution in 1988, it is possible to see that the political élites are essentially the same as in the previous governmental party. The same is true, to a lesser extent, of the administrative cadres, especially those in charge of economic policy-making. Recruitment tends to draw on groups and orientations prior to those of the economic reforms.

The system of representation – and more specifically, the party system – plays a pivotal role in this context. While the constitutional process, by and large, strengthened the system of representation, the supremacy of the executive branch over the legislature is reinforced by weakness and instability of the party system. In turn, the bases for a political culture centred in a positive attachment to the representative system do not seem to take root. The absence of a long-lasting party system deeply ingrained in the country's political culture, side by side with the diffusion of anti-party values, makes it difficult for the institutionalization of strategic mediations between different social segments and the state. The weakness of the party system lies fundamentally in its isolation *vis-à-vis* segments of the plural society that emerged in Brazil with modernization. Since the party system lacks organic links with the interests it is meant to represent – in addition to playing a limited role in governmental support – interest aggregation via parties remains dissociated from intermediation via corporative system and from other nuclei of organized interests.

Two important aspects regarding consolidation of political democracy can be derived from this scenario. The first one concerns the dynamics of the political game within the political class. The second concerns the relationship of the political class with the electorate.

As pointed out before, the pace of political reforms was especially slow regarding the constitutional process, as the latter was intertwined with the game played at the level of political élites of either assuming or holding on to power positions. However, the quick resort to a reformist strategy did take place in the context of that game. Soon after the New Republic came into being, President Sarney made a few important reforms as a means to legitimize his weak position as the heir of popularly acclaimed Tancredo Neves. Among these, the enfranchisement of the whole adult population and the legalization of parties of the left would substantially alter the parameters of the political market and the bargaining process between the executive and legislative branches. Later on, this process would be marked by the former's attempt to assure supremacy through buying off support from the latter. This was particularly clear regarding the congressional vote on important matters such as the option between parliamentarism and presidentialism and the definition of the presidential term. A clientelistic style of politics thus became the dominant currency presiding over the relations between the executive and legislative powers.

But most important, that same currency would tend to prevail in the relationship between politicians and electorate, in view of the increasing cost of elective offices through the expansion of the voting contingent. The approval in the constitution of the extension of suffrage to the population of 16 years old will certainly potentialize this trend.

Thus, the combination of a number of ingredients mentioned before, namely, the discussion and approval of substantive issues dictated by the political dynamics of executive vs. congressional hegemony, together with the absence of effective occupation of the political space by well-structured parties, and a fertile ground for clientele politics, makes it extremely suitable for the emergence and/ or comeback of populist leaders.

Again in this instance, positive and negative implications can be drawn. As long as there are institutionalized rules to frame the disputes between executive and legislative branches, competition, the essence underlying the principle of division of powers, is healthy for democracy. The same could be argued of the emergence of populist-cum-clientele politics, as long as competition through the electoral process is preserved and institutionalized over time. It is conceivable that the electoral procedures could become routine in the long run. In addition, the candidates' efforts to appeal to portions of the electorate beyond those which supported their platform might lead to an increase in their marginal efficiency, thus favouring broader segments of the population. From this point of view clientelism can even have a distributive, if unintended, outcome.

Negative implications have already been suggested. In particular, those stemming from the absence of a more articulate party system were pointed out. Additional aspects should however be mentioned. In the first place, to the extent that parties are not well entrenched, and links with different social segments not established, they tend not to function as buffers in the distributive conflict. Lacking transparency as to ideologies and platforms, parties are left with little or no room in determining the course of economic policies. Secondly, the problem of corruption as a corollary of clientelism should not be disregarded. It is corrosive of the social tissue and leads to distrust in the efficacy of institutional mechanisms. On the other hand, only under democratic institutions can some degree of accountability be assured as to utilization of corruptive practices by politicians and state officials.

URUGUAY

The Uruguayan case is unique in the Latin American context in so far as the nature of changes in the social structure and characteristics of society are concerned. It is also so regarding the previous stability of democratic institutions, the nature of the military intervention that suspended their functioning, and the recovering of the democratic path.

A fully mobilized and organized society preceded the military intervention of 1973. By then, heterogeneity of associative formats, side by side with a strong trade union movement had already taken root. By a number of standards Uruguayan society was closer to that of advanced countries, displaying a fairly high and evenly distributed GDP per capita, high rates of literacy, and an early welfare state. In addition, the country was urbanized, and the urban middle and working classes were fully incorporated in the formal economy. This similarity to the reality of developed countries expressed itself in important aspects such as the absence of crises of political incorporation of new sectors, and the central role played by the distributive conflict as contrasted with tensions over the formation of the national state. As a result, free associability and diversification of group solidarities around specific interests took place quite early (Filgueira, 1988).

In short, Uruguay had reached a stage of modernization still largely associated to the vitality of the export sector, long before the dynamics of development in other countries of the capitalist periphery had to shift to national programmes of industrialization and, from there to the new stage of deepening of capitalist modernization through internationalization.

In this context, the nature of the military intervention, from a merely programmatic point of view, was also specific. The military who took over in 1973 did so lacking a clear programme to push the country forward to a new threshold of economic development. The authoritarian intervention was then far more restricted to the political realm, the old social structure being left almost untouched.

At the same time, the 'political' slant of the military intervention proved to be very drastic, with a need to invest heavily in the repression and demobilization of the previously mature and organized society. It is within this framework that the emergence of social movements in Uruguay is to be understood. Following the stage of demobilization, in the absence of effective programmes of economic reconstruction, the Uruguayan authoritarian regime short-lived their Latin American counterparts, being defeated in the plebiscite of 1980. As is now known, it was not until the national elections of 1984 that the transition was completed after negotiations between the military and the democratic opposition. It was in that period that movements flourished, only to be rearticulated within the re-emerging party system thereafter.

Thus, social movements in Uruguay played a clearly conjunctural role in terms of reconstituting the social fabric. In this case, the absence of a relationship between the emergence of movements and changes in the social structure is quite visible, bringing the Uruguayan case closer to O'Donnell and Schmitter's (1986) description of the 'resurrection of civil society' and 'restructuring of public space' in the transitional stage. Once this stage was over, a whole array of organizations and associations which had appeared, found their way into a national coalition devised to reinstitutionalize the political space by means of a broad social pact – the CONAPRO (Concertacion Nacional Programatica). Others, basically the so-called new social movements, merely lost their specific purpose and, therefore, the possibility of representing these sectors under the democratic regime (Rial, 1988).

It is interesting to notice that, again in the case of Uruguayan movements, the same type of challenges faced by the Brazilian social movements were present regarding the dynamics of their relationship with the state. Emerging as they did mostly outside the framework of the state and as an alternative to the institutional void sustained by the military regime, very few of the movements survived in terms of their original identities. With the reconstitution of the political space, movements and social organizations brought pressure to bear for incorporation in decision-making arenas recognized by the state. Others were absorbed by traditional structures of interest representation (Filgueira, 1988).

More specific to the Uruguayan situation, however, is the role played by the parties and the pace of reconstitution of the new political order following the parameters of the old one. As pointed out earlier, and as emphasized in analyses of the Uruguayan case, this country enjoyed a situation of political stability and functioning of democratic institutions unparalleled by any other country of the region (Gillespie, 1986). From this standpoint, military intervention represents the failure of the liberal model in sustaining an efficient system of representation and intermediation. However, the century-old party system which had managed to shape political life over time, soon recomposed itself in the context of the transition, in preparation for the 1984 elections. Blancos and Colorados maintained their ability, if not so much in terms of interest aggregation and articulation, at least in terms of identification and political memory *vis-à-vis* the population.

The trade union movement, in turn, also regained its historical position, maintaining the traditional autonomy it had enjoyed *vis-à-vis* the state and apparently *vis-à-vis* the parties (Rial, 1988). The autonomy of the trade unions is such that they currently even extrapolate their specific role to act much like a party (Filgueira, 1988). The lack of a strong corporative tradition combined with a party system that was quick in regaining its place constitute two fundamental ingredients that give the Uruguayan transition a specific character.

But specificity does not apply only to the pace of transition. It also refers to the central role played by the politics of 'concertacion' in achieving the path toward redemocratization, at least until 1985 (Rial, 1988). As contrasted to other Latin American countries where wage disputes have been dealt with at the level of corporative arrangements, Uruguay has had a tradition of concertation. The centralization achieved with the merging of the PIT (Plenario Inter-sindical de Trabajadores) with the CNT (Convencion Nacional de Trabajadores) towards the end of the military regime has favoured the continuation of this tradition. While there is some doubt as to the possibility of establishing a broad social pact in Uruguay (Rial, 1988), the Consejo Superior de Salarios (Salaries Higher Council) has functioned reasonably well as a typical neo-corporatist arrangement (Streeck and Schmitter, 1985) to decide on incomes policies. It consists of an informal arena based on the ad hoc commission of labour relations of CONAPRO with tripartite representation involving the government (Executive power, Ministry of Labour and

Social Security), the entrepreneurial class (Chamber of Industry, Chamber of Commerce and Chamber of Agriculture), and the working class (PIT/CNT) (Brezzo and Vispo, 1988).

Another aspect that deserves consideration is the success of the Uruguayan economic stabilization plan. As contrasted with the Cruzado and Austral plans, based on heterodox shocks, the Uruguayan stabilization plan took place gradually, and simultaneously with the transition (Filgueira, 1988). In other words, the democratic government passed the test of governability in which the Brazilian and Argentinian counterparts disastrously failed.

Considering this combination of factors, it seems that in Uruguay a more pluralist scenario is taking ground and is bound to stabilize in the future. Even in view of a possible assymetry between the Left and the traditional parties (Gillespie, 1986), it seems that the basic aspect underlying the relative success of the Uruguayan transition and, by extension, of prospects for democratic consolidation, is the neat way in which social actors are linked to the political institutional framework. As is the central argument in this chapter, neither social structure nor political institutions alone would explain the failures and successes of democracy, but rather the bridge between the two. Mobilized actors found their institutional niches in the previously existing party system, in the trade union movement, and other organizations, old and new. Not displaying exaggerated asynchronies – which from a structural point of view means not having to deal with old and new actors brought about by rapid, concentrated modernization and social inequalities – Uruguayan society was able to return to the path of democratization after a brief detour. As the authoritarian detour was costly, consensus about the advantage of the old democratic institutions can certainly work as a deterrent to not respecting the rules of the game. This is particularly true in a society where the age pyramid is larger at the top – in contrast with Brazil, where the young population not only predominates, but also where a larger segment was suddenly brought into the political process.

ARGENTINA

Judging by indicators of social structure alone, Argentinian society would perfectly correspond to expectations as to a likely development of democratic institutions. A strong civil society was formed over a period of very fast economic growth between 1880 and the

First World War, and later acquired a very modern profile with the industrialization boom of the post-1930s. However, it is precisely in the strength of civil society, which was not followed by parallel transformation of political institutions, that the cyclical instability of Argentinian politics lies.

The first wave of economic development towards the turn of the century was essentially based on the expansion of the export sector. Massive European immigration provided the basis for a cheap and unskilled labour force which was soon organized in a strong trade union movement. Side by side, there occurred an artificial growth of the tertiary sector, leading to the formation of a broad, early middle class (Fuentes, 1987).

Industry first developed to satisfy the needs of the primary export sector and was, from the outset, turned towards the internal market. After 1930, the loss of competitiveness of primary goods in the world market further stimulated inward-oriented industrialization which, in turn, required income distribution. In that decade, Argentina already had a profile comparable to that of West European societies, with a middle class that comprised almost 50 per cent of the population. By 1947, urbanization in Argentina reached 47 per cent, a rate that Brazil would achieve only in the 1970s. Between 1955 and 1972, industrialization proceeded into a third stage with an increase from 8 to 40 per cent of foreign capital participation. By the mid-1970s, the first signs of crisis and recession began to show (Fuentes, 1987). In short, the main aspect to retain here is the early modernization of Argentina, together with the signs of limitations in its model of economic development by the time of the emergence of the bureaucratic authoritarian regime in 1976.

Instability characterized by the periodical alternation of democratic and authoritarian regimes is a conspicuous trait in Argentinian political history of this century, from the time the Radical Party won elections in 1916 with Yrigoyen, to its latest comeback in 1983 with Alfonsin. The pattern of authoritarian regimes and civilian interludes is particularly clear following Peron's downfall in 1955: the military replaced Radical Party incumbents four times, and the latter were in power for three periods including the present government. The military/Radical alternation was interrupted only by the brief return of Peronismo between 1973 and 1976. In this sense, ungovernability is a 'normal' trait of the Argentinian political system.

Much of this instability is rooted in the difficulties of incorporating the working class. The middle classes had been a traditional constituency of the UCR (Radical Party) as early as the electoral reform of 1912, which extended suffrage to the whole adult male population bringing the party to power in 1916. That basis of support was woven through the creation of a political machine tying the middle class to the state and leading to the dismantling of the oligarchic system. Just as the incorporation of the middle class was early, that of the working class was quite late, not taking place until the mid-1940s under Peron. As Secretary of Labour of the 1943 military government, Peron gave shape to the marginalized working class, bringing the strong trade unions under a corporatist, state-controlled CGT. In power from 1946 to 1955, the working classes were brought into the political process under Peron's populist leadership, much in the same way as their Brazilian counterpart under Vargas. However, as distinct from Brazil's PTB (Brazilian Labour Party) which was diluted with the first reform of the party system under the military in 1966, the Justicialista Party in Argentina became a strong source of identification for the working class beyond the populist period, and the main axis of social conflict from then on.

As can be seen, the two major forces in Argentinian politics – the Radical Party and the Peronistas – have had a fairly established tradition and stability over time. However, their rooting in society was not sufficient to establish an efficient system of representation, let alone one that could come to terms with turn-over in politics. The literature is unanimous in pointing out this aspect (Cavarozzi, 1983, 1984; De Riz, n.d.). The problem is twofold: on one hand, the inability of the parties to actually mediate the interests of their strongly organized constituencies; on the other, the absence of a truly institutionalized party system from the point of view of the relationships between parties. Thus, while in Uruguay long-established parties developed a strong system and in Brazil weak parties are further weakened by repeated breakdowns of the party system (at least four in recent republican history), in Argentina there is great continuity of the parties taken individually. Nevertheless, a real party system did not develop. Argentina's party configuration could best be described by the presence of 'strong subcultures and a weak system' (Cavarozzi, 1984).

The first democratic experiment between 1916 and 1930 did not operate towards the creation of rules of coexistence between parties. The second, between 1945 and 1955, implied an increase in the levels of political participation, but also in the levels of conflict. From then on, politics have revolved around attempts to prevent the Peronistas from taking over or the Radicals from governing, and thus making room for military interventions. In this fashion, newly elected governments take office with low levels of legitimacy which soon erode. This incapacity of the parties to act as mediators of social conflict, leading to an absence of commitment with the democratic system, has been pointed out as a serious obstacle in the way of democratic consolidation in Argentina (De Riz, n.d.). The antagonism between Peronistas and Radicals was only briefly attenuated in the short-lived, Hora del Pueblo experiment which brought Peron and Balbin to an agreement after the elections of 1973. But with Peron's death in 1974 this mode of inter-party relations detrimental to democratic competition was frozen (Cavarozzi, 1984).

In addition, another difficulty lies in the strong corporative tradition of the major interest associations in Argentina: those of the entrepreneurial and working classes have shown a tendency for the immediate, short-run defence of their interests (Sabato and Schvarzer, 1985). In so doing, they further erode the parties' ability to act as mediators.

The nature of the Argentinian transition also matters in this context. As pointed out in the literature on transitions (O'Donnell, Schmitter and Whitehead, 1986), the case of Argentina's suppression of military rule was one in which external factors mattered to a great extent. The defeat in the Malvinas war resulted in the military's being unable to stay in power and, therefore, in their decision to step down. In this sense, one can hardly talk about a transition *strictu senso* (De Riz, n.d.). It was more a case of a sudden collapse of the military regime, and rather as a consequence of their own mistakes than as a result of actions of the opposition. The parties and social actors were, thus, caught by surprise.

In this sense, again in the case of the Argentinian transition, democratization had little to do with structural changes in society. In spite of structural transformations concerning the entrepreneurs and the working class, their behaviour seems unchanged. If anything, the decline in the levels of industrial employment has led to an increase in self-employment and, hence, in atomization of the trade union movement (Jelin, 1987). The frequent 'paros' (general strikes) between 1984 and 1986 only represent the return to a route of open confrontation of the trade union movement to proposals of concerted negotiation by the state in the absence of a programme of action.

The transition prompted a relatively low level of social mobilization, except in the cases of the so-called 'vecinazos' (localized movement of protest against urban policies) and human rights (Cavarozzi, 1984). Only with the elections of October 1983 – which had an undoubted plebiscitary nature against the military – did some level of resurgence take place. The elections implied a very rapid process of re-emergence of the political parties, with over three million registrations in the Justicialista Party and one million in the Radical Party, altogether comprising 45 per cent of the electorate (Jelin, 1987). Still, to this date the parties lack a stable network of articulations with actors of civil society and they did little in terms of generating a positive programme for consolidation of democracy.

Regarding this aspect, social movements can be said to have played rather an important role. They were responsible, as in the case of Brazil, for the democratization of political culture, particularly in the sense of overcoming political factionalism (Mainwaring and Viola, 1984). But unlike Brazil, Argentina has a tradition of autonomous mobilizations vis-à-vis the state, thus resulting in quite different movements, both in terms of scope and content. The neighbourhood movements in peripheral urban areas is a case in point. While in Brazil these movements in squatter settlements have turned their action towards the state and have constituted a fertile ground for clientele politics (Gay, 1988), the 'barriales' movements in Argentina, at least in recent years, have developed a pattern of action turned towards the community and inter-family ties (Jelin, 1987). This has led to the diffusion of self-government practices, rather than confrontation with state, and therefore, to revitalization of politics at the local level. The loss of totalizing horizons and the multiplication of segmented collective practices that have tended to characterize post-transitional movements (Jelin, 1987) could in this sense be an important ingredient in de-ideologizing the universe of Argentinian politics.

Another characteristic which is more akin to the Argentinian case concerns the special place of Human Rights movements. Among all social movements narrowly defined, this would seem to be the strongest in the context of redemocratization. Emerging as a result of authoritarianism in a reaction to the disappearance of political prisoners, human rights movements, nonetheless, have had a longer tradition in Argentina, dating back to 1937. An important impact of the 'Madres and Abuelas of the Plaza de Mayo', in addition to the trial of the military, has been the autonomization of the judiciary power under the new regime (Jelin, 1987).

There are some indications of positive developments in the

Argentinian situation that have an impact in terms of altering a resilient and conflict-ridden political culture. In a context of discredit in the efficiency of politicians – especially in view of the failure of economic policies – the appointment of Menem as the Justicialista candidate can contribute towards 'softening' that conflict, to the extent that he promotes the self-image of the anti-politician. In so doing, his candidacy may overflow the boundaries of the strong party subculture, rendering the Peronistas more palatable to political society as a whole. In addition, in view of the tendency towards fragmentation of the labour movement, it would seem more difficult for a populist candidate to bypass the party and depend on a direct support of the CGT. Thus, while the spectrum of a neo-populist regime may seem frightening on a number of respects, from a strict point of view of consolidation of democratic practices, it is not necessarily so. It is in the light of potentialities for promoting consensus over political alternation and rules of the game accepted by all that the presidential choice must be evaluated.

In spite of the uncertainty and perplexity generated by military rebellions, the scheduled elections did take place. The problem that remains will be that of an efficient system articulating organized groups and the state, side by side with strong congressional power to mitigate the heavy presidential tradition prevailing in Argentina and, for that matter, elsewhere in Latin America.

CONCLUSIONS

The central argument of the present comparative analysis of the prospects for political democracy in Brazil, Uruguay, and Argentina refers to the role of the civil society and organized actors in the process. In this sense it was argued that neither social actors nor political institutions alone would give a complete picture of the process. Analyses have either emphasized the role of structural conditions or the autonomy of the state in promoting institutionalization. Instead, as suggested in a recent study (Gay, 1988), while the emphasis on the autonomy of the state represents the main advantage of an institutional perspective in terms of explaining regime change, it is not useful when the discussion turns to the process of societal transformation. That leads to the need to examine the forms of incorporation of the different segments of society into the political process which, in turn, cannot be understood only as a function of the level of economic development.

In order to specify the impact of civil society, the form and timing of the incorporation of social sectors would seem to play a fundamental role. In this sense it is the combination of characteristics of the system of intermediation allowing for such incorporation – namely, the party system, interest groups, and the new social actors – that will increase or decrease the likelihood of stabilization of a democratic system. The position of the channels for the incorporation of older social actors *vis-à-vis* the state on the one hand, and new collective identities pushing for incorporation through social movements, on the other, would have to be bound together by an effective party system.

Politics in Latin America have been characterized by a pendulum motion between the prevalence of a socio-cultural or symbolic expressive pole and the instrumental pole geared towards institutional change. The first pole corresponds to that of struggles and mobilizations against authoritarianism and exclusion, in which the assertion of a collective identity is fundamental. The second corresponds to mobilizations through more stable organizational structures, in which political strategy is central. Solving this tension through the convergence between party system and social movements would assure a smoother transit to democracy (Campero, 1988).

The comparative analysis carried out here helps specify some of the conditions associated with different probable outcomes regarding democratic consolidation in the three countries. In the first place, concerning the nature and timing of structural changes, Brazil would stand out in sharp contrast to both Argentina and Uruguay. In the former, later and deeper capitalist modernization occurred under the military regime generating, in a short period of time, a technologically advanced, although extremely unequal society. In the latter, modernization took place earlier, was more gradual, and did not produce drastic inequalities. On the other hand, both countries lagged behind, by and large, in terms of technological progress and development potential.

In so far as the form and timing of the incorporation of social actors is concerned, the three countries show remarkable differences from each other. In Brazil, the incorporation of the entrepreneurs and the industrial working class occurred relatively early under strong state corporatism. In turn, pluralization of society was protracted by state control and new collective actors outside the corporative framework emerged only in the 1970s. In Argentina, the incorporation of a broad middle class took place early in this century, but the working class was brought into the political process in the 1940s in a very conflicting way. Finally, in Uruguay the incorporation of the fundamental social actors was progressive and relatively autonomous in relation to the chapter.

As to the structures of mediation, Brazil is a case of strong corporatism, weak parties, and an unstable party system. Social movements managed to establish a significant network, in spite of limitations imposed by their relations with the state. Argentina also displays strong corporatist institutions and a pattern of direct influence of entrepreneurial and labour organizations in politics. The ideological spectrum is moulded by strong parties which are nevertheless unable to evolve into a stable system. Social movements do have a place but they are more inward oriented. In Uruguay, corporatism has not been a tradition, the parties have been strong, and the party system stable. Social movements have not taken root, being of a more conjunctural nature.

As is known, any mapping of a number of variables is bound to simplify reality. Opportunity, as pointed out in the literature, plays a fundamental role in defining the course of political events. Other things being equal, however, Uruguayan political democracy is the one, among the cases studied here, that stands the better chance for consolidation. The Brazilian and Argentinian experiences are much more complex. For different reasons, there seems to be, in both cases, a place for the re-emergence of populism, though of a distinct nature from that experienced in the 1940–50s in those countries. It appears that, even in the absence of parties that could be able to operate in a very intricate social environment, the co-existence of several alternatives of political engineering would make it difficult for the same style of personal leadership to be exerted. In the 1940s, resort to the corporatist solution was more viable. Nowadays, side by side with a state-corporatist tradition, pluralist and in some cases even neo-corporatist arrangements have taken ground. Such diversification, in and of itself, poses new challenges for the incumbents of power. In this context, an optimistic bet on the possibility of making a minimum set of rules of the game prevail would do better than the pessimistic fear as to who would win the game.

Note

1. I am indebted to Eli Diniz for comments and suggestions throughout the drafting of this chapter.

References

Boschi, R. (1987) *A arte da associação : política de base e democracia no Brasil* (São Paulo: Ed. Vertice).

Boschi, R. (1988) 'Entre a cruz e a caldeira : classes medias e política na terra da transição', *mimeo*. Paper presented at the VIII Conference on Latin American Studies, URFGS/CLACSO, Porto Alegre, August.

Brezzo, L. A. and E. Vispo (1988) 'Experiencia de la concertación de políticas de ingreso en Uruguay', in: PREALC, *Política Económica y Actores Sociales* (Santiago: OIT).

Caciagli, M. (1984) 'Spain: Parties and Party System in the Transition', *West European Politics*, vol. 7, no. 2.

Campero, G. (1988) 'Actores y movimientos sociales en Chile', *mimeo*. Paper presented at VIII Conference on Latin American Studies, UFRGS/CLACSO, Porto Alegre, August.

Cavarozzi, M. (1983) *Autoritarismo y Democracia : 1955–1983* (Buenos Aires: Centro Editor).

Cavarozzi, M. (1984) 'Los partidos argentinos : subculturas fuertes, Sistema débil', *mimeo*. Paper prepared for the project 'Political Parties and Redemocratization in the Southern Cone', November.

Dahl, R. (1971) *Polyarchy: Participation and Opposition* (New Haven: Yale University Press).

De Riz, L. (n.d.) *Partidos políticos y perspectivas de consolidación de la democracia : Argentina, Brasil y Uruguay*, CLACSO/CEDES, Grupo de Trabajo de Partidos Políticos, Documento de Trabajo 2.

Diniz, E. and R. Boschi (1987) 'A consolidação democrática no Brasil : pórocessos sociais, intermediação de interesses e modernização do Estado', *mimeo*. Projecto PNUD-UNESCO-CLACSO RLA 86/001, *mimeo*.

Filgueira, C. H. E. (ed.) (1985a), *Movimientos sociales en el Uruguay de hoy*. Montevideo, CLACSO/CIESU/Ediciones de la Banda Oriental.

Filgueira, C. H. E. (1988) 'Organizaciones sindicales y empresariales ante las políticas de estabilización : Uruguay 1985–1987', *mimeo*. Paper presented at the workshop on Políticas Antiinflacionarias y Mercado de Trabajo, Santiago, August.

Fuentes, L. M. L. (1987) *The Middle Class and Democracy in Latin America: Argentina, Brazil and Mexico*. PhD dissertation, Stanford University.

Gay, R. (1988) *Political Clientelism and Urban Social Movements in Rio de Janeiro*. PhD dissertation, Brown University.

Gillespie, C. (1986) 'Uruguay's Transition from Collegial Military-Technocratic Rule' in: G. O'Donnell, P. Schmitter and L. Whitehead, (eds), vol. II, pp. 173–96.

Huntington, S. (1968) *Political Order in Changing Societies* (New Haven: Yale University Press).

Huntington, S. (1984) 'Will More Countries Become Democratic?', *Political Science Quarterly*, vol. 99, no. 2.

Jelin, E. (1987) 'El itinerario de la democratización : los movimientos sociales y la participación popular' in: Tironi, E. (ed.), *Proposiciones : Marginalidad, Movimientos Sociales y Democracia* (Santiago: Sur Ediciones), no. 14.

Kowarick, L. (1987) 'Movimentos urbanos no Brasil contemporâneo : uma análise da literatura', *Revista brasileira de ciencias sociais*, vol. 1, no. 3.

Lipset, S. M. (1963) *Political Man: The Social Basis of Politics* (New York: Anchor Books).

Mainwaring, S. (1986) *Grassroots Popular Movements, Identity, and Democratization in Brazil* Kellogg Institute: Working Paper no. 84, October.

Mainwaring, S. (1987) 'Urban Popular Movements, Identity, and Democratization in Brazil', *Comparative Political Studies*, vol. 20, no. 2, July.

Mainwaring, S. and E. Viola (1984), 'New Social Movements, Political Culture, and Democracy: Brazil and Argentina in the 1980s', *Telos*, vol. 17, no. 3.

Maravall, J. (1982) *The Transition to Democracy in Spain* (New York: St. Martin's Press).

O'Donnell G. and P. Schmitter (1986) *Transitions from Authoritarian Rule: Tentative Conclusions about Uncertain Democracies* (Baltimore: Johns Hopkins University Press).

O'Donnell G., Schmitter, P. and L. Whitehead (eds) (1986) *Transition from Authoritarian Rule: Prospects for Democracy* (Baltimore: Johns Hopkins University Press). Four volumes (in paperback): I *Southern Europe* II *Latin America* III *Comparative Perspectives* IV *Tentative Conclusions about Uncertain Democracies*.

Pintor, R. L. (1982) *La opinión pública Espaola del franquismo a la democracia* (Madrid: Centro de Investigaciones Sociológicas).

Rial, J. (1988) 'El movimiento sindical uruguayo ante la redemocratización', PREALC *Política Económica y Actores Sociales* (Santiago: OIT).

Sabato, J. F. and J. Schvarzer (1985) 'Funcionamento da economia e poder político na argentina : empecilhos para a democracia', in: A. Rouquié, P. Lamounier and J. Schvarzer (1985) (eds), *Como renascem as democracias* (Sao Paulo: Brasiliense).

Santos, W. G. dos (1985) 'A pos-revolução brasileira', in: H. Jaguaribe *et al. Brasil sociedade democrática* (Rio de Janeiro: Jose Olympia).

Share, D. and S. Mainwaring (1986) 'Transição pela transação : democratização no Brasil e na Espanha', *Dados*, vol. 29, no. 2.

Streeck, W. and P. Schmitter (eds) (1985) *Private Interest Government* (London and Beverly Hills: Sage).

Tironi E. (ed.) (1987) *Proposiciones : marginalidad, movimientos sociales y democracia* (Santiago: Sur Ediciones), no. 14.

11 Social Concertation and Democracy in Argentina[1]

Graciela Ducatenzeiler

Democratic consolidation in Argentina has not yet been achieved. Although civilian legalism has rapidly replaced the authoritarian regime of exception, the creation of a political system based on the recognition and exercise of citizenship, and the respect for the principle of representation is incomplete.

Although the task of democracy building has been put on the agenda with the departure of the military, this process has been slowed down by the weight of political tradition. Beyond current economic and political uncertainties, structural barriers such as corporatism and weaknesses in the representational system have retarded the process of democratic consolidation. Given the lack of a democratic precedent in Argentina, the issue of consolidation must be understood not so much in terms of *restoration*, but the *construction* of a new political system.

We will examine two attempts at building a new order following the authoritarian experiences of 1966–73 and 1976–82: the third Peronist government of 1973–76 and the Radical government of 1983–89. Our analysis will focus particularly on the role of social concertation as an instrument of democratic consolidation, on the obstacles encountered, and the reasons for failure in each case. But first we will deal with theoretical and empirical conditions that make the policy of concertation viable and the break with political tradition desirable.

CLASS COMPROMISE, CONCERTATION AND SOCIAL CONTRACTS

A social contract is the creation of a cooperative mechanism of decision-making and policy formation: a class compromise between capitalists and workers organized and guaranteed by the state. This assumes the existence of institutionalized models of intermediation and agreement between governments and classes allowing for effective compromise.

> Class compromise assumes a particular (democratic) form of political relations, a specific relationship between class and state, a particular body of institutions and of relations between them, and a specific attitude of these institutions towards policy. (Przeworski, 1981, 261)

The possibility of a social contract or class compromise depends on both economic and political factors. The primary political condition is the existence of a capitalist democracy: a combination of capitalism and democracy contingent on the recognition of the right to private ownership and the ability of labour to channel its demands for resource allocation and distribution through political institutions (Przeworski and Wallerstein, 1982, 79). This also assumes that both workers and capitalists abandon their maximalist demands by accepting that class conflict is not necessarily irreconcilable. Political democracy is nevertheless compatible with different forms of interest organization and articulation. Therefore concertation, social contracts or class compromise can take on different characteristics according to the political structure of capitalist societies. Political parties and corporations are the privileged representational instruments of organized interests. A political system can be more or less democratically representational[2] or more or less corporatist according to the public status given to interest groups (Offe, 1985, 237). The centrality of parties or associations in social concertation depends on the degree of social corporatization.

Most recent literature on forms of organization and the representation of collective interests points out that the structural transformations between state and society in Western democracies over the past few decades have modified the empirical foundations of pluralist democracy. The increase in often contradictory demands by new and traditional actors has led to ungovernability. The traditional parliamentary and partisan political system has proved itself incapable of dealing with new demands. Competition between different political actors, far from producing consensus – as predicted by the pluralist theory – has resulted in conflicts, with each actor threatening to pull his resources out of the political market. Particularly since the end of the Second World War, new models of organization and representation of collective interests have emerged as alternatives to the pluralist model. The concepts of neo-corporatism, liberal or societal corporatism or of organized pluralism are used in literature to qualify changes in the political structure of advanced capitalism. This eventually leads to the establishment of centres of power outside the political system recognized by the state with a specific political status. As Offe points out (1985, 242): 'The characteristic feature of modern corporatism, in contrast to authoritarian models, is the *coexistence* of the two circuits (traditional and corporatist politics) with only a limited substitution of functional for territorial representation.'

However, this coexistence is possible under certain conditions such as the existence of a strong traditional political system and a high density of organized interests. The later condition assumes the presence of state-independent associations having a monopoly on sectorial representation (Schmitter, 1974).

Economic prosperity is one of the economic factors which can make concertation possible. Class compromise is contingent on workers being reasonably certain that future material conditions will be improved as a result of present concessions. This conviction is not simply based on confidence in capitalists' respect of the compromise, but also on predictions concerning future economic performance. In this sense both workers and capitalists are dependent on investment effectiveness: 'market fluctuations, internal and international competition, technological change, and other economic factors' (Przeworski, 1981, 251).

Most experiences in social concertation have taken place in Western Europe. With the exception of Spain[3] these negotiations occurred under very particular economic and political conditions. On the economic level, the development of social contracts took place in a climate of salary increases and an improvement of the working class's material welfare. On the political level, these experiences transpired in situations where wage earners were wholly integrated into the Western democratic political system through unions and political parties, under reformist governments and under circumstances where the government party dominated the union movement.[4] Concertation necessitated not only consensus on current revenue distribution policies, but also on the recognition of basic democratic principles. In the context of such a compromise, dissent challenged not so much the regime but the government in power. The state, having the capacity to implement and guarantee these agreements, was both judge and partner to the social contract.[5]

POLITICAL TRADITION IN ARGENTINA

Historically Argentina can be characterized as having a weak partisan system with strong pressure groups capable of blocking their adversaries' policy but incapable of imposing their own hegemony. 'Liberals' and populists took turns succeeding each other and implementing the immediate demands of their respective corporatist clientele. Economic policy was consistent with these change-overs: lifting of protectionist barriers and stabilization plans during liberal governments; increases in protectionism and public spending during populist administrations (O'Donnell, 1977). When distributive conflicts intensified because of shrinking surpluses or the overload of sectorial demands, the military intervened either as arbitrators, or in defence of the agro-export industry or big business.

Given the fragility of the traditional political partisan and parliamentary system, associations emerged as central political actors. This eventually led to the development of a political culture favouring extra-partisan and extra-parliamentary mechanisms of intervention (Cavarozzi, 1983).

Nine years of populist government (1946–55), brief semi-democratic experiences,[6] and military authoritarianism are at the roots of the development of a political mode far removed from the liberal model. Populism, semi-democratic regimes and authoritarianism rendered mediations between citizens and government ineffective or simply nonexistent. As a result when pressures were possible (which obviously excludes military regimes), they targeted the state. The absence of representation was compensated by corporatist pressure; corporatism not only replaced inefficient political institutions, but rendered them inoperable by destroying whatever small legitimacy they did have. Corporatism emerged as an alternative to liberal pluralism rather than as a compensation of its weaknesses. This is not however a state-imposed and controlled authoritarian corporatism but rather a non-institutionalized spillover of the political system.

The two semi-democratic governments (of 1958–62 and 1963–66) rendered the political system (political parties and parliament) ineffective in as much as both Radical Party victories were only made possible by the banning of the dominant Peronist Party. Excluded from direct political participation and deprived of their partisan structure, the Peronists had no other choice but to channel their demands through unions, using them as a *bona fide* political pressure group. The decision to act outside of the formalized political structure was based on the unions' characteristics, such as representational monopoly and their access to the government, making them highly visible and, by extension, more effective.

However, workers' associations had no monopoly over extrainstitutional participation. Capitalist interest groups adopted similar conduct, although for different reasons. The various bourgeois factions had difficulty expressing their concerns through established political channels and found it more convenient to act outside the political system or to exploit other political links either through their associations or through direct ministerial lobbying. In passing the Saenz Pena Law in 1912, the most powerful of these factions, the agro-export oligarchy, fell into its own trap by enlarging the electorate and thus no longer guaranteeing the representation necessary to influence policy-making. The industrial sectors were more divided: those linked to major local and international capital and with traditional alliances with the oligarchy found themselves in the same situation as the agro-export sector, while the local industrial bourgeoisie (Peronist for the most part) lost its instrument of mediation with the fall of Peron in 1955.

As a result of the generalization of this political conduct, political institutions became only marginally representative of civil society and the state became the target of pressures for which it lacked the authority to satisfy. The state was neither arbitrator, nor the executive power of a representational democracy, but one social force among others. Its role was nevertheless determinant since all political actors defined themselves in terms of state intervention, eventually leading to the inability to distinguish between the state, the political system and the social actors (Touraine, 1988).

The absence of effective democratic representation and the existence of strong societal corporatism impeded the political emergence of social actors and allowed for this institutional spillover and the establishment of a dual political system. Since democratic institutions were no longer capable of articulating general interests, almost all social actors relied on parallel mechanisms to express their demands. Democratic compromise was therefore limited to a few politicians and the middle classes. Being outside the system was not only a way of expressing dissent but also left open the possibility of challenging the regime's legitimacy if their demands were not met.

Lacking a supportive political base, the only way for a government to remain in power was to administer public capital according to the force of the non-institutionalized pressures placed on it. Governmental function was thus reduced to the impossible mediation of distributive conflicts between various associations. Following the civilian failures of 1962, 1966 and 1976, the military took over in order to resolve the conflict in favour of the capitalists. Politics gave way to inflation as a mechanism of reaching compromise, but

> Inflationary compromise had a decisive disadvantage: in such a situation it was easy for sectorial representatives to refuse any responsibility in reaching a compromise. The "Inflationary Agreement" was at best precarious and implicit and invited permanent transgression because no one was seen as having clear responsibility in price and salary increases, given the apparent automization of the process. (Cavarozzi, 1988, 5)

The responsibility for failure inevitably fell on the government in power which lost the support of those sectors least favoured by its initiatives.

The two most significant albeit very different efforts to break with this political tradition came from the third Peronist government of 1973–76 and the 1983 Radical government. On the one hand, Peron endeavoured to break with corporatism by re-enforcing the institutional political system while at the same time institutionalizing the rules of the corporatist game by way of a social contract. The Radical Party, on the other hand, focused on re-enforcing representational mediation in the civil society and distancing the state from sectorial interests. The call to *La Mesa de Concertacion* was more a concession, a pragmatic solution to interest group demands for participation than the product of policy orientation.

POLICY AND CONCERTATION IN ARGENTINA

There is obviously an enormous contextual difference between the European experience of Welfare State concertation and the political and socio-economic conditions for reaching compromise in Argentina. The Argentine experience was defined not so much by democracy or economic prosperity; it was more a question of building a democratic society, of finding new ways of mediation and conflict resolution. Concertation was seen as a solution to social ungovernability, as a way of breaking with the warfare mentality through the building of an institutional structure of collective interest representation which would allow for the achievement and the respect of compromise.

These two efforts of social concertation followed the authoritarian experiences, of 1966–73 and 1976–82; they nevertheless express two different visions of the desired political order. The Peronist *Pacto Social* can therefore be interpreted as an effort to institutionalize a new doctrine or political model while *La Mesa de Concertacion* appears to have been more of a transitory and pragmatic response to the challenges of democratic governability.

EL PACTO SOCIAL

In Argentina the most important experience of social intermediation is known as the *Pacto Social* embodied in the National Compromise Act of 1973, between the General Economic Confederation (CGE), the General Workers Confederation (CGT) and the ministries of Labour, Economy and Finance.

After eight years of proscription, the Peronists returned to power in a context characterized by the emergence of new social actors and an increasing radicalization of military and popular social conflicts. By the late 1960s, the radical student guerrilla movement had surfaced as had the anti-bureaucratic conflicts within the unions opposing various radical alternatives to political conciliation for control and distribution of social resources (De Riz, 1981, 24). In 1971, having admitted their inability to deal with the crisis and hoping for a political solution, the military turned over to Peron the task of rebuilding a political order capable of controlling the forces calling for '*la patria socialista*' from both inside and outside the union movement. Peron responded to the challenge by proposing a political accord between the two major parties (Peronists and Radicals) and a social contract between industrial management and unions. The context of the third Peronist government was that of stalemate where neither side was in a position to impose its will: for the capitalists, authoritarian rule had proved unworkable, whereas the unions and radicalized middle class were not powerful enough to impose the socialist option. If there was a reason why the military decided to pass the task of conflict resolution on to Peron and why Peron had accepted this challenge, it was because the vast majority on both sides of the conflict belonged to the same political movement: *Justicialismo*. Peron's political authority, recognized by both friend and enemy, was the foundation of hopes placed in him to resolve the crisis.

Inspired by European experiences, the *Pacto Social* was intended to complement partisan representation by institutionalizing a dualist model of interest representation. As we have shown, the political role of associations was central since 1955 but acted more as pressure groups than actual policy-makers. If we apply Schmitter's model (1981, 296), to the Argentine experience, we can describe corporatism as '*interest intermediation*' in contrast to corporatism as '*policy formation*'. Peron's intention was to establish '"*concerted*" *forms of policymaking*'.

The *Pacto Social* was primarily a revenue policy negotiated between management, unions and the state with the intention of controlling distribution conflicts in a context of economic crisis. The success of negotiations depended mainly on the ability of the business associations and unions to have the agreements accepted by the rank and file of their respective groups. The 1973 oil crisis, the virtual closing off of the EEC markets and Peron's death in 1974 resulted in the weakening of the Pact and continuous violating of the agreements. Social conflicts began to erupt outside the negotiated institutional framework: wildcat strikes, black markets, wage and price 'hikes', factory takeovers, and so on, demonstrating that the agreements reached in the Pact were not worth the paper they were written on. The labour movement found itself split between respecting the accords it had signed and defending its sectorial interests. With Peron's death, union leaders reverted back to their successful post-1955 strategy of corporative independence and extra-institutional participation. It had discovered that dealing with government as an adversary was easier than with it as a friend. 'Participation in opposition' became the motto that best described the dominant political orientation in labour circles during the post-1955 period (Torre, 1983, 150). Tensions between leaders of the central business association, the General Economic Confederation (CGE) broke out into open conflict: between internal factions on the one hand and non-member business groups that had previously supported the Pact on the other, eventually adopting a *golpista* attitude.

The *Pacto Social* never evolved beyond the framework of a revenue policy with all its inherent limitations.[7] Unions threw all of their institutional power into the negotiations while business maintained control of the economic variables beyond the scope of the bargaining agenda.

The third Peronist government's attempt to break with this corporatist behaviour by re-enforcing the political institutions and formalizing the corporatist regulatory framework ended like other elected governments, with the channelling of social conflict outside institutionalized structures. The main difference with previous experiences was the tragic outbreak of violence which supplanted traditional demands and approached the 'catastrophic' dimensions described by Gramsci (1971, 276). Following the 1976 military coup, the authoritarian government broke this dynamic and opened exclusive channels of mediation between business and the state.

LA MESA DE CONCERTACIÓN

The *Mesa de Concertacion* took place in a completely different context from that of the *Pacto Social*. The democratic transition was neither the result of popular triumph, military concession, nor a contract between the military and political élites, but the collapse of the military regime following the Falkland Islands war. No single social actor was strong enough to impose its will and the Radical Party owed no political debts to any one group. During the electoral campaign, Raul Alfonsin attacked not only military corporatism but denounced the corporatist structure in general as a cause of authoritarianism. As a citizens' party, the Radicals focused on the importance of democracy with a vision of the political arena as a space for negotiation and exchange capable of progressively rendering society more governable.

The basic principles of the Radical Party as well as its own constitution and the characteristics of its electorate rendered fairly impervious the idea of negotiation as a way of resolving social ungovernability. The Party initially sought to re-enforce the political system by distancing itself from interest groups. It was not until May 1984 that the government decided to convene the various interest groups in the *Mesa de Concertacion*. As we mentioned above, this was more a response to its failed policy of trying to govern autonomously than a political model of social interest representation.

The democratic government adopted three different strategies for the associations in general and for the labour movement in particular: first, autonomy, the only coherent strategy consistent with its political vision; secondly, concertation; and finally, co-option (Schvarzer and Sidicaro, 1987).

Autonomy

Backed by the results of the 30 October 1983 electoral victory, the Radical government of Raul Alfonsin began its fight against corporatism in trying to implement its economic programme. This first attempt at distancing government from sectorial interests was based on the belief that the government could manage the economy and resolve the crisis without making concessions to sectors affected by policy measures. This strategy was directed at both internal and external pressures and resulted in clashes with the labour movement, the majority of the business associations and international organizations such as the IMF.

This policy of state independence in dealing with social actors primarily targeted the labour movement.[8] Within six days of taking office, the government tabled a union reorganization bill aimed explicitly at internal union democratization and implicitly at weakening their power base, and thus changing the dynamic between state and labour. Along with other non-Peronist parties, the Radicals held the strong conviction that a strong union structure was a barrier to democracy. Three months later, after being passed in the lower house, the bill was voted down in the Senate, so constituting the newly elected government's first major parliamentary setback. This resulted in a resurgence in labour initiatives and the closing of union ranks, which up until then had been divided following the Radical election victory. The normalization of internal union affairs was not quite the scenario the government had planned for. In June 1984, the Senate finally ratified a bill, drafted in conjunction with union leaders, implicitly forcing the Radical government to back down on several of its initial objectives.

Concertation

The initial strategy of confrontation of the first project was eventually succeeded by a strategy of concertation which unofficially granted a certain degree of legitimacy to union leaders and business association representatives. The recognition of union leaders and business associations as legitimate negotiators for their respective sectors, paved the way for setting up the *Mesa* and the participation of the principal business associations, the CGT, and the government through the Ministry of Labour.

For the government, the *Mesa de Concertacion* was a way of forcing the various economic actors into disciplining themselves, and setting aside sectorial demands in favour of more global solutions. But above all it meant granting a legitimate space for interest groups. For the unions, participation was a way of recuperating their traditional social and political power base and confirming their status as legitimate leaders. And for business as well as labour, participation constituted not only a way of opposing government economic policy, but a warning to government that the crisis could not be solved without their input.

The *Mesa de Concertacion* was more than a simple elaboration of concerted policies; it was in effect the galvanizing of different interest group demands against government economic policy.[9]

The June 1985 Austral Plan[10] put concertation on the back burner. The government no longer spoke of concertation but of instituting a Social and Economic Conference with more clearly defined limits than those at the *Mesa de Concertacion*. The Austral Plan can in fact be interpreted as an authoritative governmental initiative to cut off inflationary inertia through *backward-looking* price adjustments and, in particular, wages (Frenkel and Damill, 1988, 274). Aside from wage and price controls, other measures included a freeze on public tariffs and exchange rates. But as Frenkel and Damill point out, wage and price controls can be only a transitory stage followed by flexibility, requiring well-determined adjustment mechanisms. The role of the Social and Economic Conference was to formulate standards of institutional treatment of distributive conflicts. However, negotiations never managed to evolve beyond salary levels and business participation was restricted to the industrial sector. 'The non-industrial sectors ... seeing that their concerns would not be dealt with beyond wage disputes, decided to distance themselves from the concertation process.' (Acuna *et al.*, 1988, 273).

The Austral Plan's initial success in reducing inflation combined with the gravity of the recession tended to muffle workers' protests; but with the first signs of economic recovery, labour conflicts multiplied. Management associations, initially satisfied with the Plan measures, began to criticize price controls and fiscal policies. Despite the split in labour and business demands, the 'Production Front' had held fast against government economic policy. Only government co-option of the Peronist CGT managed to force a clash between these two sectors.

Co-option

The failure or qualified success of the Austral Plan coincided with the liberalization of economic policy. Previously characterized as interventionist and somewhat nationalist, the Radicalist economic team, from late 1986 on, began to talk of opening up to international capital, of reduced government intervention in the economy, and of partial or total privatization of public enterprises. These changes in economic policy coincided with the incorporation of individuals directly or indirectly linked to corporatist interests. In March 1987, a union leader, Carlos Alderete, was appointed Labour Minister. The promise of economic liberalization had a reverse side in the labour camp. Through its Labour minister, the government tabled a series of parliamentary bills that addressed demands workers had advocated for several years.

None of these strategies resulted in relatively durable negotiated agreements between government and unions. The current economic pressures and ingrained corporatist traditions currently seem to be insurmountable obstacles for arriving at negotiated solutions.

CONCLUSION

We have emphasized that democratic consolidation should be understood as the building of a new political system based on the recognition and exercise of citizenship and respect for the principle of representation. Given the compatibility of democracy with different organizational forms of interest articulation, what is needed is the creation of institutionalized mechanisms of intermediation and agreement between interests and state, capable of assuring social governability.

Recent literature is generally unanimous in pointing out the political and economic destabilizing effects of pluralism. In the European and North American experiences, democratization and high levels of political participation have rendered pluralism ineffective: 'The new goods demanded may be of a kind that pluralist systems of representation have never provided.' (Berger, 1981, 22). Theorists are nevertheless divided over the effects of corporatism on the governability or stability of complex societies. Schmitter, among others, focuses on the fact that corporatism is more compatible with governability than classic pluralism, since increasing new demands on the system's regulatory capacity require a higher level of coordination. For others, the destabilizing effects of the corporatist alternative run the risk of being greater than those of pluralism.

The historical perspective of the European experiences indicates that policies of concertation occurred in situations where capitalist democracy was well established. Democratic institutions were perceived as legitimate: political forces were representational and existing interest groups were both recognized and autonomous. This type of institutional arrangement demanded the simultaneous presence of a competitive open party system and of a state-independent corporatist structure with roots in the civil society. Equally, the expanding economy permitted the positive prediction of future economic performance.

The Argentine experience occurred under different conditions. In a context of societal corporatism and insufficiently strong social actors, social concertation emerged as an alternative strategy of democratization: to pluralism – in the case of Peronism – or to the process of democratic consolidation – in the case of Radicalism. It was an attempt to transform corporatism as '*interest intermediation*' into corporatism as '*policy formation*'. Yet despite the existing elective affinity between these two types of corporatism, negotiation, with only partial access to the power apparatus, was difficult given the high level of interest group politicization in Argentina even with official recognition of the various groups as '*co-responsible "partners" in governance and societal guidance*' (Schmitter, 1981, 295).

The unique origins of interest groups in Argentina, the social and historical factors influencing their emergence, as well as their relations with the state, were certainly major obstacles in arriving at a workable compromise. But beyond these structural factors working against change, the economic crisis adds to the element of uncertainty, rendering compromise difficult if not impossible. The huge foreign debt, inherited from the military regime, and the inability to reach an acceptable restructuring agreement with the international finance sector have destroyed any chance of compromise. And much more so in as much as these international creditors, major actors in the distributive conflict, are absent from the negotiating table: 'The contradictions between the international nature of accumulation and the national character of consensus reproduction are accentuated with the internationalization of capital.' (Przeworski, 1981, 269).

Notes

1. The English translation is by Kevin Fitzgibbons.
2. We refer here to political systems where parties are privileged instruments of interest representation.
3. The Moncloa Pacts, signed in Spain in October 1977 by the parties represented in congress, involved a broader negotiation for which the main objective was the assurance the democratic transition.
4. Among the most recent experiences, one can find the *Konsertiete Aktion* (1967–77) in the Federal Republic of Germany negotiated by the socio-democratic DGB and the coalition government dominated by the SPD, the *Paritärische Komission* in Austria and the Swedish *Harpsund Democracy*.
5. Keynesianism provides the ideological and political foundations of capitalist democracy. The role of the state is to reconcile private property with the democratic leadership of the economy (Przeworski and Wallerstein, 1982, 80).
6. Between 1955 and 1983 the country had experienced only three democratic governments lasting an average of three years.
7. With the suspension of collective bargaining, unions were deprived of their only economic power: the ability to influence wages.
8. Parliamentary government intervention was easier in the labour sector due to the legislative framework and the differences between the representational structure in unions as opposed to the capital sector. Whereas the CGT held a monopoly over labour representation, the business sector had no unified representational body. Under the law, managerial associations had a civil statute of non-profit organizations and were therefore excluded from participating in the collective bargaining process. On the other hand, unions came under a legal framework which determined their functions as well as their relationship with employers (Acuna *et al.*, 1988, 210).
9. This converging of labour and business interests was formalized in early 1985 with the creation of the *Production Front*, an informal joint organization which advocated an alternative to government economic policy. The result of this alliance was a 20-point plan and represented a major compromise for these organizations with respect to their previous positions.
10. Unions were opposed to the freeze and perceived the Austral Plan not so much as an anti-inflationary instrument, but as a way of shifting the problem of the foreign debt on to the workers' backs. On the other hand, business, and in particular representatives of the most concentrated sectors of industry, gave the government their full support.

References

Acuña, C. H., M. R. dos Santos, D. García Delgado and L. Golbert (1988) 'Relación Estado/empresarios y políticas concertadas de ingresos. El caso argentino', in *Política económica y actores sociales* (Santiago: PREALC).
Berger, S. (ed.) (1981), *Organizing Interests in Western Europe. Pluralism,*

Corporatism, and the Transformation of Politics (Cambridge: Cambridge University Press).

Cavarozzi, M. (1983) *Autoritarismo y democracia (1955–1983)* (Buenos Aires: Centro editor de America latina).

Cavarozzi, M. (1988) 'De la inflación como política a la construcción de un sistema de partidos', *Plural*, no. 10–11, pp. 4–8.

De Riz, L. (1981) *Retorno y derrumbe: el último gobierno peronista* (Mexico: Folios).

Frenkel, R. and M. Damill (1988) 'Política económica de emergencia y tentativas de concertación', in *Política económica y actores sociales* (Santiago: PREALC) (Programme latino-americain pour l'emploi en Amérique latine et dans les Caraibes).

Gramsci, A. (1971) *Prison Notebooks* (New York: International Publishers).

O'Donnell, G. (1977) 'Estado y alianzas en la Argentina, 1956–1976', *Desarrollo económico*, no. 64, vol. 16, January–March, pp. 523–54.

Offe, C. (1985) *Disorganized Capitalism* (Cambridge, Mass.: MIT Press).

Przeworski, A. (1981) 'Compromiso de clases y Estado: Europa Occidental y América latina', in N. Lechner (ed.), *Estado y política en América latina*, Mexico: Siglo veintiuno editores.

Przeworski, A. and M. Wallerstein (1982) 'Capitalismo y democracia: una reflexión desde la macroeconomía', *Crítica y Utopía*, no. 8, pp. 77–101.

Schmitter, P. (1974) 'Still the Century of Corporatism?', *Review of Politics*, no. 1, pp. 85–131.

Schmitter, P. (1981) 'Interest Intermediation and Regime Governability in Contemporary Western Europe and North America', in S. Berger (ed.) (1981).

Schvarzer, J. and R. Sidicaro (1987) 'Empresarios y Estado en la democracia', *El Bimestre*, no. 35, pp. 5–14.

Torre, J. C. (1983) *Los sindicatos en el gobierno, 1973–1976* (Buenos Aires: Centro editor de America latina).

Touraine, A. (1987) *La parole et le sang. Politique et société en Amérique latine* (Paris: Editions Odile Jacob).

12 Electoral Systems and the Consolidation of New Democracies

André Blais and Stéphane Dion

Most countries that have joined the 'select' club of democracies lately (Greece, 1974; Spain 1976: Portugal, 1976; Argentina, 1982; Brazil 1986) have adopted proportional representation (PR) as their electoral system. Is it a sound choice? Which electoral system can best contribute to the survival of a new democracy? This is a vital question for the countries concerned. It is also a question of great theoretical interest for those who study the democratization process as well as for those examining the political consequences of electoral systems.

Analyses of the democratization process have largely focused on the economic, social and cultural factors which strengthen (or weaken) democracy. These factors have been clearly exposed by Huntington (1984): a strong economy, an important role given to the market, a thriving endogenous bourgeoisie, a large middle class, a culture and a religion which attach great value to individuality and equality. Lesser attention has been paid to political factors. Those most often mentioned have to do with geopolitics: the direct influence of the superpowers or the spilling effect of a democratic environment. The role of political institutions has been largely neglected. As far as we can tell, no study has examined the impact of the electoral system. Yet, the electoral system which establishes the rules of the electoral process, and is at the very core of what democracy is all about.

The great bulk of studies of electoral systems deal with Western democracies. Among the many questions raised in these studies is the relative performance of PR and majority/plurality systems with respect to such criteria as participation, stability and violence (Powell, 1982). It seems to us that this is precisely the type of question for which the experience of new 'fragile' democracies is the most relevant, as it is in those countries that the effect of the electoral system, in so far as such an effect exists, should be the greatest.

The purpose of this chapter is to determine whether electoral laws influence the likelihood that a democracy will survive. More specifically we will compare the electoral systems of those democracies which have survived with those who have fallen because of a coup d'état and find out whether proportional representation enhances or decreases the probability of a coup d'état. We will examine developing countries as well as 'newly industrialized' ones. The period covered will be 1900–85.

The chapter is divided in four sections. The first section defines the main concepts. The second reviews the debate over the merits and limits of proportional representation and plurality rule. The third presents and discusses the evidence. The last section examines in detail the link between electoral rules and political instability.

DEFINITIONS

The main concepts to be defined are: democracy, electoral system, coup d'état, developing and new industrialized countries.

There are two types of definition of democracy: substantive and procedural (Dion, 1986; Pennock, 1979). Substantive definitions refer to *what* political decision-makers do. Procedural definitions refer to *how* political decision-makers are selected. Substantive definitions classify a society as democratic or not, according to their respect for certain basic values: liberty, equality, justice, and so on. Procedural definitions use as their criterion the fairness of the electoral process. As we are concerned with the electoral system, we will stick to a procedural definition of democracy. And indeed the occurrence of a fair election is, in our view, an absolute prerequisite of democracy, since the principle of democratic equality entails that no one can make decisions which bind the collectivity unless he (she) has received a mandate to that effect from that collectivity. Democracy may imply more than a fair election but without an election no democracy. Making desirable ends part of the definition of democracy is not helpful and is even confusing, as Barry and Rae (1975, 393) correctly point out.

Democracy is defined as *the designation of political decision-makers through regular and competitive elections with secret universal suffrage.*[1] All citizens must have the right to vote, with no exclusion based on sex, race, opinion or religion. Voting must be secret so as to minimize potential intimidation. The election must be 'regular': it must be held at steady intervals, as prescribed by law, and the whole process must be fair, devoid of violence or fraud. Finally the election must be competitive, that is to say, all positions can be contested, all groups or parties may run candidates and are free to express their points of view.

The electoral system is *the set of rules which govern the processes by which preferences are articulated as votes and by which these votes are translated into the election of decision-makers.* The electoral system comprises rules about the ballot structure, the constituency structure and the electoral formula (Blais, 1987). We will be concerned here with the electoral formula, which defines how votes are translated into seats. There are three basic formulae: plurality, in which the candidate with the greater number of votes is elected; majority, in which a candidate must obtain 50 per cent of the votes plus one in order to be elected; and proportional representation, in which the number of elected candidates on a list depends on the number of votes for that list.[2] The plurality and the majority systems can be single- or multi-member districts. Proportional representation can be based on largest remainders or highest averages (Rae, 1969).

A coup d'état is defined as *an act through which democracy is overthrown by a national force.* This definition includes all forms of interruption of democracy except the following two. First, it excludes temporary states of emergency, in so far as the decision has been taken by elected representatives and citizens have subsequently had the opportunity to give their verdict on the legitimacy of that decision; in other words, democracy must be terminated and not momentarily and legally suspended. Secondly, it excludes interruptions of democracy due to military defeat and invasion. We want to understand the internal factors that contribute to the survival or death of democracies and the potential role of electoral systems in that respect. In some cases, of course, the authors of a coup d'état may have been helped by a foreign power but it remains crucial that they be a national force: the military, the party in power, opposition parties or a revolutionary movement.

Finally, our analysis excludes the most developed countries, more explicitly the 25 richest countries, in terms of GDP per capita in 1985. There is a clear relationship between the strength of the economy and the capacity to maintain democratic institutions (Huntington, 1984). There are exceptions to the pattern: Kuwait and the United Arab Emirates are rich countries which have not adopted democratic institutions, while one finds parliamentary democracies in such poor countries as India and Sri Lanka. Still, the level of economic development is probably the best criterion for identifying fragile democracies.

THE VIRTUES AND VICES OF PROPORTIONAL REPRESENTATION AND PLURALITY RULE

Proportional representation is accused of generating two evils: instability and irresponsibility. Instability is a result of the multiplication of parties represented in parliament. Each party comes to parliament with its own narrow ideology and objectives. No party has a majority of seats and a coalition government must be formed. These coalitions are extremely fragile and ephemeral; in the process, small centrist parties have great negotiating power (Taylor and Lijphart, 1985) and extremist parties, which cannot be part of any coalition, participate in the downfall of the various attempts to build an enduring alliance. Political irresponsibility stems from three factors. First, the formation of government is determined not so much by electoral results as by bargaining among leaders of the various parties and, as a consequence, politicians pay greater attention to the constraints of inter-party deals than to the demands of the electorate. Secondly, responsibility is weakened by the fact that the great majority of politicians are assured of their re-election, after having placed their names at the top of their party list (this, of course, holds only for the PR list). Thirdly, moving coalitions make it difficult for voters to determine which parties should be held responsible for policies adopted during the previous mandate. In its extreme form, these effects make democracy simply ungovernable. More often, they sustain enduring tensions which progressively undermine democracy. Parliamentary crises provide a handy justification for a military coup d'état.

Opponents of proportional representation generally argue in favour of a plurality election in single-member districts. According to Duverger (1950) this type of electoral system leads to a two-party system, but it is not so simple as that. The average number of parties represented in parliament in a plurality system is 3.8 and the average 'effective' (Laasko and Taagepera, 1979) is 2.4 (Blais and Carty, 1989; see also Lijphart, 1988). It remains, however, that the plurality formula through its mechanical and psychological impact substantially reduces the number of parties and increases the likelihood of one-party majority government (Blais and Carty, 1987). It enhances government stability as it spares the formation of alliances among rival parties. It also strengthens political responsibility. On the one hand, it is the electoral outcome, not inter-party deals, that decides which party will form the government. On the other hand, the government party may have benefited from the bias of the system, which gives more seats to the larger party, but it knows that the very same bias may penalize the party if its popularity drops. The government is therefore induced to keep in close touch with the evolution of public opinion. A stable and responsible government is well prepared to deal with the country's internal problems. The opposition party waits for the next election, disciplined and united, as internal quarrels would destroy any chances of winning that election. The military cannot use the pretence of government instability to intervene. Extremist radical groups are kept away from centres of decision and most of their members or sympathizers are gradually absorbed by the large moderate parties (Hermens, 1984, 17).

This battery of arguments is not without rebuttal from proponents of proportional representation. The rebuttal focuses on three ideas: equity, integration and equilibrium. First, it is argued that proportional representation, which gives each party a percentage of seats equal to its percentage of votes, is fair and is perceived to be fair by the electorate and that such fairness enhances political stability. The plurality system, being biased against small parties, jeopardizes the legitimacy of political institutions and threatens the survival of a fragile democracy. Secondly, proportional representation integrates rather than excludes; it permits the representation in parliament of cultural or political minority groups which, without such representation, might feel excluded and could become more radical (Carstairs, 1980, ch. 6; Finer, 1975, 30–1; Mackenzie, 1964, 75–6; Lapalombara, 1953; Milnor, 1969, 103). The plurality formula is found wanting on this criterion, as it induces parties to appeal to majority opinion and to neglect minorities; the latter feel alienated and such alienation feeds violence. Thirdly, proportional representation promotes some form of equilibrium among parties and prevents any one of them from using the state for its own individual advantage. The plurality system, for its part, concentrates power into the hands of one individual party, and it is but a step from a dominant party to a single party.

These are the two basic theses confronting each other. They are radically opposed while not incompatible. The plurality system may enhance government stability and responsibility but exacerbate feelings of alienation among minority groups and pave the way for a single-party system. Proportional representation may promote the legitimacy of institutions yet induces irresponsible strategies and tactics which threaten the survival of democracy.

Non- and newly industrialized countries have witnessed the birth and death of many democracies all through the twentieth century. A few countries have managed to maintain democratic institutions. All these cases provide useful evidence which should allow us to determine which electoral system is better able to consolidate democracy.

COUPS D'ETAT AND ELECTORAL SYSTEMS

We have defined democracy as the designation of political decision-makers through regular and competitive elections with secret universal suffrage. We therefore set out to identify which countries, during which time periods, met these conditions. Many elections in these democracies were not held under completely satisfactory conditions but were judged to be relatively fair by observers.[3] After extensive consultation of major indexes and of several monographs, we have constructed a list of 19 non- and newly industrialized countries which went through, between 1900 and 1985, 26 periods of democracy interrupted by as many coups d'état. The list of countries and periods is presented in Appendix 1, along with the prevailing electoral system. We also constructed a list of stable democracies, that is, countries which have maintained fair elections up to 1985 and for a period of at least 10 years. The list is given in Appendix 2, again along with the electoral system.

The findings are shown in Table 12.1. Among the 16 cases of plurality

TABLE 12.1 *Electoral systems and the survival of democracy in non- and newly industrialized countries, 1900–85*

Democracy	Electoral system			
	Plurality (single-member)	*Plurality (multi-member)*	*PR*	*Total*
Survives*	10	1	5	16
Falls	6	6	14	26

* Since at least 1975.

SOURCE Appendices 1 and 2.

TABLE 12.2   *Electoral systems and the survival of democracy in non- and newly industrialized countries, 1945–85*

Democracy	Electoral system			
	Plurality (single-member)	*Plurality (multi-member)*	*PR*	*Total*
Survives*	10	1	5	16
Falls	5	2	9	16

* Since at least 1975.

SOURCE Appendices 1 and 2.

formula, 10 have survived and 6 have fallen, whereas only 5 cases of proportional representation out of 19 have managed to maintain democratic elections.[4] The table has a time bias built into it: it is easier for more recent cases to persist than it is for older ones. Table 12.2 attenuates the bias by restricting itself to the 1945–85 period. The pattern is basically the same: two-thirds of PR democracies perish, compared to only one-third of plurality ones. These results suggest that the plurality system is more conducive to the survival of democracy than proportional representation. Three factors must, however, be taken into account before coming to any conclusion. First, the exceptions: 6 single-member district plurality democracies have fallen and 5 PR ones have persisted over time. Is there any lesson to be drawn from these exceptions?

The Exceptions

The single-member district plurality system failed in six cases. Three of these failures occurred in Africa: Lesotho (1970), Nigeria (1966) and Sierra Leone (1967). This is not surprising since Africa is undoubtedly the continent where democracy has had the least success. Yet it should be pointed out that the only two African countries where democracy has survived – Botswana and Gambia – have adopted the single-member district plurality system. The case of Greece (1935) is also very special; it was a plurality system when the royalist coup d'état occurred but the country had changed its electoral system three times over a period of 5 years. The mere fact of successive changes is likely to have played a greater role in the coup d'état than the specific electoral institution in place at the time. Of these six coups d'état, four were perpetrated by the military, one by the opposition party (Granada, 1979) and one by the government party (Philippines, 1972). The fear that the plurality formula may lead to a single-party system can therefore be supported by only one historical case. This strongly suggests that it is a very unlikely event. All told, the evidence shows that the plurality formula in no way ensures the survival of democracy.

Likewise, proportional representation has been successful in five countries. Two of these are special cases. The survival of integral PR in Israel surely must be accounted for by its very peculiar cultural and geopolitical context. Greece's electoral system is a much attenuated form of PR with high thresholds. In the four elections held between 1974 and 1985, the average difference between vote and seat share of the leading party is 14 percentage points (the average difference in PR systems reported by Rae, 1969, is 1.2 point). Three of these four elections resulted in a one-party majority government. There remain three 'real' exceptions (Malta, Costa Rica and Venezuela) where democracy has survived with a PR formula. The claim that PR inevitably leads to a coup d'état must be rejected.

This brief examination of the 'exceptions' shows that the pattern revealed in Table 12.1 appears robust; some of those 'exceptions' are quite peculiar cases which can be accounted for by other factors. Nevertheless there is not a perfect relationship between electoral institutions and the consolidation of democracy.

The Duration of Democracies

If the plurality system contributes to the survival of democracy it should follow that the plurality system democracies that did not survive had a rather long life. Likewise we would expect PR systems to have had a short existence. Table 12.3 shows that it is exactly the opposite. Among PR systems, the typical (median) coup d'état occurs after 11 years, whereas it is after only 5 years in the case of plurality systems. Two countries stand out in this respect: Uruguay which persisted with PR for a period of 55 years and Chile for periods of 56 and 54 years (Appendix 1). If one adds to these cases those of Costa Rica and Venezuela, which have had PR for 39 and 20 years respectively, it must be concluded that even though PR has had its share of failures in South America, it has also met with great success in some countries. It is possible for PR to survive in non- and newly industrialized countries, even for a long period of time. This being said, the overall pattern is not very encouraging. The prospect of

TABLE 12.3   *The duration of non-surviving democracies, 1900–85*

Electoral system	Duration of democracy (years)	
	average	median
Plurality (single) (n = 6)	8.0	5.0
Plurality (multi.) (n = 6)	21.2	11.5
Proportional Representation (n = 14)	18.0	11.0

SOURCE Appendix 1.

having a slower death is slight consolation when one knows that death is twice as likely to occur.

The British Factor

Appendix 3 gives the list of all non-/newly industrialized countries which have had democratic elections since their independence. Each of these countries, without exception, has been under British influences;[5] these countries, with the exception of Malta and Israel, have adopted the single-member district plurality system. The question is therefore whether it is the British culture or the electoral system that is responsible for the survival of democracy in these countries. There are three alternative interpretations. The first is that culture is the determining factor, the electoral system effect being spurious. The second is that the electoral system is the major cause, culture being at best an additional facilitating variable. The third is that both culture and the electoral system are decisive: the plurality system contributes to the consolidation of democracy by enhancing government stability and responsibility, but only when and where the political culture tolerates substantial disparities between votes and seats.

It is impossible to settle this issue categorically. It is possible, however, to determine whether democracies fall because of the reasons put forward by opponents of PR who argue that PR creates government instability, thus increasing the likelihood of a coup d'état. If the historical evidence indicates that there is indeed the causal sequence postulated here, we should be able to conclude that the impact of the electoral system is not spurious.

PROPORTIONAL REPRESENTATION AND GOVERNMENT INSTABILITY

The hypothesis to be tested is that proportional representation leads to government instability which in turn provokes a coup d'état. A coup d'état that takes place in the absence of a parliamentary or governmental crisis should not be seen as a perverse effect of proportional representation.

According to the proponents of the plurality system, the major flaw of proportional representation is that it does not result in one-party majority government. Table 12.4 shows that indeed the great majority of coups d'état in PR systems occurred in the absence of one-party majority government. Moreover, coups d'état are associated with government instability resulting from the absence of majority government. As Table 12.5 reveals, coups d'état in PR systems tend to be preceded by frequent major cabinet changes. Typically, one would have witnessed five different governments in the five years preceding a coup d'état. In Ceylon and India, two stable single-member district plurality systems, the duration of a government is three times as high. But even more significant is the fact that within PR systems there is much greater government stability in those countries where democracy was maintained over a long period of time. In this case, the

TABLE 12.4 *The status of governments in PR countries at the time of the coup d'etat, 1900–85*

	One-party minority government	Minority or coalition government
Argentina (1976)	X	
Brazil (1964)		X
Chile (1924)		X
Chile (1973)		X
Ecuador (1961)		X
Estonia (1933)		X
Greece (1967)		X
Latvia (1934)		X
Lithuania (1926)		X
Peru (1968)		X
Poland (1926)		X
Turkey (1971)	X	
Turkey (1980)		X
Uruguay (1973)		X

SOURCE Banks (1971, 282–95); Keesing's Contemporary Archives.

TABLE 12.5 Electoral Systems, Coups d'Etat and the Duration of Governments,* 1900–13, 1919–39, 1946–66

PR and coup d'état		Plurality and no coup d'état		PR and no coup d'état	
Country	Duration of gov. (months)**	Country	Duration of gov. (months)	Country	Duration of gov. (months)
Brazil (1960–64)	15	Ceylon (1948–66)	30	Chile (1896–1913)	10
Chile (1920–24)	6	India (1947–66)	40	Chile (1946–66)	15
Ecuador (1957–61)	30	Average	**35**	Costa Rica (1949–66)	40
Estonia (1929–33)	12	Median	**35**	Israel (1948–66)	20
Greece (1963–66)	6			Uruguay (1919–39, 1946–66)	24
Latvia (1900–34)	15			Average	**22**
Lithuania (1922–26)	10			Median	**20**
Poland (1922–26)	12				
Average	**13**				
Median	**12**				

* There is a change of government whenever there is a new leader and/or 50 per cent of Cabinet positions are held by new ministers (Banks, 1971, xvii).

** For the five years preceding the coup d'état.

SOURCE Banks, 1971, 3–53.

cultural explanation cannot apply since the countries involved comprise such diverse cultural areas as the Mediterranean, the Baltic region and Latin America.

Analyses of specific countries are also consistent with the broad pattern suggested by Table 12.5. In Poland, integral PR led to the representation in the 1922 Diet of 17 different parties (Rollet, 1957, 163). It proved to be impossible to form a stable government:

> 'Political parties proliferated; with their increase in number came the reluctance to compromise and the heavy need to rely upon tenuous coalitions. During the five years of parliamentary government under the 1921 Constitution ... fourteen cabinets manoeuvered for control of national affairs'. (Kefe *et al.*, 1981, 33)

The situation was more or less the same in the parliaments of the Baltic Republics in the 1920s: 'Before a coalition government could be set up, at least three – and probably four or five – parties had to agree on a common policy' (Rauch, 1970, 146; see also Sabeliunas, 1972, 7). A record was set in Lithuania in 1931 when as many as 27 parties were represented in parliament.

The governments of Chile at the beginning of the century would sometimes last only a week. Despite that, democracy survived for many years before falling after a coup in 1924; such resiliency must be attributed, according to Fitzgibbon and Fernandez (1981, 231), to a particularly strong economy and a highly educated political élite. And in 1973, a crisis situation opposing a president incapable of forming a stable cabinet and a hostile Parliament gave the military a pretext to intervene. In Greece in the 1960s, the various coalitions failed one after the other until the colonels took over in 1967. Finally, the 1968 coup d'état in Peru was preceded by four cabinet reshuffles over one year, the president being in a minority position in the two houses (Keesing's Contemporary Archives). All these instances suggest that government instability, which is often associated with proportional representation, is a threat for fragile democracies.

How can we explain, then, that some PR democracies manage to persist over a long period of time? Part of the explanation is that these countries have been able to eschew government instability. The duration of governments is fairly long in those countries (Table 12.5, column 3). In Costa Rica, one party has been able to have a majority of seats in Parliament for 24 of the 36 years between 1949 and 1985 (Banks, 1971; Seligson, 1987; Keesing's Contemporary Archives). In Uruguay, two parties (Colorado and Blanco) completely dominated the political scene until 1971 when, two years before the coup d'état, there appeared a new formation, the Partido Democratica Cristiano, a coalition of 17 parties (Keesing's Contemporary Archives). Malta has a two-party system and each election has produced one-party majority government. Finally, in Venezuela, there are also two major parties – Democratic Action and the Christian Democratic Party (Levine, 1987).

Institutions, it must be said, are not the whole story. It is quite possible to have a united and disciplined government and yet witness violence in the streets. Government stability does not guarantee social and political stability. Yet, both the quantitative and the qualitative evidence reported here strongly suggests that government stability contributes substantially to political stability in fragile democracies.

CONCLUSION

The single-member district plurality system performs better than proportional representation with respect to the consolidation of fragile democracies. Its superior performance may depend on the British culture's tolerance for vote–seat disparities, but it is also related to the plurality system's capacity to provide for government stability. A fragile democracy grappling with serious social and economic problems can hardly outlast the sclerosis of its political institutions.

Some may question our conclusion on the ground that PR has been shown to work well in Europe. Carstairs (1980) and Mackenzie (1964) contend that the adoption of PR contributed to an improved social and political climate in countries such as Belgium. They believe that PR, even though it may increase *government instability*, reduces alienation and *political instability* (political turmoil and violence) and strengthens democracy. These assertions may be right or wrong. Unfortunately, we cannot tell, since these authors have not taken care to demonstrate concretely and rigorously how precisely the political climate improved after the adoption of PR in Belgium, Switzerland, or Italy. Moreover, among Western democracies, there is no lesser political violence in PR than in plurality systems (Blais and Carty, 1989). In short, the positive impact of PR on social peace has still to be demonstrated, whereas its negative effect is quite manifest in fragile democracies.

Democracy in countries such as Spain, Greece and Portugal appears strong, and they may no longer be fragile democracies. In these countries the choice of an electoral system may depend on other criteria than consolidation of democracy. When the latter is at stake, however, the evidence suggests that the plurality system is a better choice than PR. It could be, on the other hand, that in some countries the plurality formula is simply unacceptable because it is perceived to be basically unfair. Then some form of moderate PR or a majority run-off system *à la française* could be preferred. Integral PR, however, is to be avoided at all costs.

Whatever the case, it is clear that electoral laws matter, that they have substantial effects on the party system and the composition of government and, indirectly, on the process of democratic consolidation. The social environment is of course an important determinant but political institutions have a great impact as well.

Notes

1. For a similar definition, see Butler (1981).
2. This holds for list PR; the logic is somewhat different in the case of the single transferable vote where it is opinions about candidates that are proportionately represented (Blais, 1987).
3. Most elections held before 1945 were based on universal *manhood* suffrage. Generally speaking, the criteria tend to be interpreted more strictly for elections held after 1945 (see particularly Banks, 1971). It is not an easy task to determine whether a country is or is not a democracy (Bollen, 1980). We have had to make some difficult decisions. For instance, Venezuela is often considered to be a democracy (Levine, 1987; Molina, 1988) and has had elections since 1959. Banks (1971, 295), however, notes that several parties were not allowed to run until 1966. We have therefore concluded that democracy started only with the 1968 election. Likewise, Colombia has had regular elections since 1958, but the two major parties have agreed to an equal share of seats, regardless of election results.
4. The multi-member district plurality system is most unsuccessful. The consequences of that system depend on the number of votes allowed to voters. When there is only one vote per voter, it is sometimes defined as semi-proportional (see Lijphart *et al.*, 1986). When there are as many votes as candidates to be elected, it is even more likely to produce one-party majority government (Blais and Carty, 1987).
5. The inverse does not hold: four former British colonies have had democracy terminated by a coup d'état: Granada, 1979, Lesotho (1970), Nigeria (1966) and Sierra Leone (1967).

264   *Electoral Systems and New Democracies*

References

Banks, Arthur S. (1971) *Cross-Polity Time-Series Data* (Cambridge, Mass. and London: MIT Press).
Barry, Brian and Douglas W. Rae (1975) 'Political Evaluation' in: Fred I. Greenstein and Nelson W. Polsby (eds.), *Handbook of Political Science, vol. 1: Political Science, Scope and Theory* (Reading: Addison Wesley).
Bealey, Frank (1987) 'Stability and Crisis: Fears about Threats to Democracy', *European Journal of Political Research*, 15: pp. 687–715.
Blais, André (1987), 'The Classification of Electoral Systems', *European Journal of Political Research*, 16: pp. 99–110.
Blais, André and Ken Carty (1987) 'The Impact of Electoral Formulae on the Creation of Majority Governments', *Electoral Studies*, 6: pp. 109–18.
Blais, André and Ken Carty (1989) 'The Psychological Impact of Electoral Laws', mimeo.
Bollen, Kenneth A. (1980) 'Issues in the Comparative Measurement of Political Democracy', *American Sociological Review*, 45 (3): pp. 370–408.
Butler, David (1981) 'Introduction: Democratic and Nondemocratic Elections', in David Butler *et al.* (eds.), *Democracy at the Polls: A Comparative Study of Competitive National Elections* (Washington: American Enterprise Institute).
Carstairs, Andrew M. (1980) *A Short History of Electoral Systems in Western Europe* (London: Allen & Unwin).
Dion, Stéphane (1986) 'Libéralisme et démocratie: plaidoyer pour l'idéologie dominante', *Politique* 9: pp. 5–38.
Duverger, Maurice (1950) *L'influence des systèmes électoraux sur la vie politique* (Paris: Armand Colin).
Finer, S. E. (1975) 'Advisory Politics and Electoral Reform', in S. E. Finer (ed.), *Advisory Politics and Electoral Reform* London: Anthony Wigram.
Fitzgibbon, R. H. and J. A. Fernandez (1981) *Latin America: Political Culture and Development* (Englewood Cliffs, Prentice Hall).
Hermens, Ferdinand A. (1984) 'Representation and Proportional Representation', in Arend Lijphart, Bernard Grofman (eds.), *Choosing an Electoral System: Issues and Alternatives* (New York: Praeger).
Huntington, Samuel P. (1984) 'Will More Countries Become Democratic?' *Political Science Quarterly*, 99(2): pp. 193–219.
Kefe, K. *et al.* (1981) *Area Handbooks for Poland* (Washington: American University Foreign Area Studies).
Knapp, Andrew (1987) 'Proportional but Bipolar: France's Electoral System in 1986', *West European Politics*, 10: pp. 89–115.
Laasko, M. and Rein Taagepera (1979) 'Effective Number of Parties: a Measure with Application to West Europe', *Comparative Political Studies*, 12: pp. 3–27.
Lapalombara, Joseph G. (1953) 'The Italian Elections and the Problem of Representation', *American Political Science Review*, 47: pp. 676–704.
Levine, Daniel H. (1987) 'Venezuela' in Myron Weiner and Ergun Ozbundun (eds.), *Competitive Elections in Developing Countries* (Durham: Duke University Press).
Lijphart, Arend (1988), 'The Political Consequences of Electoral Laws,

1945–85: A Critique, Re-analysis and Update of Rae's Classic Study', paper presented at the XIVth Congress of the International Political Science Association, Washington.

Lijphart, A. *et al.* (1986) 'The Limited Vote and the Single Non-Transferable Vote: Lessons from the Japanese and Spanish Examples' in B. Grosman and A. Lijphart (eds) *Electoral Laws and Their Political Consequences* (New York: Agathon Press).

Mackenzie, W. J. M. (1964) *Free Elections: An Elementary Textbook* (London: Allen & Unwin).

Milnor, Richard A. (1969) *Elections and Political Stability* (Boston: Little, Brown).

Molina, José E. (1988) 'Electoral Participation in Venezuela', paper presented at the XIVth Congress of the International Political Science Association, Washington.

Pennock, J. Roland (1979) *The Political Consequences of Electoral Laws* (New Haven: Yale University Press).

Powell, B. G. Jr. (1982) *Contemporary Democracies: Participation, Stability and Violence* (Cambridge, Mass: Harvard University Press).

Rae, Douglas W. (1969) *The Political Consequences of Electoral Laws* (New Haven: Yale University Press).

Rauch, George Von (1970) *The Baltic States. The Years of Independence, Estonia, Latvia, Lithuania, 1917–1940* (Berkeley and Los Angeles: University of California Press).

Rollet, Henri (1957) *La Pologne au XXième Siècle* (Paris: Pédone).

Sabeliunas, Lavas (1972) *Lithuania in Crisis. Nationalism to Communism* (London: Indiana University Press).

Seligson, Mitchell A. (1987) 'Costa Rica and Jamaica' in: Myron Weiner and Ergun Ozbundun (eds.), *Competitive Elections in Developing Countries* (Durham: Duke University Press) pp. 147–200.

Taagepera, Rein and Matthew Shugart (1989) *Seats and Votes: The Effects and Determinants of Electoral System* (New Haven: Yale University Press).

Taylor, Charles Lewis and David A. Jodice (1983) *World Handbook of Political and Social Indicators*, vol. 1 (New Haven and London: Yale University Press).

Taylor, Peter J. and Arend Lijphart (1985) 'Proportional Tenure versus Proportional Representation: Introducing a New Debate', *European Journal of Political Research*, 13: pp. 387–99.

Weiner, Y. and E. Ozbundun (1987), *Competitive Elections in Developing Countries* (Durham: Duke University Press).

Appendices

Appendix 1 *Coups d'état and Electoral Systems in Non- and Newly Industrialized Countries, 1900–85*

Country	Coup d'état	Democracy	Electoral system
Argentina	1930	1854–30	plur. multi.
Argentina	1943	1932–43	plur. multi.
Argentina	1976	1973–76	PR.
Brazil	1964	1946–64	PR.
Chile	1924	1868–24	PR.
Chile	1973	1932–73	PR.
Ecuador	1961	1947–61	PR.
Spain	1938	1931–38	plur. multi.
Estonia	1933	1920–33	PR.
Greece	1935	1926–35	1926: PR.; 1928: plur.; 1932: PR.; 1933–35: plur.
Greece	1967	1946–67	1946–51: PR.; 1952: plur.; 1958–67: PR.
Granada	1979	1974–79	plur.
Lesotho	1970	1966–70	plur.
Latvia	1934	1920–34	PR.
Lithuania	1926	1920–26	PR.
Nigeria	1966	1960–66	plur.
Peru	1962	1956–62	plur. multi.
Peru	1968	1963–68	PR.
Philippines	1972	1946–72	plur.
Poland	1926	1921–26	PR.
Portugal	1926	1911–26	plur. multi.
Sierra Leone	1967	1962–67	plur.
Turkey	1960	1946–60	plur. multi.
Turkey	1971	1965–71	PR.
Turkey	1980	1973–80	PR.
Uruguay	1973	1893–73	1893–1915: plur. multi.; 1915–18: maj.–PR.; 1918–: PR.

SOURCES *Area Handbooks* Washington: American University Foreign Area Studies; Banks (1971); Banks, Arthur S. (ed.) *Political Handbook of the World* New York: Binghamton; Bealy (1987); *Competitive Elections in Developing Countries; Keesing's Contemporary Archives* London: Keesings Ltd; *Parties and Electoral Systems: a World Handbook* (1962) London: The Institute of Electoral Research; *Parliaments of the World* (1976) New York: Interparliamentary Union; Taagapera and Shugart (1989): Appendix; Taylor and Jodice (1983); Weiner and Ozbudun (1987).

Appendix 2 *Non- and Newly Industrialized Countries where Democracy has Survived**

Country	Starting point of democracy	Electoral system
Bahamas	1973	plur.
Barbados	1966	plur.
Botswana	1966	plur.
Ceylon/Sri Lanka	1948	plur.
Costa Rica	1949	PR
Gambia	1965	plur.
Greece	1974	PR
India	1947	plur.
Israel	1948	PR
Jamaica	1962	plur.
Malta	1964	PR
Malaysia	1963	plur.
Papua New Guinea	1975	plur.
Trinidad and Tobago	1962	plur.
Venezuela	1968	PR

* Since at least 1975.

SOURCES *Area Handbooks* Washington: American University Foreign Area Studies; Banks, Arthur S. (dir.) *Political Handbook of the World* New York: Binghamton; *Competitive Elections in Developing Countries; Keesing's Contemporary Archives* London: Keesings Ltd; Taagapera and Shugart (1989): Appendix; Taylor and Jodice (1983); Weiner and Ozbudun (1987).

Appendix 3   *Non- and Newly Industrialized Countries which have Remained Democratic since Independence*

Country	Year of independence	British influence	Electoral system
Bahamas	1973	yes	plur.
Barbados	1966	yes	plur.
Botswana	1966	yes	plur.
Ceylon/Sri Lanka	1948	yes	plur.
Gambia	1965	yes	plur.
India	1947	yes	plur.
Israel	1948	yes	PR
Jamaica	1962	yes	plur.
Malta	1964	yes	PR
Malaysia	1963	yes	plur.
Papua New Guinea	1975	yes	plur.
Trinidad and Tobago	1962	yes	plur.

SOURCES *Area Handbooks* Washington: American University Foreign Area Studies; Banks, Arthur S. (dir.) *Political Handbook of the World* New York: Binghamton; *Competitive Elections in Developing Countries; Keesing's Contemporary Archives* London: Keesings Ltd; Taagapera and Shugart (1989): Appendix; Taylor and Jodice (1983); Weiner and Ozbudun (1987).

Index